D0437474

Praise for *Brick by Brick:*
Building Hope and Opportunity for Women Survivors Everywhere

"Karen Sherman tells her poignant story of being a mother, a successful leader, and an advocate for women worldwide in *Brick by Brick*. Her empathy for women who have been victims of violence, abuse, and disempowerment is inspirational, and her story truly has the unique power to connect the stories of women everywhere."
—Joyce Banda, former president of Malawi

"Karen Sherman's personal and inspiring account of her family's experience living in Rwanda for a year and the many life lessons that came from her work with women survivors is an easy and compelling read for anyone who strives to be a global citizen—and raise global citizens."
—Lauren Bush Lauren, founder and CEO of FEED

"Karen Sherman tells two powerful stories here, both of them straightforward yet affecting: one about her personal struggles in the first world, overlaid on another about women pushed to the brink during the Rwandan genocide. Along the way, it becomes clear that the ability to triumph is rooted in empathy and shared support. In *Brick by Brick*'s overlapping worlds, life lessons are where you find them, and heartrending and heartwarming are never far apart."
—Alan Huffman, author of *Mississippi in Africa* and *Here I Am*

"As a survivor and advocate for those suffering in neglected parts of the world, I was touched on many levels by Karen's journey. Her grit and courage are a gift to the countless women and girls she's dedicated her life to lifting up. Her fierce personal honesty will inspire all who read this wonderful book."
—Ashley Judd, actor, author, and humanitarian

"A deeply honest and moving read. Sherman weaves her own search for balance and acceptance with the courageous stories of the women survivors she works with in war-torn countries like Rwanda, South Sudan, and Afghanistan. Finding universal threads of womanhood in their shared experiences, she draws inspiration from their awe-inspiring strength and resilience."
—Zainab Salbi, founder of Women for Women International and author of *Freedom Is an Inside Job*

"A journey like no other! With unflinching honesty, badass mom and lifelong women's rights activist Karen Sherman maps her journey—and the stories of those she's met along the way—through the highest questions of modern womanhood: beauty, regret, connection, sacrifice, survivorship, and choice. From suburban dinner parties to rapid-fire war zones, long since abandoned adolescent memories to the tallest peak in Africa, this page-turner charts emotional landscapes that connect women everywhere. Sure to leave the reader with her own soul-quaking questions and a tidal wave of bravery to face them down."
—**Lisa J. Shannon, author of** *A Thousand Sisters* **and** *Mama Koko and the Hundred Gunmen*

"*Brick by Brick* introduces us to the people whose lives form the pieces of the world's most complex development puzzles. Karen Sherman draws upon her encounters with entrepreneurs and activists around the world and shows us the power of women to change their communities and their country. In sharing the stories of these indomitable women, Sherman illuminates their resilience under the most dire circumstances and shares the powerful political and personal lessons that resilience shares."
—**Gayle Tzemach Lemmon, author of** *Dressmaker of Khair Khana* **and** *Ashley's War*

"A moving, fascinating story filled with emotional highs and lows, adventures and setbacks—and a large dose of wisdom. Every woman will relate to aspects of *Brick by Brick* and be inspired."
—**Melanne Verveer, former United States ambassador for global women's issues**

Brick by Brick

Building Hope and Opportunity for Women Survivors Everywhere

KAREN SHERMAN

ROWMAN & LITTLEFIELD
Lanham • Boulder • New York • London

Published by Rowman & Littlefield
An imprint of The Rowman & Littlefield Publishing Group, Inc.
4501 Forbes Boulevard, Suite 200, Lanham, Maryland 20706
www.rowman.com

6 Tinworth Street, London SE11 5AL, United Kingdom

Distributed by NATIONAL BOOK NETWORK

Copyright © 2019 by The Rowman & Littlefield Publishing Group, Inc.

All rights reserved. No part of this book may be reproduced in any form or by any
electronic or mechanical means, including information storage and retrieval systems,
without written permission from the publisher, except by a reviewer who may quote
passages in a review.

British Library Cataloguing in Publication Information Available

Library of Congress Cataloging-in-Publication Data

Names: Sherman, Karen, 1962– author.
Title: Brick by brick : building hope and opportunity for women survivors everywhere /
    Karen Sherman.
Description: Lanham, Maryland : Rowman & Littlefield, 2019. | Includes bibliographical
    references and index. | Summary: "This powerful memoir weaves the stories of valiant
    women who survived the Rwandan genocide with the struggle of their champion,
    Karen Sherman, to recover from her own history of abuse. The strength of these
    women helped Karen find her own way—through conflict zones and confrontations
    with corrupt officials to a renewed commitment to her family."—Provided by
    publisher.
Identifiers: LCCN 2019020432 (print) | LCCN 2019022209 (ebook) | ISBN
    9781538130315 (cloth : alk. paper)
Subjects: LCSH: Sherman, Karen, 1962—Travel—Rwanda. | Women—Rwanda—Social
    conditions. | Women—Services for—Rwanda. | Genocide survivors—Services for—
    Rwanda. | Women in development—Rwanda.
Classification: LCC HQ1797.5 .S54 2019 (print) | LCC HQ1797.5 (ebook) | DDC
    305.40967571—dc23
LC record available at https://lccn.loc.gov/2019020432
LC ebook record available at https://lccn.loc.gov/2019022209

♾™ The paper used in this publication meets the minimum requirements of
American National Standard for Information Sciences—Permanence of Paper
for Printed Library Materials, ANSI/NISO Z39.48-1992.

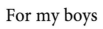

For my boys

Contents

Author's Note

This is a true story. Some of the women's stories are composites of prior interviews and new interviews that are compressed, having taken place over a more extended period of time. There are no composite characters. Some portions are not presented in the exact order of actual events. Many names have been changed, primarily to protect the identity of those individuals and their families.

Prologue

The natural beauty of the site was what drew me in on that first visit to Kayonza. The land was green and dense with leafy banana trees and other vegetation, but little of it was being cultivated. Looking down into the long, lush valley filled with formal and squatter farms, I could see it was more of the same. It was dotted with women working the land—hoeing, weeding, planting—determined to get what they could from it. At this site, and in the women, there was so much potential.

The architects of the Women's Opportunity Center in Kayonza, Rwanda, would often talk about the process of building as "brick by brick," but I always thought of it as "woman by woman." The women survivors we worked with were literally rebuilding their lives, a brick at a time. I've seen this happen not only in Rwanda but also with women all over the world—from Afghanistan, to the Democratic Republic of the Congo, to South Sudan and Iraq—some of the worst places on earth to be a woman.

In spite of hardships and restrictions beyond the scope of most people's experiences, these women confront each day with strength and determination. They have not lost themselves nor have they let go of hope. They are working, in ways both big and small, to change their lives.

Every single one of those beautiful, orange fired bricks used to construct the opportunity center, all five hundred thousand of them handmade by women, was a testament to that.

More than twenty-five years of work in developing countries and embattled parts of the world has introduced me to thousands of women like those brickmakers. Most have been taught to expect little from life, so people may assume that they have little to teach us. That is simply not true. I am more aware than most people of the inspiration and value found in the resilience, perseverance, and sheer force of will of the female survivors of war, but I had not yet internalized the lessons in their examples.

That is, until I spent a year living in Rwanda with my three boys. There, I began to see.

I

The trouble is, if you don't risk anything you risk more.

—*Erica Jong*

1

The Move

Most of us have spent our lives assuming that if we work hard, we will achieve our goals, that we will lead comfortable, meaningful lives. We start out with big dreams about what we want to accomplish in life, the kind of person we want to be, how we want to change the world. At least, that was how I started out. But despite my successes in life, I found myself in a place where both my career and my marriage were falling apart, where my three boys knew their dad better than me. On the brink of turning fifty, I had been presuming fulfillment, or at least incremental progress, but over time, I had let stress, disappointment, and the pressure of expectations blind me to the fact that I wasn't making the changes—the choices—that would deliver those expectations. Everyday life has a way of clouding our thinking and calling into question the things we were once most sure of about ourselves.

Which was why my family and I—my husband, Bill, and our three sons Sam, Eli, and Kai—landed in Kigali, Rwanda, one night in August 2012. As the five of us descended from the plane, the warm air smelled of smoke and appeared hazy, as if hundreds of families living nearby had just cooked their evening meal over an open fire. Our exhaustion masked any nerves we were feeling about our arrival and what it meant. It had been a relatively smooth travel day, all things considered, as smooth as it can be traveling with your husband, a tween, and two teenage boys, and with the bulk of our personal belongings crammed into ten assorted duffels and suitcases.

The experience stood in stark contrast to how I normally traveled in the field: light and solo. It felt new and strange being there with my family, with the boys. The country office sent two drivers to help with all the luggage and deposit us at the hotel where we were staying for the first couple of days. The boys opened their car windows to the warm breeze and view, eager for their first glimpse of Kigali. Kai, who'd asked me about twenty-five times if we were "there yet" seemed especially curious. I pointed out the bullet-riddled parliament building and other landmarks as we drove through the city's dim streets.

I'd been to Rwanda many times before but had never looked at it through the lens of a potential resident or through the lens of motherhood. This was Bill's second time in the city. We had met in Kigali three months earlier to explore housing options, tour the boys' new school, and more generally assess the lay of the land. There had been tension between us then—so much was not being said—but we were on the same page about Rwanda as a place to live.

There was good reason for the tension. For weeks now my family had been walking on eggshells around me because my bid to become CEO of Women for Women International, an organization that helps women survivors of war rebuild their lives, had failed.

I had worked there for nearly a decade. As a woman, I'd been leaning in hard from an early age, traveling all over the world for work, which often meant being away from my husband and sons for weeks at a time. Like so many people in our modern, success-driven society, the job defined me. But this work was much more than a job. Helping women who had survived war move from crisis and poverty to stability and self-sufficiency resonated powerfully with me, given my background and experiences. It felt right, like what I was supposed to be doing. This failure felt personal. It was devastating.

And then, while we were all in the car on the way to the airport to visit my brother and his family in Boston, I blurted out: "I think we should move to Rwanda," as if I'd just thought of it. As if I were saying, "I think we should go out for pizza tonight!"

Nobody said anything. It took a few minutes for everybody to understand that I was being serious.

Rwanda? As in Africa?

Yes, that's the one. *Rwanda.*

Bill kept his eyes fixed on the windshield, trying to maintain his concentration on the road ahead, but I could tell he was fuming. After all I'd put Bill
and the kids through over the past months, I had just thrown out this crazy
idea in front of the boys without even bothering to discuss it with him first.

The idea of a move had actually begun to percolate a few days before.
Though I didn't have a clear plan at first, I had been mentally cataloguing
the places where I had traveled for work: Iraq, Nigeria, Congo, South Sudan,
Rwanda, Kosovo, Afghanistan, and Bosnia and Herzegovina. Most were off
the table from a security standpoint. Bosnia was a possibility. The country was
almost twenty years post-conflict and now relatively stable, albeit dysfunc-
tional, and Bosnian women, close to half of whom were unemployed, critically needed economic-development support. It was one of Europe's poorest
countries. *I could make that work*, I thought.

There was another option, though a bolder one, a place where, not so long
ago, the rivers had run with blood during the genocide of nearly one million
Tutsi. Rwanda, a landlocked country in East Africa, slightly smaller than the
state of Maryland, was now beautiful, dynamic, and safe.

Once I'd put the idea out there, without a thought for any of the specifics, I
was frantically trying to line up arguments in favor of the move. Bill and I had
talked off and on over the years about living abroad with the kids, but it never
seemed to be a good time. Our fourteen-year-old fraternal twins Sam and Eli
were about to start high school, and Kai, our eleven-year-old, was going into his
final year of elementary school. The boys were growing up so fast, I told myself,
that this was my chance to spend more time with them. Rwanda was a place
where I could still do my job and be more an actual parent than a virtual one.
Living in Africa would be an important cross-cultural experience for them, a
chance to develop greater humility and global citizenship. I convinced myself
this was not just about me, but could I convince them? Could I convince Bill?

The fight started building silently between us, each of us knowing what the
other would say.

Bill was biting the hairs on his forearm—a longtime nervous quirk and
a clear sign that he was having a hard time processing this, that he felt am-
bushed by me raising this in front of the boys. I kept at it anyway.

The boys were chattering away in the back, more positive than I expected. Kai
loved the idea of life in a warm climate, wearing shorts every day. Sam and Eli

calculated how much their social capital would rise from a year in Africa. "Why are you being so defensive, Dad?" they pressed. The boys couldn't have known how important this move was to me—I didn't yet know it myself, but the love for them that swelled within me in this moment boosted my confidence.

At the check-in counter, in the security line, at the departure gate, during the short flight to Boston, I spoon-fed the conversation to Bill, giving him space to digest it. We talked about it on the drive to the hotel where we were staying the next three nights. By the time we were out taking our first stroll along the Charles River, Bill was beginning to warm to the idea. Rwanda. Africa. Move. Maybe it wasn't so crazy after all?

I had yet to sell the idea to the organization, but there was a strong case to be made for it. They were transitioning leadership in three of the four African countries where they worked, about to close down a program and set up a new base in South Sudan. They were also knee-deep in a large-scale construction project, building the first-of-its-kind Women's Opportunity Center in Rwanda. The project had gotten off to a late start after more than a year of bureaucratic delays and was already behind schedule for a planned June 2013 opening. With huge challenges ahead, they needed more heels on the ground in Africa. Having me there could be helpful.

When we got back from Boston, I quietly broached the idea with the board chair over coffee, and then approached my colleagues with a proposal. I would relocate to Rwanda with my family for one year to oversee construction of the Women's Opportunity Center and run point on other operations in Africa. What I didn't say was how I desperately needed an escape from my present life and time to figure things out, how I needed to be somewhere else.

My plan was approved within one week, and my head spun. Ecstatic, I called Bill to share the good news. "That's great," he said. "Let's talk more about it tonight." I could sense him being careful, trying to be supportive yet noncommittal.

I came home gushing, full of verve. It had been a long time since I'd felt such eagerness about anything. Bill, as usual, was more focused on the practicalities. Where would the boys go to school? Did we have to pay taxes in both countries? Could we get residency and work permits in-country or would we need to arrange them beforehand? He was raising all the right questions. All of them would need to be answered in good time. But for right now, for just a few moments, couldn't we simply savor the idea of moving to Rwanda without getting mired in the details of how we would actually live there?

It was then that I realized something about all this upheaval. I was at the midpoint of my life. The boys were growing up and would be going off to college in a few short years. They would be on their own before we knew it. Bill and I would, too. Empty nesting could be traumatic for any number of reasons, but the thought of it filled me with a particular sense of dread and doubt. Now that I wasn't so consumed by my career goals, I could see that my work, and the kids, had often served as a distraction from the problems in our marriage. Was Bill the person I was prepared to spend the rest of my life with?

I'd known other women whose marriages had fallen apart for one reason or another: one partner too driven by work or lust, or both partners too busy to find time for each other. Or it was a hundred little annoyances that had festered and become insurmountable. People change, they grow apart—it happens. I had prided myself on striking some sort of chaotic life balance between the demands of a high-level job, my marriage, and contemporary parenting. But I was fooling myself. Bill had been sleeping in another bedroom for months now. I was at a loss as to what made me happy anymore.

"Karen, what are we talking about here?" Bill asked that night when I told him I thought just the boys and I should go. "Are you saying you *want* to go without me?"

"No. Yes. I don't know." It was all happening so fast. "I just know that *I* need to go," I said after a fraught silence. "And I want the boys to come with me."

I'd barely formalized the thought in my own mind until that moment, but I knew it to be true. What I was asking for without saying it was almost a trial separation. Bill looked surprised, and hurt, but he said little.

Over the next week, we fought, discussed, and debated the move. Just when I thought we'd landed somewhere, Bill would raise a new strand of argument, and another late-night yelling match would erupt. He and two partners had recently acquired the communications firm where he'd worked for many years and was the new CEO. He needed to focus on managing his consulting practice, he'd said. We didn't talk about our marriage, our fights, but my last, best argument clinched it: after all these years of me commuting for work around the globe and him being in charge at home, it was his turn to do the travel and I would run the household.

So it was agreed: the boys and I would move, and Bill every so often would "commute" to Kigali.

I was thrilled, elated that Bill had agreed. But moments later, the reality of it struck hard. What the hell was I doing? What was I trying to prove? I'd been in a near-constant state of anxiety—barely able to eat or rest—for months now, as a result of the CEO search-and-hire process, which had dragged on for close to a year. Near the end, it had become unbearable. I had fought hard for the role, a position I felt I had earned, but the process had shaken me, shattered my confidence.

The board said they wanted me to stay, but with another restructuring on the horizon, I knew my time there would be limited.

Much of the following weeks had been a blur. I sulked around like a jilted lover.

Bill and the boys waited for me to get over it, to move on. "Come on, you're Karen Fucking Sherman," Bill said, more from annoyance than support. as we were clearing the dinner dishes one night. That was his way of rousing me whenever I got stuck or down on myself. But I couldn't seem to let it go.

I was ashamed to admit it, but I had slipped back into a version of my adolescent self, into the girl who feared her father's condemnation, his evident disappointment in her failing, once again, to live up to his expectations. From an early age, I had poured all of my passion and energy into work. I had built myself up, fortified myself with my career. It was a form of escape—at first from the turbulence of my childhood home and later from my problems in general.

I had grasped wildly for some kind of a solution. For Rwanda. Deep down I knew this was about more than a job. I had lost something, something essential that I couldn't quite name but could feel in its startling absence. But with so many women suffering around the world, it felt self-indulgent to be anything less than grateful for my lot, for the myriad of personal and professional choices at my disposal, for the life of privilege and abundance. But the truth was staring me in the face: I had lost my sense of joy, my sense of self. Everything, it seemed, was coming apart, my career, my marriage, my life.

But standing in our bedroom that night, having just convinced Bill that moving to Rwanda was the right thing for our family to do, all I felt was panic. What if this wasn't a crossroad at all, but my life as I knew it—everything I had worked so hard for—coming to a screeching halt?

And now, here we were in Rwanda, fractured and yet willing to try to engender some kind of fresh start, to do something big, something life changing even, whatever that meant.

2

The Country

As soon as we arrived in the country, I could hear our friends at home asking again: Why did you choose Rwanda?

My standard answer over the past few months was that Rwanda is a reasonably safe place to live with the kids, one that is hospitable to foreigners. It's clean (even bringing plastic bags into the country is illegal) and easy to get around in a small-town kind of way. It was also a fine jumping-off point to the other African countries where I would have to travel for work.

In fact, it was easy to forget that this country was still recovering. The banking system worked. Broadband was being rolled out. And Rwanda possessed an unusually large network of well-paved roads, mainly Chinese made, unlike most across Africa that were referred to as "African massage" roads because of the incessant bumping.

It is, however, a country with a tragic history—in 1994, close to one million Tutsis were brutally murdered over a hundred days of violence and inhumanity. Rwanda's story, though, neither starts nor ends with the genocide.

While ethnic tension existed in pre-colonial Rwanda, the Hutu and Tutsi were otherwise economically mobile classes. Forerunners of both people had joined the Twa, Rwanda's first inhabitants, and settled in the region over a period of two thousand years. They developed and shared a common belief system, culture, and language. The Tutsis were the pastoralists. They were rich in cattle and, hence, powerful and elite. The Hutus were the workers, the cultivators, and were considered subordinate to the Tutsis. But movement between these classes was possible. One could become a Tutsi by virtue of the number of cattle one owned.

Belgian colonialists gained control of the country in the late 1800s and, for their own purposes, worked to transform social and economic distinctions into separate ethnic identities among the Hutu, Tutsi, and Twa. Their racially charged classification system codified Tutsis' elite status and made it difficult to change groups. The seeds of future conflict were thus planted. Acts of interethnic violence continued through the country's independence in 1962 and in the time leading up to the genocide, causing hundreds of thousands of Tutsis to flee the country.

When General Habyarimana, a Hutu, took power by coup in 1973, he promised to restore order and unity. Instead, the policies he put in place led to even more division. Intense, state-sponsored propaganda served to flame the fires of ethnic hatred. The shooting down of President Habyarimana's plane in 1994 became a pretext for the swiftest genocide in history. The country was completely destroyed.

The government has been led since 2000 by former rebel leader Paul Kagame, who heads the political party known as the Rwanda Patriotic Front, or RPF. A strong and exacting leader by all accounts, he has instilled the rule of law and accountability across all levels of government and society. Kagame has purposefully driven the country forward through careful implementation of Vision 2020, and now Vision 2050, both blueprints for its advancement. Although Kagame has garnered criticism for his authoritarian leadership, including his 2017 election to a third seven-year term after a referendum to extend limits on his term—a referendum that Rwandans had asked for—the country has indeed developed, even thrived. Poverty rates are down, life expectancy is up, and there have been dramatic improvements in areas such as maternal and child mortality. Rwanda ranked first among forty-eight African countries in progress toward the UN's Millennium Development Goals and has set its sights on the new Sustainable Development Goals. The country has been working to slowly wean itself off foreign aid in favor of a robust private sector, trade, and investment. Today it has one of the fastest growing economies in East Africa and serves as a model for human development across the region.

Some of the biggest gains have been for women. Upward of three hundred thousand women were sexually violated, tortured, and mutilated during the genocide, systematically used as weapons of war. Women fought alongside men in the Rwanda Patriotic Army to bring an end to the genocide, and in the aftermath, so many men had died or were incarcerated or in refugee camps that women bore a disproportionate burden to rebuild their homes, families, and country. Yet it also put women in a position to renegotiate their rights and roles, and they have progressed at a remarkable pace ever since.

Yet there is another side to the country. There is still work to do to enable more citizens, especially women, to thrive. I wanted the boys to see both sides of Rwanda, to experience its harshness and its beauty, beyond what could be gleaned from a two-week vacation. Listen and learn, I told them as we were packing to leave, form your own impressions of the people and country. I hoped they would gain a better appreciation for how and where they lived and the breadth of choice they had back home but took for granted, as so many of us do. I was shooting for more enlightened and engaged young men.

We were staying at Hotel des Milles Collines, also known as "Hotel Rwanda." In 1994, when the genocide against the Tutsi began, the hotel's Belgian owners abandoned Kigali—as did the diplomatic corps, international aid groups, and most foreign governments. The movie version of the story is dramatic, but in truth, it was a handful of UN soldiers, not the hotel manager himself, who kept the Interhamwe (a Hutu paramilitary group that committed the genocide) at bay, enabling the survival of more than a thousand Tutsis and moderate Hutus who had taken shelter at the hotel.

Other than a dorsal fin–shaped water sculpture engraved with the words *never again* on the edge of the hotel's parking lot, there was almost nothing to remind us about the 1994 events. The hotel now caters to upscale tourists and business people interested in a manageable African experience. The night we arrived, a local cover band was playing kitschy Afro-American pop music at the thatched-roof, poolside tiki bar. Congolese kuba cloths hung decoratively from the high wood-beam rafters above the noisy and crowded bar. The three boys, glassy eyed with exhaustion, observed the colorful, merry scene from our third-floor balcony. I couldn't imagine what they must have been thinking—how different this all looked from Bethesda.

That night, Eli had a tough time settling. Perhaps the most sensitive of all our boys, Eli suffered from intense separation anxiety. I knew he was apprehensive about Bill's leaving and my having to travel for work. Even with his brothers there, the uncertainty of being apart and alone made him feel unsafe. It had been like that from the beginning. He was also facing a scary time of transition—his first year of high school. He was the one I was most worried about.

In the dark of the hotel room, our suitcases and duffle bags heaped in a corner, I realized with sudden panic just how much I was asking of them, forcing them to jump into this vastly new environment. As usual, I'd rushed in without thinking any of this through. Bill would be leaving soon, and I'd be working full time, which meant taking trips away from the boys. I kept my growing fear under wraps, but I think they could sense my anxiety.

Remember to breathe, I told myself, as I had on so many occasions, in the field and at home, when reality seemed too daunting. "Just take it one day at a time."

We rose early on our first morning, still groggy, and headed to the bustling commercial district in search of furniture for our empty rental house. Downtown Kigali's congested streets were already awash with shoppers, professionals, and day laborers. We passed street sweepers in bright green jumpers, smartly dressed workers on the way to their offices, women sellers in vibrant African prints, some with babies swaddled around their backs, balancing baskets laden with mangoes and pineapples on their heads. Snippets of Kinyarwanda were barely audible above the din of passing motorbike taxis (motos) and blaring music emanating from long rows of narrow shops on both sides of the road. At some point, Kai leaned over and said: "Look at all the African Americans."

"Kai, they're not African Americans. They're Africans, hon," I replied.

"Ohhh," he said.

Hot and tired a few hours in, we finally found a small woodworking cooperative that made basic but well-made pine furniture. Interested in several pieces, we asked the furniture maker for his best price, one that we knew included the standard *muzungu*, or white person's, markup.

Bill and I had learned to negotiate together in marketplaces around the world through years of foreign travel. I mostly play bad cop to Bill's good. This was one of those moments when our natural, well-honed roles at home worked in our favor. After some back-and-forth number crunching, and a few strained looks between Bill and me, we concluded the deal. The boys, who hadn't seen us negotiate before, were fascinated.

"Wow. I didn't know you could do that," Eli said as we were leaving the shop.

"That's how it's done, E," Bill said. "The guy wouldn't have sold it to us if he didn't get the price he was looking for."

"Dad and I had to do this all the time in the former Soviet Union," I added, knowing that we both felt decidedly less team-like than we once did, despite our joint negotiating skills.

On our way back to the hotel, several aggressive street vendors approached us, peddling maps and magazines, flash drives, phone cards, belts, even knives. The boys glanced nervously at me, unsure what to do. Bill deferred, too. I was used to being on my own in the field. But it hit me that I would now be navigating this kind of situation regularly with my kids in tow, and it would all fall to me. "No, thank you," I said on our collective behalf as I protectively put an arm around Kai and hurried them all past. "Don't engage with these guys unless you want to buy something," I urged. It seemed like a teachable moment, though the same could be said on the streets of New York. It had to be overwhelming for them. Once we moved into our house in a real neighborhood, we would be away from the hustle.

Situated in a mixed neighborhood of locals and expatriates (expats) in a part of town called Nayutarama, our cream-colored stucco, tile-roofed rental sat on a paved road across from a grove of pines in an undeveloped valley where some neighbors had set up garden plots and were growing their own food. The Tanzanian Embassy had been renting out the house to successive embassy staff, who would simply pack up and leave when their postings were finished. Not far away was a neighborhood pool and tennis club, a shopping mall boasting a foreign exchange bureau, dry cleaner's, grocery, hair salon, and Bourbon Coffee, the Rwandan equivalent of Starbucks. While the woodland views from the front patio were lovely, I did worry about how my Rwandan colleagues would view things like this house. Maybe there was a major divide between local and international staff, but I didn't want to further it, to be one of *those* expats who come to Africa with oversized benefits packages and claim the best real estate. The house was not as big or ostentatious as some we'd seen, but it was not exactly a hardship post.

Bill, as usual, handled the logistics around the move. A field organizer by training, he was in full campaign mode—problem identification, strategy, tactics, resource requirements. He seemed to enjoy figuring out how to make everything work, although the house didn't come with a single appliance. In the kitchen were a few wood-veneer cabinets and a basic sink, above which was a window with a view of the water tank and clothesline on the narrow back patio. The living room was bright and open, though, with freshly painted white walls, but it also stood empty except for three tiny, speedy lizards, who the boys quickly nicknamed Alpha, Beta, and Omega, and a few bloated cockroaches accustomed to having the place to themselves.

That night, with the furniture yet to arrive, we pulled our bare mattresses into the common room and slept side by side. Having Bill and the boys there, sprawled out around me, was comforting. It made me feel safe. It was a wonder they still wanted to be near me after how I had behaved in the previous months. Eli stirred and I recalled how I had railed when, in the midst of the CEO search process, he had showed me a half-baked writing assignment, full of misspellings and incomplete sentences. "What the hell, E," I had said. "There's no way you could have read this over. If you had, you'd see that it's crap. Come on, buddy!" At the time, I was startled by my harshness, by the vicious words that had come out of my mouth, but I hadn't been able to stop myself. Eli recoiled, his eyes filled with tears, and slunk away. They all did. Instead of the normal morning banter getting the kids up and out the door for school, or taking turns sharing our day around the dinner table as usual, Bill and the boys scattered when I was nearby. I had been driving my family away.

Planning for this massive change had been an excellent distraction, keeping me from falling into a deeper funk, but I wondered now if I'd simply exchanged one emotional rollercoaster for another. If it was even possible to make things right. I'd been having little moments of both panic and elation about settling into a routine without Bill, just the boys and me. Bill would be returning to the US in about two weeks, and I would be back to work full time after the weekend. Fortunately, that night my concerns only lasted as long as I could keep my eyes open.

The next morning, we climbed the steep hill to the main road and walked the mile or so to the shopping center that housed Bourbon Coffee, a common meeting place in Kigali. Located on the third floor, the coffee house had a pleasant outside balcony with a hillside view that would soon become a post-weekend-morning-run tradition. In addition to serving locally grown coffee and tea (the country's two main export crops) and a decent breakfast, Bourbon had a fairly reliable internet connection, which at the time was hard to come by.

Breakfast was followed by a trip to T-2000, the Rwandan equivalent of Wal-Mart, where we loaded up on silverware, plates, glasses, bedding, towels, mosquito nets, a few pots and pans, cleaning supplies, and a white plastic table and chair set for the front patio. By the end of that day, we had installed local satellite television and bottled gas to fuel our tiny new cook stove, the kind you might find in an RV or studio apartment.

The house had a few problems from the beginning. The water pressure was weak, the showers didn't work properly, and some of the toilets didn't flush. Power was intermittent, and there was no internet connection. The area was quiet and woodsy, though, and everywhere we needed to go was walkable: my office; a few restaurants off the main road; the shopping mall, where a constant swarm of motos gathered in pursuit of passengers; and the International School of Kigali (ISK), the boys' new school. My only concern was about the boys crossing the busy streets. Pedestrians never seemed to have the right-of-way, even in crosswalks.

Over that first week, the boys were still adjusting to their new environment. Though they had all been excited about the move, they were admittedly a bit "freaked out" now that we were here. Kai, our blondish, not-quite teenager, was great all day but got anxious around bedtime. He'd been crawling into bed with me every night, relegating Bill to Kai's slim twin bed in his room down the hall. Eli had trouble sleeping, too, probably a combination of jet lag and anxiety. That one didn't deal easily with change. It was a lot to take in, even for Sam. Naturally self-possessed, Sam was the only one who had prepared for the move by reading several books on Rwanda. Sam, like his father, had worn glasses from the age of five. He liked to take things apart, figure out how they worked. He wanted to understand and asked lots of questions, largely about the genocide.

I understood what it meant to be away from friends and family, everything familiar. I hoped they would feel better once school started and they met some of their new classmates and we began to develop a routine. Eli, whose thick curly hair and facial features most resembled mine, needed constant reassurance. "Don't worry, bud. It's gonna be fine," I said, but I had no idea whether it was helping. I'd taken a couple of days off to set up the house but was still working a few hours while Bill was focused on troubleshooting multiple problems; our move was the equivalent of a weather emergency. Mostly we tried to stay out of each other's way. Kai, thankfully, still had his sense of humor. After going out in his Barcelona #10 Messi jersey and being stopped by about thirty people to discuss soccer's "great one," he announced he would never wear his jersey in public again. Soccer was close to a national obsession in Rwanda.

Our first weekend in Kigali, Sam and I took the first of many runs together in the neighborhood, something we started when he joined the cross-country team at school, though I'd been at it since my teens. Beyond sheer physical release, running had long been a calming outlet for me, helping to relieve anxiety, restore perspective. The silence was precious; a chance to think things through away from life's challenges and distractions. In addition to that, we had already started to prepare to climb Mount Kilimanjaro later in the year, and we needed to train.

The early morning was clear, cool, and sunny as we ran along the sand-colored brick sidewalk toward the golf course at the end of the long road. We passed women street sweepers in neon green safety vests using handmade stick brooms to remove debris from the sidewalks and gutters, a backbreaking job done almost exclusively by women; a couple of clay tennis courts and a vast swath of blue corrugated metal shielding an active construction site, one of many in this fast growing country; a block of partially built apartment complexes next to several mansionesque gated and barbed-wired homes, hotels, and chanceries, all with luxuriant, well-kept gardens. Traffic was light then, and the chatter and song of unseen birds in the red and yellow flowering trees filled our ears. We saw a few other runners, but we must have been something of a novelty, given the stares in our direction.

We also noticed that several of our neighbors were out before the start of *umuganda*, or community service day, held on the last Saturday morning of every month. *Umuganda* had its roots in Rwandan culture, predating colonization, where friends and neighbors were called upon to help those in need with large tasks like farming or house building. Today participation in *umuganda* is mandatory for all Rwandans as part of the country's reconciliation and rebuilding efforts. Businesses remained closed and streets emptied during *umuganda*: motorists found on the road could be stopped and questioned by the police.

We decided to participate in *umuganda* as a family. We had always been service oriented and were eager to make inroads in our new community. It was good for Bill and me, too; we were at our best when we were doing for others. The five of us walked the paved road to the meet-up spot nearby, passing men and boys walking down the street with machetes and hoes casually thrown over their shoulders. I gasped involuntarily at the sight. These implements were for hacking weeds or cultivation, of course, but on a total gut level, knowing how they were once used to hack life and limbs in the genocide—when going to work meant going off to kill for the day—made it almost impossible to look at these former weapons benignly.

We joined the neighborhood group of about fifty men and women and were welcomed with a handshake by the local district "coordinator" who, coincidentally, worked for a University of Maryland HIV/AIDS and TB project. He explained that after this month's work project, there would be a community meeting to discuss the upcoming school year and security issues for the neighborhood. Then we got started on the field-clearing work, the five of us taking turns with a borrowed machete to hack at the overgrown brush. Our new neighbors mostly stood around and watched, humored by our earnestness. Within ten minutes, our miserable attempts to whack the brush away began to look like a *Saturday Night Live* skit.

We shrugged and lay down our machete, choosing instead to pick up trash, putting small bits of paper, plastic water bottles, and other garbage into neat piles for collection, just as we had done on Potomac River cleanup days along the canal near our home. There was a surprising amount of litter on the side paths and trails, given that most public spaces were litter free. No one came to help out, but we didn't think much about it until one woman, who had been watching, approached, clearly agitated. She kicked over our neat piles of trash, re-scattering it everywhere. We assumed that she, like the others, was poking fun at us. But confused, and a little embarrassed, we finished up quickly and walked back to the house.

A few months later, while running along the golf course road—none of the roads and streets had names or numbers at the time—I would suddenly understand why the woman didn't want us to handle all that trash. The trail we were clearing served as a bush toilet and the trash had been used as toilet paper. "Guvnor—there's a cleanup on the poop deck!" Kai would've said in a perfect-pitch British accent, with his usual wit. Knowing him, he would find this both disgusting and hysterical. I probably shouldn't tell him about it. The woman who re-scattered our trash was trying to stop us from humiliating ourselves. It had been a kind and generous act, one of many we would be recipients of during our time here.

Just a little over a week after we arrived, the boys began school and I went back to work; Bill did his best to make us functional. A couple of good hires helped a lot. Back home we'd had a series of nannies as well as someone to help with house cleaning and yard work so I felt comfortable enough with the support, and grateful for it. It was customary for expat families living in Africa to have staff but, as more of a transplant from the US, Bill and I made a point of covering these costs ourselves.

Joseph, the gardener, came with the house. He was single, in his late twenties or early thirties, with a nearly shaved head and thin mustache. In most houses for rent to expats or successful Rwandans, a caretaker or houseman lived next to the front gate. That was Joseph. He had lived beside our green front gate for eleven years, since the house was constructed. Joseph's first job in Kigali had been to guard the construction material and equipment as the house was being built. And so, Joseph the gardener was also Joseph the "guard." His only weapon was the machete he used to maintain the yard's hedges and flowering shrubs, including the one banana tree on the property. He also grew his own vegetables on a garden plot above our house. He seemed to have a life of his own in the neighborhood. Friends of his would often drop by, and he paid a family up the street to prepare his meals for him, a routine that continued even when we took over the house.

He was a kind and gentle soul who spoke only a few words of English. Kai was disappointed at first that we didn't use one of the uniformed security firms employed by other expatriate families. He knew all of them by name: RGL, Excel, TopSec, Agespro, Intersec, KK, Warrior, and Fode. But he grew to love our own J-Security. We all felt better, safer with him there.

In his daily uniform—blue jumpsuit, gumboots, and red stocking cap with an Arsenal Football Club logo, a favorite team in Rwanda, Joseph would greet us with a "Murning" in a low voice, then set to work washing the car inside and out, watering the plants, hosing down the patio. He seemed to favor any job that involved water. "Tell Joseph to turn off the hose," one of the boys quickly learned to yell down when their shower stream turned to a trickle, indignant about the finite water supply. *Welcome to the developing world,* I thought.

Joseph's tiny room by the gate resembled a jail cell with one small cracked window covered by metal bars. Its only amenity was electricity. He slept on a stack of cardboard with a quilt on top. One of his few possessions was a small wooden stool that doubled as a nightstand. Another was his cell phone. He listened to the radio on his phone day and night—music, soccer matches, Radio La Benevolencija, which broadcasted a hugely popular radio soap opera called Musekeweya, meaning "New Dawn." The storyline dealt with pre- and post-genocidal themes like hate speech and violence, healing and reconciliation.

"Why do we sleep on mattresses and not Joseph?" Kai asked. He said it made him uncomfortable that Joseph didn't have a real bed, so Bill went out and bought him a mattress. Joseph was shocked when he saw it. No one had ever given him something like that before. It was a small gesture, but we made sure he knew it was inspired by Kai. Kai was just as pleased as Joseph. He liked that he had righted a wrong.

Our nanny/shopper/cook was named Innocent, a common, telling name in the country. We found her through a woman who advertised "nanny training and placement services" on the Kigali Life website, a vital source of information for expats living in Kigali, or so we were told. We met at her pop-up office, which seemed to double as a small travel agency. She claimed to do thorough background and reference checks on all of "her girls." We were inclined to believe her, as her husband was a highly placed officer in the military.

The boys didn't require babysitting, just someone to keep an eye out while I was at work or traveling. Innocent fit the bill: She spoke fluent English and was willing to spend the night while I traveled out of the country. We learned that she had spent the genocide in Burundi, where she had family. After that she had lived in South Africa with another family, taking care of their kids, so she was an experienced nanny. Yet underneath her competence was an aloofness that was hard to warm to, an indication that this might not be her preferred employment.

Still, everything seemed to be going well, better than expected, in fact. The boys loved their new school. In its third year and in the midst of the accreditation process, the young school offered a blended curriculum based on American and international standards. The hundred or so ISK families hailed from all over the world, including many other African nations. The students were, for the most part, the offspring of diplomats and development types who had been posted to Kigali.

Kai said he liked the smaller classes and organized soccer matches, and the chance to meet kids from so many other countries. Sam was taking a photography class and practicing his new skills on Joseph, who was a willing subject. He loved having his picture taken and insisted that Sam print out each photograph for him; these were probably the first pictures he'd ever seen of himself. The twins were taking classes together for the first time since preschool, after which we'd intentionally separated them. It helped that there were only five kids in their chemistry class.

Kai, ever sociable and outgoing, was making the transition to the new school with ease. He walked into the house that very first day raving about his new classmate, the son of Sudan's ambassador to Rwanda. When we met his mom at the Parent Teacher Organization's annual ice cream social a few days later, she told us she couldn't bear the thought of Kai walking home, so she'd nabbed him in her four-door Mercedes.

The week's highlight was Kai's play date with his new friend. We worried all afternoon that he would mention my work in South Sudan, the other Sudan, or disclose that Bill was a leader of the Save Darfur campaign and had once been arrested at a Darfur protest in front of the Sudanese Embassy in Washington, DC (evidently the ambassador was a deputy there at the time). We were invited in to meet the family when we went to pick up Kai, and the embassy residence was stunning: high ceilings, major artwork, top-end furniture imported from Dubai, a kitchen with two sub-zero freezers and granite countertops, a sauna and infinity pool that overlooked Kigali. The ambassador made quite an entrance down the spiral staircase in his flowing white robe and warmly greeted us. And his wife could not have been more hospitable. She gave us a tour of their home, pointing out the art and artifacts she'd brought with her from Sudan, offering us homemade snacks and fresh hibiscus juice served in crystal goblets.

There was an element of irony to our visit, given Sudan's wretched history of war and genocide. The former president of Sudan was an indicted war criminal. This would be just one of many incongruous experiences we would have in Africa. I wondered how different the boys' experiences this year would be from my own. Aside from the time Bill and I spent in Russia, we hadn't lived outside of the United States before, outside of our suburban enclave, where the boys were shuttled between in-school and out-of-school activities that consumed their busy lives. In Bethesda—one of the country's most educated and affluent communities—they'd never had to fight for anything. Their lives were predictable, cushy. They were safe. In many countries like Sudan, kids did not get a childhood at all. Boys their age were already men. Our boys didn't even think like that. They were still kids.

3

The Work

Though my time with the organization was uncertain beyond the year, I grounded myself in the place and started to settle into my new role. I liked the early morning walk from our house to the office compound in a part of town called Kimihurura, watching the city come alive as I made my way along Kigali's crowded streets and sidewalks. Both the walk and drive there meant dodging heavy traffic. The two-storied building sat on a long, steep cobblestone street, one of only a handful in the city. Expats flocked to the area in spite of its pot-holed, dirt roads for its multiple restaurants, American-style fitness club, and spacious gated homes.

A freestanding metal sign with the organization's logo, an orange circle above a forest-green Nike-like swoosh meant to symbolize a woman's head and outstretched arms, was visible from the top of the road. The sign had become so familiar that it barely registered as I slipped through the painted metal door into the brick enclosed compound that morning. A couple of the drivers were there, readying themselves and their vehicles for a long day in the field with the trainers. I greeted them on my way into the building and up the short flight of stairs to my office, one they'd kindly freed up for me by shifting a few people around. Several early-bird colleagues raised their heads and bade me good morning as I walked past, not quite used to me being there yet.

The staff, numbering close to fifty with the life-skills trainers, was warm and welcoming, and delighted that I'd brought the family with me to Rwanda.

There was Teddy, who headed up monitoring and evaluation; Clemence, the lead on income generation; and Joie Claire, who ran human resources and admin. They had been with the organization for several years and seemed equally committed to its mission. We'd gotten to know each other over regular visits to Rwanda. Joie Claire had taken on an interim leadership role during the search for a replacement country director. Others I knew less well—some of the more recent hires and junior staff.

My office was small but bright, with a view, through the covered porch, of the surrounding courtyard and gravel car park. Antonina, the new Rwanda country director, had also just joined the team, having built her career in strategic management and microfinance. Pretty and elegant with shoulder-length hair, Antonina was a single mom with an adorable young son. She was Rwandan but had lived most of her life in Kenya. We were acclimating together.

Living in the country, as opposed to visiting it, was an altogether different experience. I liked being closer to the action, to the work. Because I didn't have to cram in meetings and site visits over one or two weeks, I could be more thoughtful and deliberate with my time, really dig in. I'd already begun to delve into the question of legal marriage—a serious issue for the women who participated in the organization's year-long social and economic empowerment program. It was clear that it was a source of multiple domestic conflicts, including gender-based violence. Many of these women had lived with their "husbands" for years without the protections afforded by a civil union, which meant they had no legal standing on issues such as land registration and property rights if the relationship ended, nor did they have a say when it came to child custody and inheritance. Even obtaining a loan was difficult for "unofficially married" women.

I went with Teddy and one of the trainers to the Gasabo District's Ndera Sector on the outskirts of Kigali to discuss this issue with a few program participants and take down their stories. I'd been doing that for years as part of my job—collecting the personal stories of the women who were ready and willing to share. Those interviews were a means of data collection and an important part of program monitoring and evaluation. But it was more than that. So many survivors had never spoken about their lives, about what had happened to them. The chance to do so in a safe space was a form of therapy, a way to break that silence. For me, their stories were a window to another world, a far crueler one, where women were pushed to the margins or marginalized on an everyday basis. I had notebooks full of their stories, close to a decades' worth, from all of my visits to the field.

There was Remzije in Kosovo, who became the head of household when her husband died after the war. Until his death, she had never left home without a male relative at her side. There was Elizabeth in South Sudan, who took her marriageable daughter away so that she could continue going to school. When she told the authorities that she didn't know where her daughter was, they beat her, broke her leg and four ribs and threw her in jail for a year. And Habiba from Bosnia, a thirty-year-old mother of three who lost her husband to war. She described herself as "hopeless" because she didn't think she could learn a skill and support her family.

Other stories were sent in by the country offices each month. Evanne in Iraq lost her husband and father the same night while trying to flee the bombing in Baghdad. When their car was attacked, Evanne had to drag both her husband and her father away from the car, and in the process, some of her husband's internal parts were splayed in the street. He was the first to die, and her father died soon after. Evanne, grief stricken, was left to raise their six-month-old son alone. And Safeta from Bosnia. She lived a comfortable life with her husband and his parents before the war, awaiting the birth of their first child. When the city fell under siege, her husband was taken as a prisoner of war and forced into hard labor. One night Safeta's once-friendly neighbors-turned-soldiers kidnapped her and brought her to an empty house where they repeatedly raped and tortured her. One of them suggested they kill her, but another said no, that she would kill herself. After she was released, the only thing that kept Safeta alive was her infant son. "I had to live for him."

There were so many more. Christina in Rwanda, who watched as her husband and five children were killed with a machete in the genocide; Fadila in Iraq, who walked her children to and from school every day, two hours each way, because it was too unsafe for them to go alone; Azema in Bosnia, who lost everything when Serb forces took over her home and forced her and her children onto the streets; Zulatkha in Afghanistan, who lived in a crowded storefront with no windows or sanitation. She had nowhere else to go.

Philomena from Nigeria. Adele from Congo. Hanifah from Afghanistan. These were only the stories that had come to the surface. There had to be hundreds of thousands more. Though the grim details differed from country to country, conflict to conflict, woman to woman, a consistent thread ran through each of them. All of these women, in one way or another, had managed to survive. Remzije formed an association with other program graduates and lobbied the local government to bring Heifer International to her village and give each woman a cow, a vital source of food and income; Elizabeth was rescued by her daughter and landed a decent job cleaning airplanes, making one hundred dollars a month; Habiba made a living doing piecemeal knitting and embroidery. I felt as if I knew these women through their raw and intimate stories.

I had several stories in hand when we arrived in Rwanda from women I had met and interviewed before. I had also read the stories my colleagues had collected in Rwanda and hoped to be able to meet a few of the women who were new to me. I planned to write a series of blogs about their lives, hoping to raise both awareness and support. On a personal level, though, I was starting to think about story collection in a different way. Now that we were living in Rwanda, I thought maybe if I could sit and talk with some of these women, learn more about their perspectives and choices, it might help to bring me back to myself.

Teddy had arranged for us to meet two women, Shantel and Lydia, inside the sector's compound, a sprawling set of single-story brick offices that housed the sector's administrative services and officials. When we arrived, the two women were standing in the grass courtyard. The three of us and a trainer/interpreter followed Teddy, who walked with a slight limp, into a small room on the compound where we could sit without being disturbed.

Shantel, a soft-spoken woman in a pale yellow dress, told me that she had been living with her "husband" for two years, raising their three-year-old daughter. When she tried to ask him about formalizing their marriage, he said he was "still thinking about it." Lydia, wearing a colorful headscarf, had also been living as "husband and wife" with her partner for four years. They had a son together. She thought of them as a family. She understood that without a legal marriage, she would have no recourse if her husband decided to officially marry or cohabitate with another woman. Lydia added that victims of domestic violence who were legally married could report the abuse to community leaders, who would take action. Without a legal marriage in place, those same leaders would do nothing.

Lydia was right. In the absence of a civil union, the women could be viewed as concubines or visitors in the home. Unmarried women also ran greater health risks: potential exposure to multiple sex partners and increased chances of disease and domestic abuse.

Legal marriage—described in the Rwandan constitution as a civil union between one man and one woman—had become a government priority in recent years. Yet some men were still resistant because of the freedom and protections afforded to legally married women. As civil unions were still considered to be relatively new—having been legalized in 1999—traditional men often balked at the idea of no longer being free to have as many "wives" as they wanted.

Legal marriage could be cost prohibitive for poor women and couples because of the custom of gifting cows, cash, or other assets to the woman's family as a dowry, and the obligation to host expensive engagement parties and wedding celebrations. Most young men could not afford to build a house for their new brides, which made it even more difficult to marry.

The issue was widespread. In the Gasabo District's Ndera Sector alone, 40 percent of the adult population were not legally married. This was not by choice, we learned, for the majority of women. We also knew there was strong resistance to legal marriage in other communities around the country. The executive secretary of the Ndera Sector acknowledged that while women were working to change traditional practices, it was an uphill battle that would take time.

The program addressed the issue by focusing on the benefits of legal marriage for women and men. Women learned about Rwandan family law and how to protect and claim their rights. For many women, the majority of whom were in their thirties and forties and considered themselves "married," this was the first time they understood that they actually had rights, and for some, that they didn't have to accept violence as a part of life. Men learned the advantages of creating stronger families and protecting their children.

To draw attention to the legal-marriage question, we asked the mayor of Gasabo to consider cosponsoring a mass wedding ceremony as one of the district's accountability week events that year. Accountability week was intended as a forum for development partners to showcase their tangible contributions to the communities they serve. He agreed.

The very next week, we attended a community meeting in which women were encouraged to bring their partners. Held in the courtyard at the sector's offices, the event drew more than one hundred women and about twenty men who came to hear the sector's legal affairs officer and other leaders extol the benefits of legal marriage and refute common objections—men's freedom and control, the expense, and inheritance rights.

"Women are doing everything," the officer said, addressing the men. "If she were to receive pay for what she has done for you and the family, how much would you pay her?" I watched the men, who were mostly standing on the periphery, shift uncomfortably.

He went on. "Men think women will undermine them if they are legally married, or that it's expensive to get married. But it's not about money, it's about rights. It's about character. Children get their rights through the legal marriage. Give your children a better future." He paused, then asked, "Who's ready?"

Twenty-one couples registered to become legally married that day. One of the couples, Francoise and Fidele, explained their decision: "We have been 'married' for nine years and have two children together. We've wanted to do it but thought it was too expensive," said Fidele. He added that it was important to "give value to himself and his wife" and enable his children to inherit should anything happen. Francoise said that once she is officially married, she can "feel empowered and enjoy her rights." Mediatrice and Donat, another couple convinced of the benefit of legal marriage that day, thought they would have more opportunities to live a better life as a family. "It will bring us closer," said Mediatrice.

Back in the office after the community meeting, I couldn't help but feel the personal irony under the surface of what I was working on. Bill was leaving in another week. We both knew the next several months were going to be difficult, potentially more than just difficult. I don't think either of us was sure of where we stood with the other. Unlike the women of the Gasabo District, unlike so many women in Africa and in other parts of the world, I was fortunate not to need marriage to assure my rights. But did I even want marriage? There was something about the institution itself that made me feel, I don't know, contained. Bill and I had had our problems over the years, and yet our marriage had also made me feel empowered at times, and it *had* given us more opportunities to live a better life as a family. I had never before felt so conflicted.

4

Activists in Debt

When I was twenty-two, a year before meeting Bill, I left Oregon for good. Portland was great, it was home, but the thought of rejoining the family I had escaped from after college made it impossible to stay. I threw everything I owned into my light-blue Ford Granada, a hand-me-down from Mom, and drove across the country to Washington, DC, for an internship with a non-profit working on human rights in Central America. I'd always been drawn to helping others. As a kid, I sold Van Dyne chocolate bars door to door to send underprivileged kids to summer camp, collected canned foods for the hungry with my little red wagon, raised money for "Jerry's kids." In my teens, I led a boycott of Nestlé for marketing expensive baby formula to women in the developing world, claiming it was better than breast milk. Every cause was my cause. With the house often in turmoil because of Dad's fighting with Mom, or with all of us, I'd channeled my energy into helping others in need. It felt good, validating, to be able to tackle problems bigger than my own.

Two months into the internship, I was hired by an organization called Peace Links to educate women about the consequences of the nuclear arms race. Peace Links was my first real experience with purposeful work. It paid the rent and little else, but I loved it. While there, I was invited to join a group of women leaders in Geneva for the first Reagan-Gorbachev summit. We went to counter the ultraconservative Phyllis Schlafly crowd, with their mink coats and pro-SDI (Strategic Defense Initiative) buttons, and to ensure that women's voices were well represented in the arms control debates. Shaking General Secretary Gorbachev's hand only confirmed what I knew in my heart—when it came to world peace, I did not want to be a bystander.

Bill was in DC working as a field organizer with a consumer watchdog group founded by Ralph Nader. We were set up by his favorite aunt, who ran a business with my sister Laura's mother-in-law in Portland. She thought we were both "activist types" and would have a lot in common. He called one day and invited me to a lunch he was hosting for Rosh Hashanah, the Jewish New Year. We connected immediately, though he accused me right off the bat of making a "chaotic" salad. When he casually asked me to join him and a few friends at the movies a few nights later, I accepted but failed to show up, having made other plans. He persisted, and we had our second date ten days later on Yom Kippur, the Jewish Day of Atonement. After breaking our fast over pizza at Armand's, we shared our first kiss on the Calvert Street Bridge. He was a nice guy, a great guy even, and I had dated enough to know the difference. As predicted, we had a lot in common. Both of us were middle children, raised Jewish in middle- to upper-middle-class homes in Oregon and Oklahoma. We had a shared passion for exotic travel. There was a comfort and ease to the relationship from the very beginning.

During our quick courtship, we visited his parents, who were living at the time in Puerto Rico, where his father owned a leather-goods factory. We found that we traveled well together, enjoyed the same things—snorkeling, tennis, a quiet walk through the rainforest and finding that *one* hole-in-the-wall restaurant that served *real* local food. At home, we spent weekends on day-long hikes or biking around the city, the shrill song of the seventeen-year cicadas as our backdrop, or wandering around Eastern Market on Capitol Hill, or the Italian Market in Philadelphia, where Bill was working to launch a home heating-oil co-op. Bill had learned to cook alongside a friend, a chef in Paris, and prepared luscious, elaborate dinners for us—fresh pastas topped with creamy sauces and succulent, roasted meats. It felt like love. It felt like coming home, or what home ought to feel like.

On the drive down to DC from New York, where we'd spent the winter holidays, we talked about traveling somewhere neither of us had been, maybe to South America. The conversation evolved, and the trip became a honeymoon destination. We became engaged in his apartment later that night, on New Year's Eve, just three short months after my chaotic salad.

A year later, the theme of our rehearsal dinner was "Activists in Debt," so named because our two jobs at the time gave us a combined income of about $28,000. The program for the evening depicted Bill standing on a soapbox gesticulating and me carrying a placard that read "Peace Not War" with an arrow pointed toward the USSR. We were married in my hometown synagogue in the suburbs of Portland and spent our three-week honeymoon traveling around Brazil. I was twenty-five, and Bill was a few years older. We were young, idealistic, full of ourselves and of life.

In 1987, the year we married, I started traveling in earnest to the Soviet Union, escorting groups on experiential tours for a start-up in exchange for the paid flight over and field experience. Still, I had grandiose visions of changing the world. I joined an organization called International Peace Walk, which paid even less than Peace Links, and later participated in two month-long American-Soviet Peace Walks. The first was a 450-mile walk from Leningrad to Moscow. The walkers were 230 peace-loving Americans and 200 Soviets, hand selected by the government's Soviet Peace Committee. Over the carefully choreographed walk, billed as a citizen-led effort to build bridges of peace amid an escalating nuclear arms race, we lived in tent cities along the road to Moscow. We walked up to fifteen miles a day through remote towns and villages where they had never actually seen an American, except on *Dallas* reruns on state-controlled television. We were greeted as heroes by the waving, cheering crowds lining the streets, and were offered bread and salt, a custom of hospitality.

The Cold War, like the genocide in Rwanda, had also been fueled by divisive, state-sponsored propaganda, echoed strongly by the media. With large numbers of nuclear weapons trained in each other's direction, bent on our mutually assured destruction, Americans and Soviets had to see the enemy as an implacable one. A public opinion poll at the time showed the majority of Americans believed that Soviet people loved their children less. Loved their children less? The Cold War played on our fear of those who are different from us, our fear of otherness, and was used by both sides to present something as abhorrent as nuclear war as a viable option.

We knew that some of the Soviet walkers were informants and that the KGB was monitoring all of our movements, but we didn't care; it actually made us prouder. We felt as though we were making a difference. The day we marched into Red Square and formed a peace circle across from the Kremlin, we believed we were making history. The walk culminated in a Fourth of July rock concert at Izmailovo Stadium in Moscow, a first, featuring the likes of Carlos Santana, James Taylor, the Doobie Brothers, and Bonnie Raitt.

"I bet you've never seen a woman do this in the Soviet Union," bellowed Raitt, jamming on her guitar in front of a wildly cheering crowd.

The second walk took place in Ukraine, from Odessa to Kiev, the following year. Ukraine for Bill and me is home country. Bill's Grandpa Louis, his Zaide, was born in Odessa and my Grandma Lilly in Ekaterinoslav, now called Dnipropetrovsk. They lived a mere eight hours apart by car. Fleeing her *shtetl* before the start of World War I, Lilly emigrated with her mother to the United States when she was seven years old, traveling via Ellis Island to Portland, where she had a cousin. Life was not easy in America. It was difficult to assimilate. Her mother, who suffered from depression, finally committed suicide at age sixty, jumping out of a window at a Portland hospital.

Tough and opinionated, with a unique sense of style, Grandma Lilly was a working woman, a partner in my grandfather's wholesale business. Under five feet tall with large breasts and thin ankles, her daily smear of fire-engine-red lipstick stood in sharp contrast to her tanned, deeply lined face. I adored her. This walk through Ukraine felt personal—it was for my grandmother.

In 1989, Bill and I walked through Checkpoint Charlie into East Berlin, when the Berlin Wall was coming down. I hacked at it myself with a rented sledgehammer. Those small chips of painted concrete are among my most treasured possessions—each of them a little symbol of freedom. They meant the world was opening up, shifting, moving away from proxy wars and "us versus them." They meant there was hope. Both of us felt fortunate to have a front-row seat.

Later, in 1992, Bill quit his job as field director at People for the American Way to move with me to Moscow, where I was running an independent travel company while pursuing my graduate degree in Russian studies.

Under *glasnost* and *perestroika*—openness and change—everything was up for grabs, especially with *blat*, the word for influence or hard currency, cash. Land, state-run enterprises, oil, babies, you name it. Every Russian with a state job seemed to have a "joint venture" on the side. There was a host of jokes about the new Russians, a good number of them mobsters, who paid more for already expensive imports just for bragging rights. These were reckless days, the kind of days when you could just stick out your arm to flag down a car, any car, and a willing stranger would take you wherever you wanted to go for a few rubles.

Stunning, impeccably dressed prostitutes, who earned a great deal more in an evening than doctors, lawyers, and scientists earned in an average month, scoured the lobbies of Western hotels hoping to meet wealthy European or American *biznismani*, as dates or future husbands. Women had little room to define themselves, professionally or otherwise, in Russia's patriarchy, despite extraordinarily high education, literacy, and workforce participation rates. Women also carried the double burden of work inside and outside the home but, excepting prostitution, were mostly confined to lower paying professions.

Domestic violence against women, exacerbated by the prevalence of alcohol, was rampant. Vodka bottles still came with throw-away foil tops, despite Gorbachev's so-called alcohol ban. When people couldn't buy it, they made their own *samogon* (moonshine) with anything they could find, some of it deadly.

There was an odd cadre of academics, get-rich-quick scammers, and financial types looking to cash in on the change and instability. There were also the activists, including Bill and me.

The travel company's clients were venturesome Americans who shunned Intourist, the official state travel agency, in favor of a customized, off-the-grid living experience anywhere in the former Soviet Union. Hosts were paid in then hard-to-come-by dollars. Visitors came with their own agendas: to meet a professional counterpart or trace their family roots, conduct business or journey along the Trans-Siberian railway. One middle-aged traveler spent his entire homestay interviewing potential brides. The young women themselves wanted out, a chance at a better life, particularly in America.

While I negotiated planes, trains, and homestays, Bill combed the open-air ruble markets for fruits and vegetables or greeted guests and helped them change money on the black market. We were on our own private adventure, living on the edge and trying to make a difference.

In the first years of our marriage, we faced the challenges of long distance, and then of living together in Russia. After I completed my graduate degree, we spent another couple of months globetrotting around Eastern Europe, Greece, and the Middle East before heading home in time for the presidential election and my thirtieth birthday.

We returned to the US without money, work, or prospects. I'd quit the travel business after earning my degree in hopes of transitioning to development work, but I had yet to start paying off my student loans. And, with our credit cards maxed out, we were even more in debt.

Bill borrowed $10,000 from his father to launch his own public relations consulting business. While he was out hustling up clients, I volunteered a few days a week at President-elect Clinton's presidential transition office, answering phones and correspondence as I searched for work. Everyone there was talking about the developing crisis in Bosnia, and whether or not America should intervene. There were widespread reports of ethnic cleansing and of thousands of women being held in camps as sex slaves for Serbian soldiers.

It was in 1993, in the transition office, when I first learned about rape as a weapon of war, the same year Women for Women International was founded by Zainab Salbi and her then-husband Amjad. With the money they had been saving for a honeymoon, Zainab and Amjad traveled to Bosnia to help women held in "rape camps" begin to pick up the pieces of their shattered lives. They initially worked with seventeen rape victims, although they didn't see or treat them as victims; women to be pitied. To do so would be another way of robbing them of their dignity, according to Zainab. Instead, they viewed them as potential agents of change, capable of transforming their lives and, in turn, the lives of their families and communities. Each woman learned about her rights, received a small amount of cash and was matched with a sponsor-sister, a lifeline, in the United States.

It wasn't long before Counterpart International, a nonprofit organization focused on global development, asked me to travel to Ukraine to lead a new-project assessment, which led to a full-time position. Around the same time, just as his consulting practice was taking off, Bill was asked to join the new Clinton administration as head of the Office of Consumer Affairs at the United States Department of Agriculture. Both of us now had good jobs and steady paychecks, which we expected would lead to long and meaningful careers.

We began moving up the ladder. Bill left the USDA for a consulting firm, where he worked to advance national and international causes. He eventually acquired the firm with two long-term partners and became CEO. I progressed from project officer to executive vice president over ten years at Counterpart, focused mostly on helping women in the former Soviet Union make the difficult transition from a planned to a market economy.

But while our careers were on track, even thriving, we struggled almost from the beginning with our marriage. At least I did.

I saw firsthand how women in the former Soviet Union were dichotomized. They were either objectified as professionals or revered as mothers, a whore, or a socialist hero. There was no middle ground for women when it came to their personal and professional identities, no balance. I struggled with this, but even more so with the concept of being a wife, being the one responsible for so-called wifely duties like grocery shopping and cooking, when we were both working. I used to tell Bill that a baked potato and broccoli, my standard college meal, was fine for dinner. If he wanted something different, he could make it himself. Bill didn't seem to mind or push back much, claiming to be attracted by my unconventionality.

My attitude was a reaction to my image of marriage growing up. My parents had a common one for white families of their generation. Mom didn't attend college or work outside the home. Other than Dad's Sunday morning breakfasts and the occasional barbecue, she did everything around the house. I watched her struggle through the daily grind of caregiving for my siblings and me and cater to her thankless, belligerent husband. His contempt and lack of respect for her were obvious; he demeaned her constantly, at home and in public. To avoid being like her, the object of such enmity, I refused to even learn how to cook.

Though Bill did not impose them, I found myself in a constant battle against the invisible tethers of marriage. In graduate school, I would pretend to be single, either not wearing my wedding band or discreetly moving it to my right hand, when I went to class or out for beers with other students. It was the same when traveling abroad for work. "Geographically single," we called it at Counterpart. Most of my colleagues were still unattached, unencumbered. I wondered if getting married so early was a mistake. I couldn't wait to shake things up, do something that mattered. I didn't want to be constrained, even by a supportive husband, as I explored the world and my own potential.

"I've changed," I announced after one of those first trips to the Soviet Union. Bill had no idea what that meant. I just felt different, more conscious and alive from my experiences. I was only beginning to grasp the scope of my ambitions, but I had realized with startling certainty that those ambitions meant more to me than my marriage, than being Bill's wife, at that time.

Of course we fought, mostly about silly stuff. He complained about the burdens of my travel, how we could never talk about it because I was perpetually on a trip, recovering from a trip, or preparing for one. I complained about him being the most disorganized of organizers. His discarded clothes were stacked high in one corner or another; drawers were stuffed to overflowing with financial statements and misplaced records. Instead of trying to balance his checkbook, he would just close an account and start over. His weight was a more serious problem; both his father and grandfather had died early of heart disease. It would fluctuate, mainly up, until either he was so frustrated with himself or I said something hurtful. Then the cycle would start all over again.

Quick to ramp up like my father, I got loud and angry at the first sign of conflict. I could hear Dad yelling "stupid bitch" at my mom. So in the heat of an argument, I yelled at Bill. "Fucking asshole!" When I got loud, Bill got quiet and shut down.

These moments of rage were the most difficult to reconcile within myself. I had been on the other side of my father's outbursts, so I knew Bill found me intimidating at times, found my intensity overwhelming. At the time, I needed someone who wouldn't hesitate to call me out, to tell me when I'd gone too far, was too much. If not my husband, then who? I wanted him to stand up so that I could stand down. To give me the chance to be the softer one.

Still, there was a certain comfort, a refuge, in the sweet familiarity of our rituals: lingering over a vodka rocks after work in our favorite pair of cushy green chairs by the corner window, the ones that once belonged to Bill's parents; our Sunday morning banter over veggie omelets and the *New York Times*. Sometimes that felt like enough.

We had intentionally waited to have a family so we could focus first on building our two careers. But by the time I was in my early thirties, seeing other happy couples and young families made me desperate for more. I wanted that, all of it, steadfast in my determination to have it all, in spite of our problems.

After more than a year of failed attempts, I finally went to the ob-gyn and, following exploratory surgery, was diagnosed with endometriosis. They put me put on a nasty, menopause-inducing drug that made it impossible to get pregnant or pursue infertility treatments, and I was a tangle of night sweats, mood swings, sleeplessness, and depression.

Our relationship went from tolerable to worse. I asked myself if it was worth it. It might be better to cut my losses and walk away clean, I thought at the time. Maybe it was a sign, a blessing even, that no children were involved. Still, there was something, a stick-to-itiveness or simply the fear of failure, that kept us both hanging in there.

Completing the course of treatment but still not pregnant, we decided as a last resort to see a fertility specialist. With two painful and expensive cycles of fertility drugs, we got the news that I was pregnant at last. With twins! Both of us were overjoyed. Ready to leave the anguish of the past few years behind, we committed ourselves to starting fresh.

Rwanda wasn't the first time our marriage had been in trouble. But now, at this critical transition point and having moved my family halfway around the world, the same questions were hounding me.

Over the years, Bill and I had learned how to organize our hectic lives, but in practice, that meant that we would organize around each other. He was coming while I was going and vice versa. "Us time" was very hard to find, and when we did find it, there was so much pent-up emotion that we fought. I had so often blamed Bill, or my past, for these ugly blots in our marriage, but it was no longer enough to explain away my anger. I hoped this year in Rwanda was the shake-up we needed. But in truth, I had no idea if this move was more about me or him or us.

With the house almost set up, and Bill about to leave, I once again thought that a change of scenery would do us all some good. Still without a car, we rented a beat-up Toyota RAV4 for the day from affable and entrepreneurial Patrick, a self-proclaimed "fixer" for expats, a man who could help navigate the local bureaucracy and acquire all kinds of goods and services. Patrick, like many, fled the country as a teen to escape the rising ethnic tension and violence; he was one of the lucky ones with family in Kenya. His mother was Tutsi and his father Kenyan, so he grew up speaking Kinyarwanda and Swahili. He'd returned after a decade in Kenya, married another returnee, and now ran several businesses with his wife.

We got a late start leaving Kigali and headed north for the two-hour drive to Volcanoes National Park, which borders Virunga National Park in Congo and Mgahinga Gorilla National Park in Uganda. The park is home to five hundred of the world's eight hundred remaining mountain gorillas, made famous through the work of Dian Fossey in the 1960s to 1980s.

The paved road out of town passed through a busy commercial district, past the Nyabugogo bus station, a major transit point in and out of the city. A throng of weekend pedestrians picked their way through the congested streets, weaving in and around the traffic. We joined the dense, slow-moving pack of cars, motos, and overloaded trucks, impatient to get moving but eagerly taking in the sights.

The scenery opened up once we cleared the area. We passed women walking on the side of the road carrying large baskets of pineapples and dingy yellow water containers balanced on their heads (water collection was almost always a female responsibility) and young men from the villages with overstuffed hemp bags slung over their shoulders on their way to the city market. The metal-roofed houses gleamed in the midmorning sun as we passed a lone biker in a racing jersey, a children's pickup soccer game in one of the few open fields, and twenty or so men in army fatigues waiting in the back of a pickup truck fitted with bench seats.

Climbing through the steep mountain passes afforded us views of bustling village life alternating with lush, vertically terraced farms and banana groves—a rich patchwork quilt of earthy greens and browns blanketing the many hills. I had been to Rwanda several times before and seen a little of the countryside, but this was the first time we were seeing it as a family, the first time I was experiencing Rwanda through the curious eyes of my children.

"What kind of trees are those?" Kai asked, pointing off to his right.

"Those are banana trees, bud," I answered. "Remember, we have one in our front yard, over by the fence. It's Joseph's baby."

"Why are they farming like that, up those hills?" Sam wanted to know.

"Because land is scarce here. It's called terrace farming and it allows them to take advantage of the limited space to grow more vegetables, feed more people," I replied, happy to answer all their questions as they took in the surroundings. The weather was turning quickly as it does in the rainy season. It had started to drizzle by the time we reached the park entrance. Then it began to pour. Other than a crafts cooperative that sold the typical souvenir baskets and gorilla-themed kitsch, everything had been shut down. We stubbornly walked around the parking area anyway and took a few perfunctory photos. But it was getting colder and wetter by the minute, and we didn't have the proper gear for a real hike into the mountain jungle. Disappointed but resigned, we decided to pack it in. At least we got to see more of the country, we told ourselves, trying to salvage the day.

The storm increased in fury as we zigzagged up and down the mountain switchbacks, lashing us with torrential rain and close-up lightning. At one point, the fog was so thick we were forced to pull off onto the narrow shoulder and wait for it to lift. Other cars soon joined us there. The boys were okay, but Kai, not a fan of thunderstorms, was visibly anxious. We were all unusually silent. As we inched along behind a line of heavy trucks, Bill drove carefully and kept his cool, the way he did under circumstances that often flustered me.

Our non-adventure was making me even more aware of my own anxiety about Bill leaving. I hadn't taken care of the boys on my own for more than a week or two; from the time they were born I'd been an in-and-out mom. It wasn't only that. The intense focus on my career, this notion of being an independent woman, had left me uncomfortable with my role as a mother. I had no idea whether I could be the kind of full-on mom the boys surely needed. And could I do it without Bill?

Again, I asked myself, *what was I thinking, bringing them here with me to Africa? What was I trying to prove?*

5

Tag, You're It

"Tag, You're It" was Bill's aptly named memo transferring responsibility for managing our home in Kigali to me. The memo was eleven pages long and spanned everything from key contacts and shopping lists to sample menus and play-date options. He also addressed the fact that if we didn't closely monitor our electricity usage, the power could go out unexpectedly. (It did anyway, often for an entire day.) Sprinkled with advice on where to shop and bank and other logistical matters, the memo was a thoughtful and thorough handover. It was also exhausting. The women I worked with managed in the roughest of circumstances—farming from dawn to dusk with babies tied to their backs, collecting firewood and water every day in order to prepare a meal, assuming there was food. I'd had enough with the planning.

"Okay," Joseph said, as in "It's all going to be okay."

Bill had, in fact, done everything possible to ensure we were well set up before he left, including leasing an old, barely functioning Toyota RAV-4 from Patrick, only a little worse than the one we'd taken on our recent excursion to Volcanoes National Park. The boys were ecstatic, having repeatedly complained about the thirty-minute trek back and forth to school with heavy backpacks, embarrassed to be arriving on foot just as their new friends were driving up in large, expensive SUVs with hired drivers.

Their parents likely all had generous support packages through the United Nations, the World Bank, or one of the many aid organizations working in

Rwanda; there were several large-scale, government-funded development projects underway. International transportation, moving, education and child care allowances, housing, uniformed security, cars, generators, and paid visits back home were only a few of the potential perks. Hardship pay, for working in a place where the living standards were below the United States', was also common. With the exception of a modest housing allowance, we had none of these enticements. I didn't mind being an outlier.

The whole *business* side of development made me uneasy at times, given *why* we were there and *who* we were there for. It was one of the things that attracted me most to the organization. They hired local nationals where possible for their in-country leadership, set limits on government funding, and spent the majority of their resources on the women they served.

Despite all he had done to prepare us, Bill had become more and more agitated as his departure date neared, running again and again through the litany of things I would need to be responsible for when he left. What would I do if the car stopped working or what was my backup plan if the nanny got sick or failed to show up when I was out of the country on a work trip, he pressed, losing patience with my noncommittal answers.

"Karen, you *have* to be ready. I need you think through all of this stuff," he snapped.

"It's impossible to plan for absolutely everything, Bill, and you know that. You're driving me crazy with all this grilling," I countered, exasperated.

Then finally, more coolly, he said, "I am starting to get really anxious about leaving and being without you guys. That's why I keep lashing out at you."

I knew just how he felt.

He was getting a small taste of my last twenty-plus years of international departures. Wrapping up, handing things off, letting go, saying good-bye. Over and over and over again. The pain of separation diminished over the years but had never completely disappeared. Immersing myself in meaningful work simply made it more palatable.

The worst part was the anticipation of leaving. My pre-departure rituals involved madly tidying the house and yard in an attempt to leave everything just so, a clean hand-off, so to speak. But it never worked out that way, not by a long shot. Bill and I invariably would have one of our pre-departure fights, usually about something ridiculous, like the clothes being left in the dryer or the mail left unsorted. These clashes stressed the kids out as badly as they did us.

I eventually stopped helping the boys with homework assignments or school projects during that frenzied, pre-departure rush. Tears would ensue, followed by a series of frantic text messages from the departure lounge, trying to soothe hurt feelings, theirs and mine, before takeoff. I'd spent more than a few long plane rides regretting my poor choice of words, or my lack of self-control. Bill would soon learn what it felt like to be the one who is there and then gone, the one who is missed and is missing.

Three weeks after our arrival in Kigali, we said our good-byes to Bill. The boys sent him off with big bear hugs as he left the house for the airport and his evening flight; naturally they were sad and a little worried to see him go. Bill and I met for lunch earlier in the day at a restaurant near my office, talking through final logistics over steaming bowls of carrot-ginger soup. There, with a quick peck on the lips, we went our separate ways, both of us ready to get on with it. Our good-bye seemed to underscore the point we had come to in our marriage—it was almost professional, businesslike.

Excited but nervous about the chance to solo parent, I'd hustled back to the compound to prepare for my afternoon calls and meetings. We were all determined to make it work—no one more than I. The next morning, however, it didn't. In fact, nothing worked. The gas cooker exploded, there was no internet, and the damn car wouldn't start. The boys looked reproachfully at me, as though I had caused all these problems. I couldn't blame them. I somehow felt that this was my fault, too. Bill and I had our respective spheres of influence, and these kinds of fixes were outside of mine. After a few minutes, the boys bitterly exited the car sitting idle in the driveway and trudged off to school, and I walked the few miles to work, more than a little defeated.

How I envied Bill's long plane ride then, the one I was usually on, going *away* from home. All the little and big things that needed tending to would gradually give way under those softly dimmed cabin lights, my pressurized containment. At times, it was almost a relief to be unreachable for hours and hours, beyond the limits of space and time. Instead, I was now faced with a full day's work and had to restore some measure of functionality to the house.

My main focus in Rwanda was to oversee the development and completion of the new Women's Opportunity Center in Kayonza, in the country's Eastern Province. Situated on a major traffic artery from Kigali to Akagera National

Park that connected Tanzania to Rwanda and to neighboring Burundi and Congo, the center would serve as a multi-use facility for learning and commerce for women and the community, and as a destination for passing tourists and truckers.

Talented, New York City–based architect Sharon Davis had designed the center, which was being built with hundreds of thousands of fired clay bricks made by graduates of the program, several of whom were involved in the construction. Like the country itself, considered to be a leader in sustainability, the center boasted environmentally friendly features like rainwater harvesting, biogas cooking fuel, and solar power. Composting toilets would generate fertilizer for the onsite kitchen gardens and a nearby demonstration farm; organically grown vegetables from both would be used for healthy-cooking demonstrations and in the center's restaurant. An eco-lodge and catering and event services were designed to generate income for the women and revenue for the center, which aimed to be financially independent within five years.

I had come to know Sharon well over the course of the project. She had initially built a successful career in finance on Wall Street but was far happier now in architecture. I admired her for the resolute way in which she had reinvented herself, turning away from a lucrative but ruthless profession to a more personal and meaningful calling, creating purposeful architecture that was beautiful and ecologically sound.

Sharon Davis Design's onsite manager, Bruce Engel, was my partner on the project. Uber tall, thin, and decidedly quirky, with a retro-urban kind of vibe, Bruce was a fine Cornell-trained architect and all-around great guy. He'd relocated from New York City and was spending the better part of each week living in a tiny room out in Kayonza, returning once or twice a week to Kigali to lecture at the Kigali Institute of Science and Technology and to spend weekends with his fiancée.

I had begun to make biweekly visits to Kayonza to review construction milestones with the team and ensure the project was on track for a June opening. It wasn't. The construction company we hired, while competent and committed, had clearly underbid the job and, as a result, was beset by planning and cash-flow problems from day one. Prices for labor, transport, and imported materials like steel had increased dramatically since the contract was signed, exacerbating the company's already precarious financial situation and causing us to scale back on some of the planned design elements. It took weeks to secure the required ministerial sign-offs for repeated customs clearances, which was both frustrating and time-consuming and resulted in even further delays. We needed to catch up.

"Please, Edward," I pleaded, shouting to make myself heard over the din of the midday rainstorm. The sound of it hitting the metal roof of the makeshift onsite office was deafening. "We need more workers. We're going to run out of time, and money." Edward, the company's unflappable construction manager, a Kenyan, was responsible for ensuring the project was finished on time and on budget. His job was also to liaise with the firm's owners when there were problems.

"The problem is we need more *skilled* workers," said Edward, his voice calm and reasonable. "We will have to source them outside of Rwanda, maybe in Nairobi."

"Do whatever you have to do," I said in an exasperated tone, knowing how far behind we were on the monthly targets. I told him we might be forced to withhold future payments or, if things didn't seriously improve, take legal action against them.

Bruce, as unflappable as Edward, quietly suggested adding five night shifts a week to get the project back on schedule.

"I will try my best," said Edward, in a way that didn't inspire confidence.

In spite of the challenges, the project was a labor of love for all of us. More than twelve thousand program graduates, many of whom lived in walking distance of the center, were eager for it to open so they could take advantage of its services, which would include business incubation and mentoring, vocational skills training for income generation, health and nutrition counseling, and even a roadside café and crafts market from which the graduates could all benefit. Euphraise, a graduate from 2007, immediately came to mind. She had been born in Congo, where her parents had fled during the war in Rwanda in 1959. Like other refugees, Euphraise and her family returned to the country after the genocide. She had recently opened a small crafts shop in downtown Kigali that sold the usual souvenirs: paper bead jewelry; hand-woven baskets; and black and white *imigongo* panels, geometric patterned art traditionally made with cow dung and ash by women. Her products would be perfect for the center.

Euphraise and I had met several times over the years. She would often drop by the office to sell products or meet staff, who asked her to lead trainings sometimes. Euphraise was waiting in the reception area of the office one morning after Bill left, and I'd gone over to say hello. We greeted each other warmly, with three kisses on alternating cheeks followed by a handshake, the traditional greeting for a friend. Quiet and unassuming yet fiercely determined, Euphraise shows the pain of her troubled past on her scarred face, behind her hooded eyes.

This time, I asked if she would be willing to share her story and what first brought her to the program. She agreed and actually seemed eager to talk. One of the life-skills trainers in the office volunteered to serve as our interpreter, and the three of us walked over to the tin-roofed gazebo in the courtyard, where we would have privacy and shade against the late-morning sun. I had a copy of Euphraise's story in hand, but I told her I also wanted to hear it from her.

Euphraise began to speak in her soft-spoken but unbowed way: "I have never had a happy marriage for my husband used to beat me. When I was pregnant with my first child, he beat me with all his strength until I had a miscarriage. I have a scar from being chased in the street in broad daylight, which made me fall on a stone and hurt myself. My husband continued hurting me with his insults and his words. Because he was the one providing for the family, he kept on repeating to me that I should be fed like a bird. All this happened in Congo where we used to live before coming to Rwanda."

"Did you ever consider leaving your husband?" I asked gently.

"Our culture says you're supposed to be patient and not divorce, and I had no means to take care of the children by myself."

When they were back in Rwanda, Euphraise's family gave her a little money, and she started to sell tomatoes in the market. She also received assistance from a church every few months. When the local authorities were handing out small plots of land several years later, Euphraise was among the recipients. She used her earnings to employ people to make bricks for a new house, which she had half built by the time she joined the program.

"In 2006, one lady who worked at the sector asked me to enroll in a training program. I was happy to have such an opportunity. In my mind, I wanted to learn a skill that would sustain me economically. During the life skills training, the trainer gave an example of a woman who is always beaten. I felt moved to fight for my rights. The trainer continued saying that without a husband, one can survive. This encouraged me to acquire a skill and use it as a tool to survive. I was enrolled in beadwork training.

"During the training, I walked hills all the way from Gacuriro because of my desire to be there. I could also make a necklace and walk in town to look for a buyer. I opened a [savings account], which assisted me a lot. At the end of the program, the money I had saved amounted to 60,000 RWF (about $100). All this time, I survived on selling necklaces. Then the time came when I decided to go for a loan. The loan was used to construct my house. Apart from my house, I have two more houses at the roadside that were constructed through other orders. They provided me rental income each month.

"My husband always insinuated that I took loans and soon would be arrested for not paying, for I am a useless woman. But this did not discourage me, for he had left us. But, God works in miraculous ways and we survived without him. For the loans I took, I used to bring my son as a second signature (co-signer). He was also hated by his father because he took my side.

"Later, I was informed about Goldman Sachs' 10,000 Women Initiative and I applied. Luckily, I was enrolled at the School of Finance and Banking in Kigali. During the training, I met prominent business people, and I studied with them. I went through many topics that I will apply to train others and improve my career."

Euphraise said that her husband had come back and was treating her better now, as she was the main income earner in the family, although he continued to insult, and at times beat, her until she finally reported him to the local authorities. She taught all five of her children how to make and sell crafts. "I feel proud," she said. "My children will not have to wait to find a job. They can do their own business."

She spoke of her plans to help other women facing the same struggle she did. "Women should not feel discouraged," she said. "If you get an opportunity, don't let it go. It might help you to survive."

I had listened to Euphraise's story with interest and awe. I knew other women saw her as a role model; even the trainers looked up to her. But it was the truth of that final statement—"If you get an opportunity, don't let it go. It might help you to survive"—that hit me at a gut level, now that I'd uprooted the family in search of a better place. Euphraise was such a great example of how important it is to seize an opportunity for change, to be willing to jump even if you don't know exactly where you will land. I felt inspired by her honesty, her relentlessness in the face of such adversity.

My thoughts returned to the opportunity center, how it would be a space that women like Euphraise could call their own, one dedicated to their renewal and progress. I pictured the half-built brick walls of the training pods, the piles of construction materials stacked around the site. There was so much work to be done, I barely had time to think. For a moment, though, I let my mind linger on the concept of renewal.

The first few days had been hectic without Bill. On the Saturday of my first solo weekend with the boys, they woke up famished as usual. My plan was to take them to breakfast at one of Kigali's most popular hangouts for expat families, the African Bagel Company or ABC, but the car still wouldn't start. We waited at the house for an hour or so for Patrick to come by and give us a jump, and then we got thoroughly lost. The boys were ravenous now and cranky, to the point that I was ready to give up and head for home when I made one last effort to find the place by employing Bill's strategy of flagging down a moto and following him there. By then it was lunchtime.

The narrow strip of dirt road fronting ABC was lined with so many Land Cruisers—as it was the only day they made fresh doughnuts—that ABC actually employed parking attendants. Part café and grocery, ABC started as a Christian charity project to provide job training and placement services for poor women, teaching them the baking and problem-solving skills they would need to find work or start their own enterprises, but it had evolved into a real business. The women who trained there had somewhat higher levels of education and English-language facility than the organization's participants, which gave them a leg up in terms of their ability to secure employment beyond manual, farming, or domestic work.

ABC had a relaxed, family-friendly vibe, with funky, hand-woven papyrus tables and chairs scattered around a grassy courtyard that encouraged lingering. After downing our thick bagel sandwiches, we decided to check out the Kicukiro Centre Market up the road, which had a large selection of local fruits and vegetables. We strolled around the covered market, taking in the stacks of purple beets, eggplants, and passion fruits, as well as several aisles of fabric and used clothing, more interested in looking than shopping.

The four of us clearly stood out as the only *muzungus* there. That meant that we had cash. When a few of the women sellers rushed up and grabbed my arm and attempted to pull me over to their stalls, where neat stacks of green onions, radishes, and tomatoes were on display, the boys grew alarmed, unsure about what to do. They huddled in close as if to protect me.

"Guys, it's okay. Really," I said. "These women are just trying to make a sale."

"Can't we just go home?" Eli asked, speaking for all of them. He looked as if he expected to be pounced on at any moment.

"How about we give it a few more minutes?" I said, wanting to push them a little more out of their comfort zone.

"Mom, please," Eli said again, almost in tears.

"Okay. Let's get out of here," I said.

We left hurriedly, in uncertain moods.

Things hadn't gotten much easier, when a week later I received a call at work from Eli. "Mom, we won the season opener."

"That's great, E," I said, not quite focused on the conversation.

Then, "Mom, you have to come right away. Sam's hurt."

"What?" I glanced at my desk, not seeing the piles of work, my heart starting to race.

"He's hurt bad."

"Oh no! I'm coming, bud. I'll be there as soon as I can."

Unbelievable. New to solo parenting and already I had a man down. Shaky with the news and unsure of the way, Antonina, the country director, offered to lead me to Circle Sportif, the big sports complex where the boys were playing, while I followed in our crappy car. We went racing through Kigali. When we got there, Sam was in serious pain, his arm wrapped tightly against his body with an impromptu cloth bandage.

Sam's coach was apologetic as he helped load him into the car, then the boys gave me a quick rundown: Sam had been dribbling past a huge player from the other team, Ecole Francaise (French School). He was shoved to the ground. He got up and kept playing, but then headed to the sidelines, his arm surging with pain.

"When did it happen, Sammy?" I asked.

"Like right away. In the first fifteen minutes," he said, visibly distressed.

"What?" I cried out. "And I didn't hear about it until after the game?" Never mind, we had to keep going. Still tailing Antonina, we sped toward the hospital. Sometimes parenthood made fieldwork look like a piece of cake.

From the outside, King Faisal Hospital looked more like a small hotel or a government admin building than a hospital. Flower boxes adorned the concrete three-story structure, which had two winding external staircases and a wrought-iron top-floor railing. Surrounded by a well-manicured yard with several nice grassy spots and evenly trimmed shrubbery, the emergency room was on the bottom floor, below street level. A lone ambulance sat parked in front.

The waiting area, with a single row of chairs and small intake window, was clean and orderly. A quick fifteen minutes later, Sam was being examined by a foreign doctor and sent off for x-rays, and I was politely directed to the hospital administration office to pay for the consult. That's when I remembered the final bullet in Bill's Tag memo, which was to "keep lots of cash around" since everything in Rwanda was pay-as-you-go. I silently thanked Bill then.

The x-ray machine was a rustic, lower-tech version of what we were used to, but it seemed okay, and there was no other option. Sam howled through all of it. A few minutes after the x-ray, I was asked to return to hospital admin. What? Why? "To pay for the x-ray, ma'am." Thank god we had money. What if we didn't and this had been a more serious emergency? What did Rwandans do?

I called Bill, leaving him a short, "nothing-to-worry-about-I'm-on-it" message. The doctor came in later and confirmed a broken clavicle.

"These bones practically heal themselves in kids," he said. His English was perfect. "There's not much more I can do."

Dispatched to the onsite pharmacy with two prescriptions—one for pain medication and the other for a basic arm sling—I returned to the hospital administration for the third time to pay for both. Three and a half hours and 34,000 Rwandan francs later, about sixty dollars, we were back at home. I felt drained but pleased, as though I had just cleared my first real parenting hurdle in Rwanda. Bill was empathetic when we did connect; we even joked about the differences between American and European soccer and how the latter is more of a contact sport.

Sam was back in school the next day and returned to the soccer field two weeks later.

We were approaching the end of our first month in Rwanda. Feeling a little more confident now after managing through the first few bumps, the boys and I were still trying to get into a routine without Bill there to fill in the gaps. Joseph was a huge help, tending to us as meticulously as he tended the garden. He made all our beds, mopped the floors, and did the laundry. His preference was to iron every single article of clothing, including our socks and underwear, until we begged him to stop. He would even scrub our dusty shoes and then line them up on the porch when he finished. Despite the language barriers, we managed to communicate. Though you couldn't see our car coming from the road, Joseph seemed to know intuitively when we were close to home. He would be there, waiting for us at the front gate.

Through Patrick, the fixer who doubled as an interpreter, Joseph told us that he was from northern Rwanda, the sixth child in a family of ten. With no land to speak of, his parents could no longer afford to support all of their children. He came to Kigali in search of unskilled work. He had not once in eleven years returned to his village near Byumba, about an hour's bus trip from Kigali, nor seen his family, yet he continued to send money home to pay his younger brothers' school fees.

Joseph was exceptionally loyal to his family, and ours. We had heard stories of other guards from the big security companies who actually let thieves in or stole, themselves, because they were poorly paid, but we trusted Joseph. His constant and reassuring presence gave me an early sense that, with so much at stake, Rwanda was the right place to be with my family.

I had contemplated what a reinvention might look like more than a few times since our arrival. What I kept coming back to, oddly enough, was a speech I had heard a few years back by the TV news host Mika Brzezinski at—yes—a reinvention convention. Dispatched there to fly the organization's flag on International Women's Day, I didn't typically go for this kind of thing, but her personal reinvention story had stuck with me. "Insecurities were my best friend," said Mika, who recounted the pain of losing her job, her sense of identity and affiliation, nearly hitting rock bottom before being forced to reinvent herself. It was bad, bad, bad . . . and then it was so good.

"How do you know if it's time for a reinvention?" a woman from the audience asked.

"How do you wake up?" Mika responded. "If you don't wake up happy, it's probably time for a reinvention."

Two other points stayed with me as well. You can't change your wiring—
that is, who you fundamentally are—and rejection is hard. To gain traction,
she recommended, "Reinvent yourself in stages." Progress, not perfection.
Progress, not paralysis. This, I knew from the survivors I worked with, was
possible. Margaret had done that.

When Margaret's village outside of Rumbek, South Sudan, came under
attack, she was forced to flee her burning home. She traveled by foot for days
to reach Yirol, another county in Lake States. When I visited Margaret in her
newly constructed mud hut, which other women had helped her to build,
she showed me the few possessions she'd managed to bring with her, among
them her graduation certificate from the program. To rebuild her life there,
Margaret joined with several other women to pool their meager resources and
start a café, launch a piecemeal knitting and embroidery business, and begin
to cultivate a few plots of land. They weren't earning much, the equivalent
of about ten dollars every two weeks for each of them, but in the context of
South Sudan, it was progress.

Tikkun Olam, the concept in Judaism of repairing the world through acts
of kindness, resonated with me from an early age, though our family, except
for my father, was not especially observant. And it was almost the High Holidays, beginning with Rosh Hashanah, the Jewish New Year, and ending ten
days later with Yom Kippur, the Day of Atonement. It seemed like the right
time, the right place, for a reinvention. Rwanda was a country that had to
completely reinvent itself post-genocide.

Jews are supposed to spend these ten days seeking out those we have
wronged and amending our behavior so that we can make it into the Book
of Life for another year. The meditation professes: "Every word, every act
inscribes itself in the Book of Life. Freely we choose, and what we have chosen to become stands in judgment over what we may yet hope to be. In our
choices we are not always free. But if only we make the effort to turn, every
force of goodness, within and without, will help us, while we live, to escape
that death of the heart which leads to sin."

To escape that "death of the heart," we are told to ask for, and find, forgiveness. Rwandans knew more than most about forgiveness. Forgiveness was the
only way the country had been able to rise above its horrific circumstances; it
was the only path forward. There is no collective forgiveness, Rwanda's for-

eign minister has said. By its very nature, forgiveness is personal. It is a choice. The Jewish faith teaches the same.

Who had *I* wronged? I thought back to my conversations with Erin, the coach who had been offered to me as part of a transition package after my failed CEO bid. A petite and attractive blond, Erin was there to guide me through the next stage of my professional development. After interviewing several of my colleagues, she laid out several areas where it was possible to have a greater impact, as she put it—opportunities to work more collaboratively and better empower the team, to build stronger, more trusted relationships, to hold myself and others more accountable.

I'd thought of myself as an accountable person—at work, certainly. "Above reproach" was my modus operandi. But what about my accountability as a partner and wife? Or as a mother for that matter. Everything that Erin said about me professionally could apply to my personal life as well: those oft-repeated sins of commission and omission on Yom Kippur, that is, what I did, but also what I didn't do or could have done differently. Had I really acknowledged my own parenting failures, taken responsibility for my share of the problems in our marriage? I'd probably put more energy into assigning or deflecting blame than to fixing our relationship.

That instinct to blame had been honed over my childhood. Dad blamed Mom for everything that was wrong with his life: his financial concerns for the business, his frustrations working for his harsh and condemning father. He blamed us kids, too. My siblings and I walked on eggshells around him, anticipating the swift and severe rebukes that could follow even a small mistake or casual remark. My brother Kenny would cower in terror, unable to move or speak, as Dad stood over him as he did his homework. Ken blamed it all on him. I blamed Mom for never taking our side, for not shielding us from Dad.

Blame, unspoken and pervasive, inundated our house like a flood or fire. It came out in a hundred little ways; the cause itself, rightness or wrongness, had very little to do with it. "Above reproach" was my modus operandi for that reason. Even though I'd fought the tide of similarities that I shared with my parents, I found myself repeating some of the same mistakes.

I was trying to learn how to do things differently, to reinvent myself in stages as Mika had advised. Progress . . . not perfection. Progress . . . not paralysis. It was a good time to start fresh here, with the boys, with work. I had committed myself to it.

We managed to find some expensive, imported apples at the German Butchery so that we could celebrate Rosh Hashanah the traditional way: with apples and honey, meant to usher in a good, sweet year. After the sadness and disappointment of the past year, this next one could only be sweeter. It had to be. The holiday also marked the day that Bill and I first met, the day of my chaotic salad. Those twenty-five years had practically slid by without either of us noticing, when most of our energy had been directed to building our careers, raising the boys, attending to all the details in life except our marriage. We, I, should have been paying closer attention. Who knew, maybe we would have a chance to start fresh as well?

We were invited to the home of one of Kai's classmates to celebrate with her family. We had just started to meet other expat families, most of them ISK parents. Some were in Rwanda running multiyear development projects or businesses, but many were on shorter stints like ours. Their family was also visiting for one year, with a group of doctors. The husband was an anesthesiologist and the wife a former opera singer, now a "trailing spouse."

Motherhood and marriage can be especially challenging in the international development field. According to insiders, the World Bank doesn't publicize their divorce rates for exactly that reason. Most women I know with careers in this line of work are either single, divorced, married without children, or empty nesters. Even if one partner is willing to forgo their own aspirations to play a support role at home with a traveling spouse or to move overseas, it's tough to make it all work, and last.

In online forums devoted to mothers working in international development, women chat about relationship and parenting difficulties in a profession that involves extensive travel or postings to insecure countries, where children and families are perceived as limiting career progression. I had heard stories of women forgoing jobs that required too much travel or were not family friendly. I knew others who had spent time as a solo parent, or were separated from their spouse and/or children for long stretches, or raising their children in a foreign culture away from extended family and the comforts of home.

I'd always felt that if you were willing to work your ass off and accept the tradeoffs, anything was possible. I'd chosen to forgo overseas work to build a life with my family in the United States, until Rwanda. Maybe this *had* limited my own career progression, but it had been worth it in terms of sustaining two careers, a family, and a marriage, however messy. Now I was beginning to wonder if I should have made different choices for my family.

What had I missed out on? Family milestones mostly, too many to count: Kai's fifth birthday and Sam and Eli's eighth, Bill's fortieth, the opening night of Eli's junior high school play, and pretty much every back-to-school night, music recital, and baseball game. A thousand good-bye and good-night kisses. Those, I knew, could never be reclaimed. There were no do-overs here.

The work, I knew now, would still be there. With years of practice and some amount of discipline, I'd learned to walk away. To leave things undone.

When I first convinced Bill that this move would be good for all of us, I told him that living in Rwanda with the boys would allow me to bring work and family into focus at the same time, without that constant feeling of sacrificing one for the other. But it was more than that. It was a chance to pause, to reconfigure my thinking and choices.

6

Sometimes Together,
Sometimes Apart

Despite all the adjustments, and my own internal conflict, the boys and I finally settled into a more or less comfortable weekly routine. Mornings, I would confront the rush-hour madness— horns blaring, choked intersections and roundabouts—and drop them off at school on my way to the office; they had to hustle their own rides home, or walk. Everything else got squeezed in before and after work. Unable to defer to Bill on all manner of household management, it now fell to me. Delegation, however, proved to be key. Each of the boys was assigned a scope of work—in executive-management speak— with a set of deliverables.

Kai's job was to clear the dinner dishes, wipe down the kitchen table, and put away the clean clothes. Eli had to straighten up the living room before school, sweep up after meals, and help with Sunday night dinners. Sam was tech support, in everything from uploading pictures to laying out Excel spreadsheets. They'd had chores back home, of course, but rarely did them without major prompting, if at all. I'd set the bar higher here, and the boys fell into line. Their reward was an allowance of 5,000 RWF, or about eight dollars a week.

Sam and Eli had a weekly poker game going with some classmates, so most Friday nights they would gamble away their week's earnings. They liked to play at their friend Alex's house, mostly because his kid sister loved to cook and prepared multicourse dinners for them. Alex's family had moved from

New Orleans around the same time as us when his mother, a professor at Tulane, accepted a temporary teaching position in Rwanda. He was one of five seniors at ISK and basically coasting after receiving early admission to college. He was more than a little reckless (his driving motto being "the faster you go, the less likely you are to have an accident") but also smart, savvy. He had brought his own poker chips to Kigali.

The twins had quickly formed a tightknit group of friends—a diverse mix of kids from around the world, some of them girls. Aside from poker, they played a raucous, often mud-soaked game of football on Friday afternoons when school let out early. Kai had also made friends and was pretty good at setting up his own play dates, once he got a cell phone. They were with ISK classmates mostly, a number of them from other African nations. And there was always Joseph for one-on-one soccer matches on the front lawn. He was Kai's frequent soccer mate, not minding that the boisterous play sometimes tore up his precious flowers.

The boys were spending more time together than they ever had in Bethesda. Yet they still managed to get on each other's nerves. It might have been a twin, brother, or age thing, but Sam and Eli were always in competition over grades, sports, friends, who got to ride shotgun. Even their friends back home had stopped wanting to hang out with the pair of them because of their constant bickering. I thought living in closer proximity to each other might improve things, but so far it hadn't helped. Just leaving the house meant there would be an argument about who saw the car or touched it first.

Personality-wise they couldn't have been more different. Born twenty-nine minutes apart, Eli was our "Baby A." As Samuel's teacher in the Bible, Eli showed Sam the way out and had been leading the way ever since. He was the gregarious one, full of drama, singing and acting in all the school plays. Sam, whom we affectionately call "the literalist," listened to a "Stuff You Should Know" podcast to lull himself to sleep each night. They'd been like that since they were toddlers and spent their early years devising new ways to torture each other.

I'd had to step in to break up their fights on several occasions, usually by yelling at them to stop fighting or sending them outdoors to take a run or do push-ups, anything to burn off the excess hormonal energy.

Solo parenting definitely had its own set of challenges, but there were upsides as well. There was none of the second-guessing around parenting approaches or the daily judgment calls. For better or worse, I was forging my own path here. The boys and I were also having a lot of fun together exploring Kigali. We walked practically everywhere, stopping when we found a new or unusual place to eat or rest. We'd spent an entire afternoon at Juru Park, kicking the soccer ball around, eating french fries and grilled tilapia from one of the fish farms on the fringes of the city. The downtime with them was precious; we'd had so little of it at home. It felt intimate, like the four of us were on our own private adventure, even if we were just playing cards or listening to music or watching old movies or reruns of *Chopped*.

Despite the occasional bouts of loneliness when the boys were off with their friends and the house was still, being on my own felt okay; the same, but also different. Weekends were less structured, more flexible; there were none of the obligatory get-togethers or work functions. And I could cook without judgment. Nobody was there to stealthily turn down the burner or ask, "Are you really going to use *that* saucepan?" Eli, it turned out, was an easy and able cooking partner. Sundays, we would shop for groceries and make dinner together. We looked forward to it.

Bill and I continued to check in by email and had a weekly Skype call. Mostly we talked about what the boys were up to, how they were faring. The distance somehow rendered both of us kinder, less caustic with each other. It had been like that from the time I started commuting to the Soviet Union. Whatever issues or arguments we had while together seemed to dissipate across the miles, and I felt these gushes of love for and from him. Though stories of missed birthday parties and family outings were bittersweet to read, those electronic family memories also represented some of the strongest bonds between Bill and me.

I had traveled enough throughout our marriage, though, to be wary of the palliative that distance sometimes provides. Stress and loneliness had a way of making things seem rosier back home. For now, I was appreciating the extra distance.

My first work trip to Congo came about three weeks after Bill's departure. I realized then how apprehensive I still felt about everything, especially about not having Bill there to provide backup. With oversight of the country offices in Rwanda, Congo, South Sudan, and Nigeria, travel was always part of the job, but in truth, I hadn't thought through the implications. Bill had always been there to watch the boys.

I asked Innocent, our cook/nanny, to sleep over so I could quietly leave for the airport without waking the boys. She hadn't thawed much, but I reasoned that she could take care of them just fine for a few days. "My Rwandan cell phone still works in Congo, guys," I assured them. "You can call me anytime." Still, I was wondering how Kai would do without being able to climb into bed with Mom for almost the first time since we moved in. He seemed fine, though. They all did. *They must be so used to me leaving*, I thought.

The early morning flight to Kamembe, a Rwandan town on the border with eastern Congo, took just forty minutes. A driver from the Bukavu office met me in the parking lot right outside of the airport's pristine, newly modernized terminal. We caught a stunning glimpse of vast Lake Kivu on the steep drive down to the border crossing, which serves as a major gateway for trade between the two countries. A long line of Congolese—mostly day laborers and traders and an odd flock of nuns in white habits—waited at the border to pass through into Rwanda. I quickly received my exit stamp, and we crossed over a wood-plank bridge spanning a narrow strip of the Rusizi River and drove another half kilometer along a dirt road crowded with traders carting bags and cartons of goods from Rwanda into Congo to the border checkpoint.

The Congo border crossing was always unpredictable. I'd been stopped a few times before to answer questions about my visa. I was usually directed into a ramshackle government office filled with a few simple wooden desks and chairs and half a dozen or so uniformed officials; one of them would slowly flip through the pages of my passport—there appeared to be no formal document-review process—deciding whether to approve my paperwork. Once, when I couldn't produce my yellow immunization card, I was told to wait in the car as they considered my situation. After an hour or so of fruitless haggling, including the threat to reimmunize me at some nearby clinic, a modest bribe facilitated entry. On a good day, I would join a line with mining company executives and other development types, cramming in under a small overhang in front that provided virtually no relief from the harsh sun and wait for that passport stamp.

This time, there was no problem with my entrance papers. But this time, my family was back in Kigali. My cell phone started to ring almost as soon as we left the border for our office in the center of Bukavu. All three boys had awakened sick and miserable with the flu and couldn't go to school.

"You have to come home, Mom," each of them said, their voices sounding weak and strained.

"I'm sorry, guys. I know it sucks, but I can't come home right now," I said, feeling horrible about leaving them in that state, with the less-than-nurturing Innocent as backup. I felt guilty, too, for prioritizing my work commitments, for being away when their dad was gone, for being away so often.

I'd been to Congo many times before, but the stark, depressing contrast between the Rwanda and Congo sides never ceased to amaze me. Rwanda was smooth and efficient; Congo was gritty and chaotic. And it wasn't only the contrasting landscapes. There was a sharp-eyed edginess to the people in eastern Congo, long accustomed to marginal, off-the-grid living. The entire population seemed to be in perpetual survival mode.

Congo is a country ravaged by war and conflict. Millions of lives have been claimed over the past twenty-plus years due to the continuous violence and resulting humanitarian crisis, and even more people have been displaced. Both Joseph Kabila, who ruled the country from 2001 until 2019 after a controversial presidential election, and the government in Kinshasa, about a thousand miles from Bukavu, are notoriously corrupt. They hand out favors to global mining companies that exploit Congo's vast reserves of tin, gold, tungsten, and coltan and have a personal stake in the economy. Local and foreign militias, many ethnically based and operating with American-supplied weapons and training, vie for control over the mineral wealth, while residents sink lower on the misery index.

Brown mud and stick houses with plastic or tin roofs climb up Bukavu's hillside, a typical urban slum. Most people live on less than one dollar per day, with limited access to food, basic services, and medicine; hunger is prevalent while security and rule of law are almost nonexistent. From a development, security, or public-health standpoint, worse conditions are hard to imagine. It is especially difficult for women. Congolese families average six or more children, owing in large part to Catholic culture combined with a lack of health infrastructure that limits knowledge of and access to family planning. Maternal and child survival rates are among the lowest in Africa. Poverty, inadequate education, early marriages, and restrictive norms compound the threats to women, who suffer daily occurrences of sexual and domestic violence.

Congo has the unfortunate dual distinction of being the rape capital of the world and one of its poorest countries. The *American Journal of Public Health* estimated that four women are raped every five minutes in Congo. More than two million women have been victims of rape over the country's protracted war, a number so staggering it defies comprehension. Beyond the devastation of individual lives is the wake of shame and humiliation that has torn families and communities apart, destroying the very fabric of Congolese society.

It is unimaginable to find ways to live day to day, and yet women do so because they must. More than sixty thousand Congolese women had participated in our twelve-month work- and life-skills training program, including widows, rape survivors, single heads of household, returnees, and the internally displaced: thousands of women each year. Some are so traumatized when they first join that they cannot even say their names out loud. "We resurrect the dead," the director of programs here once said.

Dr. Denis Mukwege, a gynecological surgeon who has devoted his career, his whole life really, to caring for victims of sexual violence, sees the wounds of such trauma every day. His hospital, Panzi Hospital, provides holistic care that includes medical, psychological, legal, and socioeconomic support to patients, and treats about three hundred rape survivors each month. Seventy-five percent are minors under the age of eighteen, some of them, unfathomably, toddlers and babies, according to Panzi's director of medicine. Many suffer from rape-induced fistula, a condition that causes urine and feces to leak through the vaginal canal. Dr. Mukwege himself performs multiple fistula repair surgeries every day. "I think our work is to transform these women from victims into survivors," Mukwege has said. "Not just survivors, but to empower them, and to have this power turn into genuine leadership of their communities." We had met a couple of times to discuss setting up a cross-referral system between the hospital and Women for Women. A statuesque and big-hearted man and an outspoken critic of the conflict, Mukwege is among the most brilliant of upstanders—a person who sees wrong and acts. He is the kind of man I hoped my boys would grow up to be.

Organizations working to bolster women were especially needed in Congo. But the places most in need were often the most difficult ones in which to work. Congo was a shining example of that. The elusive Mwami, or traditional king of Walungu, had finally reemerged and requested an in-person meeting with us. Traditional authorities like the Mwami administer land on behalf of local communities, which meant that he had decision rights over all land and commerce matters. The country office had negotiated a long-term land lease with him months earlier that allowed several hundred women to set up a commercial farm on his property for income generation.

The land-tenure system is complex and opaque in Congo. Though the state legally owns all land, and formal legislation governs land use, a large percentage remains subject to customary law. When it comes to land rights, both sets of laws discriminate against women. Most can only access land through male family members or chiefs; a married woman must have her husband's permission to lease or buy land. Husbands, on the other hand, enjoy full rights to their wives' property.

The Mwami's land had been overgrown and dormant, and swampy in parts, before the women stepped in and took on the labor-intensive work of land clearing, planting, and basic irrigation. And now, it seemed, he wanted to renegotiate terms. If the land was lost to us, it could devastate the likes of Josephine, one of the women farmers.

I'd met Josephine on another visit to Congo a few months earlier. She was a remarkable woman who'd had a difficult life. On the day we had met, she was wearing a sleeveless black shirt and head wrap, a swath of faded, red patterned fabric tucked in at her waist; her face was unsmiling, resolute.

Orphaned at age seven, Josephine and her four-year-old brother had been separated and sent to live with families in different villages—food was too scarce to keep them together. She didn't see him again for eleven years. It was only by chance that she was reunited with her brother when he came to her village near Walungu in search of food one year during the long, dry season. He never left. For the past twenty-two years, they've lived in the same village and raised their families together.

Josephine had been married off at eighteen and had twelve children, four of whom died, all of them girls. When her husband proved unable to support the family, they divorced, and Josephine became the sole breadwinner. Even with the familial support of her brother, Josephine, now forty, was desperate to earn an income to feed her children, but also to secure their future. She'd approached a landowner in her village to rent one hectare of land for four years with payment of a goat. She'd already taught two hundred other women from her village how to cultivate beans in straight lines, a skill she'd learned in vocational training.

These same women had organized themselves into groups of twenty-five, formed a cooperative, and elected Josephine president. They were working together to produce clay tiles and cooking pots, make honey, and cultivate seedlings. Two volunteers from the group were teaching the women how to read and write, skills they would need to grow their businesses. The group was using their income to rent additional plots of land, send their children to school, and feed their families.

Josephine's dream was to have a small house and "continue to give birth" by passing on her learning to other women in her village. She had been walking to the commercial farm twice a week, eight kilometers each way, to tend her plots.

After our meeting on the farm, we'd given Josephine a lift back to her village. There she gave us a tour around, pointing out where she lived and where they made the tiles, bee boxes, and honey. Her industriousness was astounding. It was hardly enough to keep her family afloat. And yet, that alone was a triumph in this environment.

Over the next few days, I tried to keep Josephine and her fellow farmers in mind as I worried about my sick boys in Kigali and prepared for what was certain to be a tense meeting with the Mwami. In our previous meetings, he proved to be a highly skilled negotiator, polished and immaculate. We had heard he was spending most of his time in Kinshasa, the capital, running for elected office. And like all good politicians, he needed to show his constituents that he could bring home the bacon. Foreign bacon was even better. The last time we met, he had asked for a brand-new Land Cruiser. "Impossible," we all said.

The boys, meanwhile, were calling and texting me several times a day, letting me know just how bad they felt.

"Mom, Sam just threw up again. When *are* you coming home?" Eli groused.

"Just a couple more days, bud. I'm sorry," I repeated, again.

Immersed in operational planning with the entire Congolese staff, and in an intense session with the interim country director around some serious management issues involving a complicated web of family, tribe, church, and politics, I excused myself and stepped out into the corridor to take their calls. *There's no way to get this right*, I thought at the end of one of our calls. Either I was disappointing the boys, the team, or the women. Right then I was failing on all fronts.

I called Innocent to make sure that she was on it, providing at least basic care.

"How are our guys doing?" I asked her.

"They're fine," she replied.

"Are they able to eat anything?" I pressed, looking for details.

"Not much," she said.

"Maybe you can make them some soup," I suggested.

"I don't know how to make soup," she said.

"Hmm. Well, see if you can try and get them to eat a little," I continued, growing annoyed.

"Okay."

"I'll give you a call a bit later."

Okay then, no soup. I Skyped with Bill and filled him in, and then he spoke with the boys. He started a round of emails and texts to rally our nascent support network in Kigali to go over to the house and check on them. Among them was a practicing nurse from Connecticut whose three sons were ISK classmates.

Why was it so hard for me to ask for help? Josephine walked sixteen kilometers a day to give her children a real future. She had taken the initiative to join the program and learn a new skill, which took great courage. Euphraise had done the same. All I had to do was make a simple phone call or two. Josephine and Euphraise set a great example. Their ambition to not only survive but to thrive in such difficult environments, to put everything on the line for the sake of their families, made me want to do better.

I remembered then how good Bill was at this kind of stuff. I don't know why it made me think of the night of our second date—that romantic, post-break-fast kiss on the bridge. We had laughed about it being Yom Kippur and told each other we were atoning for all our sins past and yet to come. There was a nearly full moon that night, and I remember thinking: *I actually like this guy.* Funny that I hadn't thought about that in all these years, not until I found myself in Bukavu trying to take care of my kids in Kigali, with Bill in Maryland.

The boys' health steadily improved over the next three days, and they were able to return to school, but I'd caught whatever bug was going around—achy joints, nausea, fever, chills. I couldn't eat and, with a packed schedule, there was little chance to rest. Feeling sick and sluggish, Bill's Yom Kippur email came at just the right time:

> Team WaSherman. I'm at the tail end of my fast, listening to Mom's favorite CD. I've taken on the responsibility of atoning for the whole family to ensure we're all marked for another year in the book of life. I realize this wasn't the most traditional way to spend a holiday with family. However, I couldn't feel more connected to all of you.
>
> It hurt to get the call from Eli yesterday morning alerting me that everyone was barfing up their cookies and much more. Stomach bugs Rwanda-style. It sucks. However, thanks to Skype, MTN minutes, Innocent and our new friends, we're all connected and you seem on a glide path to an easier week.
>
> I'm proud of how you boys handled the minor adversity. This year is just different. We're all confronting challenges and fears, and adjusting to a different way of living. Sometimes together, sometimes apart, but always knowing that we've got each other's back.
>
> Rabbi Roos gave one of his stem-winder sermons today. He referred to last year's sermon where he and Rabbi Oleon committed to renew the Temple's commitment to social justice. You might remember that last year he gave a shout out to Mom for her leadership in global development and human dignity. Well, he reported that the Temple has done a good job at committing to projects like Sinai House and several other important causes.
>
> After services, he came down to greet me and was thrilled to hear how well you are doing. I know we will talk again over the weekend. I can hardly wait to see you guys next month.
>
> Love, Dad

Bill knew just how to fill me up. He'd supported and encouraged me like that for years, without hesitancy or rancor, even when I'd looked at him with contempt, unable to take it in.

We had a long-standing pact that if anything were to happen to me overseas, he would do everything in his power to get me home. He had made good on that promise a few years back. It was International Women's Day, and I had been marching with hundreds of Rwandan women to the border at Goma to join our sisters on the other side. With ongoing hostilities between Rwanda and Congo, the symbolic walk was meant to demonstrate our commitment to building bridges of peace. Excited and proud to be doing something important to mark the day, I held up a large white placard that read, "We wish women to have rights all over the world."

It started to rain as the group made its way to a hotel just inside Congo where the formal celebration would take place. My wallet and passport were stolen in the crush of people entering the hotel, eager to escape the downpour. Stranded without money or identification, Bill was my first call from the border post, where I had returned to give a statement to the police. He rallied our congressman when the American Embassy in Rwanda was slow to respond and made sure I received an emergency passport in time to make my flight back to the United States.

As I shut down my computer for the night and crawled into bed, shivering, my head throbbing, I couldn't help wondering what would happen if we didn't end up staying together. Who would look out for me the same way Bill did? He'd been my lifeline while I was out of the country, my caretaker when I returned home exhausted and spent.

Home had become a place of sanctuary compared with the disorderly and insecure places I worked. An image of what, and who, was waiting for me there came with me wherever I went: in Afghanistan, in Congo, in South Sudan, in Bosnia, in Rwanda, in Kosovo, in Iraq, in Nigeria. I once walked with a group of Nigerian women for what seemed like hours to get to the tiny stream where they wash their clothes and bodies and collect drinking water—a trek that many of them must make every day. Soon I would get on a plane and go home; these women were home, this was their reality. Welcoming me with flowers and a vodka rocks, Bill would nourish me back into family life; stock the cabinets with my favorite potato chips, grill or smoke a pile of meat on one of his three outdoor cookers. I knew how fortunate I was to return to our life in Bethesda.

On hyper alert during my travels, I wanted nothing more than to let down my guard and give myself over to him. And yet . . . I couldn't.

The house was often a mess by my standards, and I would start to nitpick about the piles of clutter, unsorted mail, and stacks of clothes yet to be put away. That first hour or two at home was spent re-marking my territory and putting things back where they belonged: clean clothes into drawers, mail into the recycling bin or bill folder, furniture righted. I yearned for order after the disorder, to be in an environment that I could control.

But it wasn't only the house. It was us. While we were apart, I'd often fantasize about our reunions, about being kissed deeply, melting into Bill's arms, yet I couldn't seem to get there when we were together, when my outsized expectations from weeks alone in the field met the reality of our married life. We were back to the same old issues, the same unfinished arguments.

Switching gears was never easy: alone in the trenches one day, then back into motherhood and married life the next. And I wasn't the one doing the fighting; I was doing the cleanup. How difficult it must be for combat soldiers to reenter civilian life, knowing that you could never fully reconcile where you'd been or what you'd seen and done with where you are now. The transition alone from one's military unit to the family unit had to be devastating.

Those first few days at home were always the roughest. Alcohol helped to smooth over some of the initial awkwardness and discomfort, for both of us. There'd been a large bottle of vodka in the freezer for years, our drink of choice from the time in the Soviet Union. Just the sound of those ice cubes hitting the bottom of the lowball glass was enough to cheer me up: a reward for making it through the day. We would slowly return to "normal" until the next trip and reentry cycle.

Bill had built up his own resentments over time about our marriage. He was angry with himself, too, for bringing his father's passivity to the relationship. When his dad was asked about the secret of his long and seemingly happy marriage, his response was: "Always give in." If his parents fought at all, they did so quietly, behind closed doors, away from the children. We were polar opposites when it came to conflict.

Bill and I committed to working out our differences through individual and couples' counseling. Though therapy helped us to understand and diffuse some of the pent-up anger, our marriage was still heading over a cliff. We both knew it. Was travel the source of the problem or the only reason we were still together? I couldn't say for sure.

Bill was a good man and a wonderful, engaged father. Other than the usual parenting concerns, I never worried over the boys' health or well-being during my frequent absences. I should have been satisfied with my "great" life, especially compared to other women's lives. I wasn't being beaten or poor; I could make my own decisions. But had I chosen safety and dependability at the expense of my own passion? Did I need to be with a different kind of man to be a different woman? I loved Bill, and though I desperately wanted to be, I didn't know if I was in love.

That's what I was grappling with four years before Rwanda, when I had to see what it was like to live on my own. It was only for a few months, I told myself, but I consulted an attorney anyway, thinking of the boys. Bill was totally against it, but then, he knew it wasn't his choice. We were practically living apart anyway: separate floors, rooms, beds.

As if I were leaving for the developing world instead of a high-rise ten minutes away, I found a one-bedroom corporate apartment, rented it for an initial three months, packed my usual travel bag, and left.

Now, here we were again, in another separation of my own making. Bill was the most decent of guys. I depended on him, but my unhappiness persisted. Contentment was just a state of mind, I berated myself. We had our problems, sure, but they were little nothings, blips, compared with those of the survivors I worked with. Having seen the worst, I knew in a very real sense how much I had to be grateful for. Maybe that was the moment when it started to dawn on me that all of this upheaval had less to do with our relationship and more about something I had yet to resolve within myself.

I was starting to see that I had been blaming my parents for my hardness; it wasn't just a legacy. It was easier than acknowledging my own deficiencies. But the women around me hadn't done that, even though they could have easily, and perhaps rightly, blamed others for the condition of their lives and the tethers that were holding them back. How had they avoided falling into that trap? What was I missing?

Still feeling unwell, I pulled myself together for the meeting with the Mwami on my final day in Bukavu. He arrived wearing a dark, pressed business suit, starched shirt, orange power tie, and, despite the dusty streets, perfectly shined European-style leather shoes. We greeted each other with the proper formalities.

"So nice to see you again sir," I said. A colleague served as our interpreter, translating my English into French.

"Yes. It is good to see you as well," he said.

"We are so appreciative of your generosity, allowing the women to cultivate on your land. They are doing quite well, as I expect you've heard," I said. Usually I try to minimize the formalities and get on with it, but he was a king, and protocol mattered.

"Yes, well, I have not been involved. I do not know these women," he replied.

"You should come by and see the land, sir," I enthused.

"You know, it is my responsibility to monitor the land, to assess how it is being utilized. I could be harmed by the project if it is not well managed," he said.

"What do you mean?" I asked, knowing exactly what he meant and where the conversation was going. We'd been down this road before. King or no king, the man had shown himself to be more attuned to his own interests than the interests of his people. I didn't trust him.

"You have not followed up properly, by allowing me and my people to visit the land," he said, as smooth as glass. As satisfying as it would have been to rip into him, wipe that smug look off his face, it wasn't worth it. The Mwami held all the power here, and he knew it.

"But sir, you can come and see the land and talk with the women anytime you like," I countered, playing the naïve foreigner.

"Unfortunately I cannot. I do not have a vehicle that would enable me to see all of my property," he said, looking directly into my eyes. "How can we establish trust if I cannot even visit my own land?"

So there it was. We were back to the damn car. He didn't care, had never cared about helping these women to earn an income. This was a business deal; a quid pro quo: a new car for their livelihoods.

There was more dialogue. I reiterated that a car was simply out of the question; he implied that we were keeping him from his Mwami duties. And if he couldn't fulfill his responsibilities, he might have to terminate the agreement.

"Please send me your proposed terms in writing," I finally offered, frustrated to be back at square one. "We already have a signed agreement with you, but I will get in touch with our lawyer and see what we can do."

"Yes, I will do so," he said, rising to shake my hand. Our session had come to a close.

After he left the room, my colleague and I sat there for several more minutes trying to process what had just happened and thinking through our next move. If those women were removed from the land, they would have no means of generating an income. They were counting on us, and that land. The situation didn't look as though it would resolve itself anytime soon. We would have to look for another place for them to farm. We would have to start over again.

7

Rumbek

The boys were already at school when I landed in Kigali. *Would it be too weird to drop in on them at school?* I thought, impatient to see them. What was happening? I was usually more focused than this. Was it just because it was easier to be in the field when my family was so far away? My ability to compartmentalize work and the rest of life had been totally thrown off with the boys sick and right across the border, with being *the* parent. Maybe that wasn't such a bad thing.

Unfortunately, there wasn't time to see the boys. I had to rush from the airport to the office to get ready for the mass wedding later that day. The team had been working toward this since we first arrived, and it had finally come to fruition. The mayor of Gasabo was presiding over the ceremony, which was being held at Kigali's Petit Stade, or small stadium. Preparations were well underway when a small group of us from the office showed up. A large, open-sided shade tent had been erected and filled with white plastic chairs for the couples and more than three hundred expected witnesses and guests.

We saw the couples arrive by hired bus. The men wore jackets and ties, if they had them, and the women were dressed in their best *mushanana*, traditional Rwandan ceremonial attire; some wore bridal headpieces. The tenor of the event was serious and formal, with officials offering both legal advice and premarital counseling in advance of the ceremony.

When it came time for "I dos," fifty-two couples came forward to make their commitments. The men came first, followed by the women: one hand

Mass wedding.

raised in affirmation, the other touching the blue, yellow, and green Rwandan flag as they each said their vows.

Donning a borrowed *mushanana* for the occasion, I stood and congratulated the assembled group of newlyweds. At a brief reception after the wedding, trays of warm sodas and straws were passed around for the requisite toasting, and there were four round wedding cakes, each one white with writing in orange frosting that read "Civil Marriage Ceremony." The wedding was a big success, so much so that there was talk of replicating it in other districts across the country. I loved being a part of it, even if seeing all those couples left me wistful and thinking about my own marriage. It represented a major victory for the women there, one that could be life changing.

Florance and her new husband, Emmanuel, said the wedding was everything they had dreamed of when we spoke after the ceremony. "Now we are more motivated to work together," they said. The beaming bride in a traditional white gown gushed: "I am valuable now that I am legally married."

When I came through the door that night, I hugged the boys tight. They were fine and eager to hear about Congo and the mass wedding over dinner. The concept of it was so bizarre to them. Sam, our budding photographer, helped select several photos to send to HQ along with the blog I'd written on legal marriage. I usually didn't talk much about my work with them, but it was fun to rave about the ceremony.

This mood, however, did not last through the weekend. The rest of it was consumed by a new crisis, this time in Rumbek, South Sudan, where we had a field office. The security situation there was deteriorating fast.

It wasn't a total surprise. The country was home to the longest civil war on the continent, at a cost of well over a million lives. The violence was not only linked to the North-South conflict that had lasted for decades, with its own political, ethnic, and religious dimensions, but also deeply embedded in the culture and its people. Fighting continued even after a peace treaty backed by the United States officially ended the brutal war in 2005 and guaranteed the South's right to secede. It had become a way of life.

The capital of Lakes State and former capital of the country, Rumbek is an area dominated by the Dinka tribe, the largest ethnic group in South Sudan. Tribal disputes between the Dinka and Nuer, roving militias, and revenge killings were status quo in Rumbek. The Wild West, with its lawlessness and vigilante justice, seemed tame by comparison. Most people were grateful just to survive each day.

There were growing fears for our team's safety there. Once the organization formally announced plans to move its program base to Yei, via a letter to the governor, several highly placed officials turned nasty over the departure. They began to make false allegations against the staff, accusing them of being in the country illegally and attempting to move property out of the state. Work permits for regional staff were being held on the charge that their photographs were changed, constituting a criminal offense. The police and other authorities were instructed to "monitor" all staff movements. Several of the staff had been detained at police headquarters for questioning, and others had been threatened with violence. These were not idle threats, not in Rumbek.

On an earlier trip to Rumbek in 2011, the year before we moved to Rwanda, some colleagues and I had hosted a lunch for the staff there as a gesture of thanks for being on the frontlines of the work. South Sudan was on the cusp of independence then; the pivotal vote to create their own state was about to happen. A driver was dispatched to the local animal market to buy us a goat for the midday meal; a local dance troupe made up of program graduates had been invited to perform.

The hearty smell of roasting meat permeated the compound as we danced in a loose circle with drums, rattles, and tambourines, with me awkwardly trying to follow their dance moves. The smell of yet more war was also in the air; Khartoum had been inciting tribal violence, arming militants, and selectively bombing strategic areas in advance of the vote. But nothing could quell people's optimism and excitement for independence. They could taste it, and if need be, were ready to die for it. As one woman said, "I want my rights."

As we feasted on goat, one of the dancers got a call informing her that her brother and his two wives had been pulled off a bus and had had their throats slit by the side of the road, in what was described as a revenge killing. Her anguished cries transformed the smell of meat filling the air into a greasy, sickening stench. She collapsed in a heap on the ground. Two of her fellow dancers drag-carried her limp body out of the dirt compound back to her family.

Now, citing orders from "above," the national intelligence service's criminal investigation department demanded that all program assets be confiscated—two cars, several computers, a broken tractor, and a generator. A motorbike had also been stolen from the compound during the night—the security guards were suspected of being in on the theft. Everything seemed to be spiraling out of control. Our well-thought-out security plans were useless against these kinds of threats. The country director, normally composed, was becoming more and more distressed; there was a new remoteness in her voice, as if she were removing herself from the havoc. Given my own experiences there, I privately feared the worst. I was spending several hours a day on calls with her and trading emails with the regional team in Kenya.

The plan had been to finish training the women and leave Rumbek at the end of year. That was impossible now. There was no choice but to move ahead with an accelerated departure. The staff, tense and afraid, were holed up in the compound, in lockdown.

We just had to complete the program handover to the local community and authorities and get the hell out of there. It was going to be rough, though. It wasn't clear who to trust. Those in a position to help—the police, the military, the government, even some "trusted" former staff—also had the most power to hurt. Some of them were full-fledged criminals; others were simply on the take.

But the women would be the ones who lost out. South Sudan ranks among the worst places in the world to be a woman. Thousands have been terrorized, tortured, and repeatedly raped, with no access to medical care, or any form of justice. Many have had to flee their homes and endure extreme poverty and hunger. It is a place where food, shelter, and education—the most basic of human rights—are considered negotiables for women. Men hold the power in South Sudan and exercise all the levers of control.

South Sudan's deputy minister of gender, child, and social welfare considers the devaluation of women and girls as one of the main obstacles to the country's stability and forward development. Over decades of war and conflict, women and girls have increasingly become targets of sexual violence and remain so today. Once considered collateral damage, women are used by the warring parties as a deliberate means of destroying families and communities. Rape is endemic and goes unchallenged. Women are raped when they leave their homes to search for food and firewood, to access essential services, and even on the way to the trainings. Then, and now, there is no safety for women in South Sudan.

On that first trip to Rumbek in 2008, I had the chance to talk with multiple groups of program participants about their lives. Sitting on mats and scarves under a large shade tree, they spoke of soap making and being responsible for keeping the children clean and fed. And how the training, especially in the areas of health and hygiene and women and the economy, was opening their eyes and minds. "Before we were victims of war. Everything was closed to us. We were sleeping . . . now we are awake," said one woman.

The women also talked about knowing their rights, having a better home life with less domestic violence, and learning to set goals and plan ahead. Most were using their monthly training stipend to bring home little things for the family, a bunch of bananas or a tool, to demonstrate the program's value or to pay school fees for their children. Some were saving it in a "black box," away from their husbands, for emergencies. Before this program, the main occasions that women could leave home were for deaths and marriages, they told me. Men would do the shopping to keep women from going out. Now they were freer to come and go. It was like their very first taste of liberation.

Though some of the men were skeptical or angry at first—one woman's husband beat her and called the program a "training for prostitutes"—many were supportive, thanks to the stipends and the women sharing with their families what they had learned. The husbands had paid a lot of cows for the women and came to see the training as "adding value" to them, that their investments were paying off. In a place where women were valued beneath animals, that was progress.

The women in that community gave me the nickname *Yar*, which means *cow* in Dinka. This was meant as a compliment as cows are revered for their beauty as well as their ability to provide food, clothing, and milk to orphans whose mothers have died in childbirth. A man's wealth and status is largely determined by the number of cattle he owns. "You're old, but you have good teeth," the women said, assessing my value at 120 cows. I suspected it was my tooth gap that merited those few extra head.

Cows are more highly prized than women. Both are treated as property whose ownership can be transferred at will. I will never forget the look on the face of a fourteen-year-old girl who had been sold into marriage for 130 cows. Pure innocence mixed with sheer terror. Her mother wanted her to stay in school but was unable to intervene, and the daughter, whose wedding was planned for the following week, could not disappoint her family; she was the only girl, and they needed those cows. The marriage meant not only the end of her education, but likely immediate childbearing and a life of domestic support to her husband's family.

In a country where child marriage is already widespread—UNICEF estimates that more than 50 percent of girls in South Sudan are married when they are still children, some as young as nine years old—war places added pressure on poor families to marry off their daughters at a young age. Although the legal marriage age in South Sudan is eighteen, enforcement is weak, and traditional norms usually triumph.

Once the organization left, who would look out and offer support for these women? All I could hope was that the program had already done some good, that the women there had begun to realize their worth and how to push back against those constraints, even in small ways. At least they would have each other.

I was thinking about going there to finish closing down the office myself. But Rumbek was so volatile—like Kabul, maybe worse. Or Nigeria. When I was in Nigeria a few years earlier, before the world learned of stolen girls and Boko Haram (which means "Western education is forbidden"), there'd been a massive street protest in Enugu over a Danish cartoon satirizing the Prophet Muhammad. The controversy had raged for weeks, resulting in bloody riots, church burnings, and a significant loss of life.

The angry crowd-turned-mob had become out of control, and the police had responded, first with tear gas and then bullets. The country office was right in the line of fire. My colleagues looked frightened but were doing their best to stay calm. They urged me to take cover. I'd crouched beneath a desk for ten or twenty minutes, heart pounding, frozen, unsure whether to wait it out or run. Bill and I had lost touch during the incident when our usual modes of communication failed. Then my colleagues and I had to leave Enugu quickly; it wasn't safe.

But the situation in Rumbek was different. Life there seemed to have little value, and the thought of becoming yet another development professional killed in some random—or not so random—act of violence unnerved me. It happened all the time, those murders, kidnappings, and jailings. Maybe there'd even be a small news article, tucked away at the back of the international section, reporting my death. Or maybe it would just be my boys growing up without their mother.

Over the next few weeks, I was in full crisis mode, working almost around the clock to get everyone out of Rumbek as fast as possible. The boys could sense that something was wrong and instinctively gave me a little more space. There was no reason to explain what was happening; it would only make them worry. Bill was adamant that I not go to Rumbek when we spoke.

Every morning, I woke with a familiar roll of the gut, bordering on nausea, about what might have happened overnight. It reminded me too much of those unbelievably tense weeks when I learned the Taliban had issued a death threat against the country director in Afghanistan. Sweeta and I had worked together for years. She was a friend. They warned her that if she didn't leave her job, they would kill her son and baby girl.

"My husband and I were watching TV when I got a call from one of our guards advising me not to come to the office because of a death threat they received," Sweeta explained to me later. "In the morning I decided to go anyway. I never trusted these kinds of letters. . . . I was not the person to be scared or give up. I worked in very difficult circumstances such as the Taliban time," she said. "The year of my birth, 1973, was the same year Afghanistan was established as a Republic and welcomed its first President, former Prime Minister Mohammed Daoud Khan, a man whose progressive politics encouraged women's education and protected their human rights. A woman of the times, my mother was a doctor and a professor who for seven years served as the chairperson for the Kabul Institute of Medicine. I followed in her footsteps to become a doctor of medicine, nearly completing my studies until I was forced to withdraw from school after the rise of the Mujahidin."

Exhausted by the endless violence on the streets of Kabul, Sweeta and her family fled to Rawal Pindi, Pakistan, where they were refugees for the first time in their lives, though it wouldn't be the last.

"Following the Mujahidin, many greeted the Taliban with hope, though it was short-lived. The Taliban regime implemented a heavily restrictive, fundamentalist interpretation of Islam that rendered Afghan women far less free than before. Access to education remained out of reach for me and my Afghan sisters; we were not allowed to leave the house by ourselves and were relegated to the position of animals, forced to walk behind, rather than next to, our husbands.

"Returning to Kabul the year the Taliban took power officially, I withdrew inside my home where I did not wear the *burqa* and could do as I pleased. Inside the relative security of my own home, I taught English to other women, a crime and a heresy at that time but a personal duty to my sisters and my sole source of stimulation."

After an especially dangerous threat against Sweeta and her family, they had no choice but to again flee to Pakistan, where they remained until 2001, just before the September 11th attacks. When they were able to return home, it was to prepare again for conflict. As they lay in wait of the American invasion that eventually deposed the Taliban, they hoped for a new beginning.

"Since the fall of the Taliban, issues such as mandatory marital sex, forced marriages, self-immolation, and honor crimes continue to plague rural communities and exclude women from the sphere of influence," Sweeta said. "We have 25 percent women in parliament but extremists retaliate, threatening the brave women who do seek leadership. We are building bridges and schools every day, but women do not feel safe enough to walk across alone, nor are girls sure that they will not be attacked if they dare to fill the schools."

Sweeta often spoke of two Afghanistans: one in Kabul, where women and girls have access to an education, economic, and political opportunities, and another outside of the capital, where they are subject to a different set of rights and laws that restrict their freedom and endanger their lives. As a rule, in more remote areas of the country, women are still not permitted to work, study, or stand on their own. Those in the program, through the dual perils of conflict and oppression, had truly suffered. Eighty percent were illiterate and innumerate. Many of the women did not know their own age or the ages of their children. A number of them were single heads of households with seven, eight, ten children to care for. It was not uncommon for these women to marry off their daughters at nine or ten in order to reduce the economic burden on the family. The same had been done to them. There was little choice.

One of the first women I met in Afghanistan was an eighteen-year-old girl who had been living her life as a man. At the time, the only people who knew her story were her family and a teacher, who had confidentially contacted the country office on her behalf. When a rocket hit and demolished their home, her brother was killed and her father, the family's sole support, became partially paralyzed and mentally ill. She herself was scarred and disfigured from the fire that followed the attack and had lost an ear. Her mother was in urgent need of medicine, and her sisters needed food, but she was not allowed to leave the house without a male. Desperate to help, to do something for her family, she donned her brother's clothes and went out to search for work. It was the only way.

The year we moved to Rwanda, Afghanistan's Independent Human Rights Commission registered more than three thousand instances of violence against women. And those were only the cases that came to light. There were no laws in place then to protect women from domestic violence, sexual harassment or rape; rape victims themselves had been the ones charged with extramarital sex. Eighty-seven percent of Afghan women are reported to have experienced at least one form of physical, sexual, or psychological abuse, at least half of them at home. Women like Sweeta were essentially putting themselves on the frontlines of conflict simply for trying to help their own.

"I went through [that death threat from the Taliban] ten times, and as I read it again and again there was a growing fear inside me," Sweeta said. "It was about my little son who was seven and little daughter, only one year and six months. They warned me that if I didn't quit the job they will kill my daughter and son and I would be responsible for their deaths. As a mother of two kids, I could not believe these two innocents were the ones who should pay [for] the cost of my work."

Following the initial death threat, Sweeta received two phone calls from the Taliban. They seemed to know where she was at all times, to be tracking her movements. No place felt safe. I used every political connection I could think of to try and get Sweeta and her children out of Afghanistan, knowing how difficult it would be to live with myself if anything were to happen to them on my watch. I spent weeks calling congressional staffers, lawyers, those with influence, running down tenuous links to make contact with people who could put me in touch with other people who could connect me to those who might be able to help.

The problem was that post-9/11, the United States was letting few Afghans into the country. Those they did allow first had to undergo rigorous security screening designed to flag potential terrorists. That took time, precious time Sweeta and her family didn't have. Finally, we received word that their visas had been approved, except for her husband's, whose case was pending. Afraid to delay any longer and at her husband's urging, Sweeta and her children boarded the first available flight to the US. He joined them a few weeks later.

The situation in Rumbek didn't look as though it would escalate to this level, but then again this was Rumbek. Anything could happen. There was no question that the staff members were in a precarious situation, their safety in no way guaranteed. And I felt just as responsible for them as I did for Sweeta and her family.

Needing some kind of diversion from the crisis over the weekend, the boys and I headed to a roadside market near our neighborhood in search of a few plants to spruce up our still under-furnished house. As I was paying, Sam and Eli carried a heavy potted cactus back to the car; it was then that I realized I had left my cell phone in the car with the window down—a rookie mistake.

Then I got angry with the women who sold me the plants, raising my voice in an accusatory tone. A man who had appeared to be working with them had suddenly disappeared . . . maybe with my phone, but maybe not. No doubt they were thinking: "That *muzungu* woman is crazy." It didn't help that I had called the police in a rage (thankfully the call didn't go through).

The boys were visibly embarrassed. They tugged at my arm, urging me to calm down. "Let's go, Mom. It doesn't matter," Eli pleaded, speaking for the three of them, a spark of apprehension in his eye. I was still trying to return that damn cactus, but the boys had already loaded it into the car. I took a deep breath and saw that the women who made the sale were all smiling, thrilled with the extra cash. I relented and drove home in a huff, while the boys silently stared out their windows. I wondered what lesson they were taking from this little incident other than that Mom sometimes loses it. But they knew that already—not that that made it okay.

I thought of how many times I'd avoided eye contact with onlookers when my father had one of his explosions. It was bad enough at home but public places were even worse. My siblings and I would cringe in our seats as Dad shouted down my mother, or a waitress, in a restaurant or on family outings. Here I was doing the same thing to my kids.

I'd taken pride in my "on it–ness," in my ability to keep my problems at home away from work and my work challenges away from home, but what if that firewall wasn't as failsafe as I thought it was? Of course these work-life boundary issues were nothing compared to the life and death struggles of so many South Sudanese, Afghan, and Rwandan women, but I still grappled with them. Those lines seem so clear and clean in the abstract, and then one of your kids gets hurt or sick, or you hear pain or fear in their voices, and that line instantly dissolves. These were my kids, but they were people, too. As much as I wanted to shield them from the uglier parts of my work, maybe trying so hard to keep it all separate was not the answer. Without Bill here, I couldn't just retreat into myself or work late into the night. But I found that I didn't really want that, not anymore. Losing it in front of the boys was inexcusable, no question, but it was also part of understanding me and what I did for a living.

The boys had started to call me out on my behavior, just as I called them out on theirs. This pushing back was new, and it was good. Unlike my parents, who rarely apologized or acknowledged wrongdoing, I'd strived for mutual accountability.

It was around this time that I started having flashbacks to my time in the Soviet Union and Russia. Despite Rwanda's undeniable beauty, cleanliness and civility, striking development gains, and fast-growing economy, there is an underside to it not apparent to the average visitor. I don't know why I hadn't noticed it, or made the connection, on previous visits. This latest crisis in South Sudan probably had something to do with it.

I'd heard the usual criticisms leveled at Rwanda over the years and could see, at least on the surface, where there were similarities in the two countries. Both had dominant party systems allowing for only limited opposition and dissent. Both were led by popular leaders who, following traumatic upheavals, had been able to restore stability and pride in their nations. Both presidents shared a penchant for order and organization, in terms of their governance.

The Rwanda Patriotic Front, or RPF, is involved in nearly all aspects of daily life, from the news headlines to the performance plans of every cell, sector, district, and province. Government agencies, local officials, even businesses, work according to a master plan designed to move the country along a defined path toward a better future. The "national solidarity" camps, aimed at developing Rwanda's youth, are reminiscent of the Young Pioneer camps from Soviet days. The country's firm suppression of ethnicity, intended to build unity and a common identity, called to mind the Soviet's Russification strategy. No official references to ethnic groups are tolerated in Rwanda.

Running counter to that is the near-constant use of the Swahili word *muzungu*, literally translated as "aimless wanderer," but used to refer to any foreigner, specifically someone with white skin. Everyone uses it, including the *muzungus*. Even two-year-olds point and call out, "*Muzungu, Muzungu.*" Harmless, even amusing in some respects, the label had a deeper, depersonalizing aspect that was troubling, perhaps because of my Jewish background. I'd never before experienced such a distinct sense of otherness, at home or abroad.

Human safety was paramount in Rwanda. Nightly military patrols as well as large-scale police deployments across the country kept close tabs on locals and foreigners alike. Drivers communicated through a series of well-known hand signals to show when the police were nearby, which was often. In Rwanda, though, the police were there to guard and protect—unlike in many countries, including Russia, where they were feared and/or used their position to line their pockets. There were few places in the world where a woman could walk alone at night and feel perfectly safe. Rwanda was one of them. That said, there was a Big Brother quality to all the watching and checking, an overriding sense that if you stepped out of line or said the wrong thing, someone would notice.

For a country so recently traumatized by the horrors of genocide, and the threat of insecurity looming within and around its borders, the compulsion to keep a very tight lid on things is understandable. A necessary evil, some might say. And who am I to judge? I cannot even begin to account for the difficulty of the country's choices. I was simply a guest.

The Rwandan government is not only functional but also seems committed to tackling its social problems, and to investing in its people. In a meeting with the Ministry of Gender, the permanent secretary there spoke candidly of the country's persistent challenges: drug abuse and alcoholism, domestic violence, prostitution, and family feuds. Her openness was both surprising and impressive. Many countries confronted these same challenges but were loathe to share them with outsiders. It was akin to airing one's dirty laundry in public. Even during Gorbachev's "openness" tenure, and in the new Russia, the leadership whitewashed its problems, either pretending they didn't exist or shifting the focus to the United States. Meanwhile, tens of thousands of women were dying in their homes each year from domestic abuse while the oligarchs and mafia robbed and terrorized the country.

History, though, as well as my own experience shows that sooner or later, people push back against rigidity and rules—in one way or another.

The crisis in South Sudan, the flashbacks to the Soviet Union and Russia, and the plant market were all connected in my mind. The adrenaline-pumping, high-risk-and-reward nature of the work—the extremity of it—had allowed me to effectively block out or work around my other problems. Work in general had been a steady bulwark against those personal issues; it was the one thing I could always fall back on and do. But here in Rwanda, trying to meet the dual demands of work and motherhood, my career uncertain, my marriage uncertain, those issues had forced their way to the surface.

The incident at the plant market, in particular, jarred me, even more than usual. That hair-trigger temper, inherited from my father, had been an albatross since childhood. In the face of Dad's rages I seethed with my own. *Stupid. Bitch. Cunt.* Though meant for my mom, I wore those words as if they belonged to me, defined me. But I rebelled against them, too, from the indignity of it. I would race up the stairs to my room, slam the door, and swipe everything off the dresser, upturn the mattress, or start to clean furiously. The only control I had was over that room.

Why would she tolerate such demeaning behavior, or stay in a marriage that clearly wasn't working? Why didn't she do something, say something? Where was her voice? I threw tantrums, screaming fits, most of them directed at her. Mom was the one nearest; Dad was untouchable.

She told me after one of those tantrums that, if I wasn't her own daughter, she wouldn't like me very much, that she hoped I had a child just like me so I would see how horrible it was. The sense of shame was too great. I hid myself away in the bedroom closet. Didn't she understand that my anger was on her behalf?

I'd tried and tried to manage my temper, rein it in, but the impulse was still there, like a thunderclap threatening to explode. I made sure to offset my volatility with loads of affection so the boys knew for certain they were well loved, to make sure I did it differently from my dad. But that consciousness, that intentionality, hadn't made it easier to curb it.

Now that I was playing the role of both parents, I could see myself more clearly through their eyes and I didn't like what I saw: the way they looked at me sometimes, that look of fear. I'd looked at my father exactly the same way. They had no idea how much I'd agonized over my own victim mentality, how often my upbringing was used to explain away my bad behavior, not only with my family, but, I wasn't proud to admit, with colleagues as well. How was it possible to be so in control in some parts of life and so out of control in others?

Back at work, the "handover" to the local authorities in Rumbek was uneventful, although "takeover" was more like it. Everyone seemed to want a piece of the action: the police, government officials, even some of the former staff. All program assets were turned over the Government of South Sudan Relief and Rehabilitation Commission (RRC). The next morning, however, a colleague from the regional team in Kenya, who was there to help troubleshoot the situation, called to report that things were starting to get ugly.

Eight male community leaders with their armed security guards arrived at the compound on motorbikes and demanded the new Hilux, a car that had already been given to the women by the former governor. They claimed that the women never used the vehicle and that it had been given to the women without their being consulted. A ferocious argument ensued, and one of the community leaders slapped my Kenyan colleague several times; the country director, shaken, refused to leave her room at the compound.

Meanwhile, four security agents assigned by the governor's office came and demanded two hundred dollars each, claiming that the former country director had been paying them that amount on a monthly basis. The Asset Verification Team from the RRC also came to search every packed box to ensure that no assets were being taken out of the country. A formal letter of clearance from them, a release, was required to leave Rumbek. The insistence on protocol seemed ludicrous amid this free-for-all, but it had to be done.

A former staff member then called to inform the country director that the remaining staff would not be allowed to leave Rumbek unless she was paid $1,000 in cash. She knew what she was doing—her husband was a national intelligence service agent. Four other security agents were posted at the airport to flag the names of staff to immigration officials to halt their departure.

I frantically paced the house, cell phone in hand, desperate to hear from my colleagues on the ground. Hours went by, and still nothing. It was painful being on the sidelines, responsible yet powerless, anticipating the worst but hoping for the best. That sense of impotence once again took me right back to my teens, when I stood by and watched as my father discharged his fury, incapable of helping my mother, or myself. That was a time when I was a bystander. I never wanted to go back there.

Feeling useless but determined to help, I repeatedly called the UN's Office for the Coordination of Humanitarian Affairs (OCHA) in Juba to plead for their support. OCHA is supposed to advocate on behalf of NGOs with local governments. They affirmed that this level of harassment was not uncommon, and while sympathetic, the situation was "too political," and they would not get involved. With more pushing, they did agree to "monitor" the airport so that the staff could be evacuated from Rumbek.

The country director was dragged from her room and forced to sign a document stating that when she returned to Rumbek, an unspecified amount of "cost share" funds would be paid to the community. This was never going to happen, but it was the only way they would release her to travel. She ultimately paid $300 to remove the threat of detention at the airport and ensure the team's safe exit from the country.

When the call finally came through with the news that every staff member was on the plane bound for Nairobi, I whooped with relief.

8

Grace

The black fog that had descended over me before we came to Rwanda was starting to lift. The broad shapes and outlines of the past were becoming clearer, more visible. Maybe it was being alone with the kids, or the new environment, or the people around me, but my experiences were serving to break down what I thought I knew about myself. It made me want to reexamine everything. I had come to Rwanda needing a change yet clinging to the person I was instead of the woman I wanted to be. Unpacking decades of heavy baggage was not easy. To get serious about a reinvention, though, it was a necessary part of the journey.

As I reflected more on my own sense of being a bystander growing up, my thoughts naturally turned to Rwanda and the genocide. Through my own fieldwork as well as twice-yearly visits to the country for almost a decade, I had come to believe there was blood on many hands—on those of the perpetrators, certainly, but also on those who knew what was happening and stood by, did nothing, to intervene. The entire world was watching. The United Nations, national governments, and countless diplomats and individuals were in a position to change the course of events in big and small ways, and they did not. This was not supposed to happen again. *Never again* was supposed to mean *never again*.

Yet there were upstanders as well. The worst of humanity brings out the best of humanity, or so they say. There was Father Borile, a Catholic priest from Italy who had been living in Rwanda since 1987 and ran the Centre Saint Antoine Orphanage, a place of refuge for 830 Tutsi and Hutu children during the genocide. Again and again, he managed to turn the Hutu killers away from the orphanage gates, protecting those kids as if they were his own. And Carl Wilkens, who delivered lifesaving food and medicine to hundreds of trapped children. Carl was the only American to remain in Rwanda then. A number of Hutus also risked their own lives to save friends and colleagues, even total strangers, from almost certain death.

One such person was Grace, a Rwandan woman approaching thirty to whom I was introduced through Aegis Trust, a UK-based charity focused on genocide prevention and that runs the Kigali Genocide Memorial. Aegis's peace education initiative told the stories of Rwandans who had to make "impossible choices" as children in 1994. Grace, whom they'd been assisting for years through their social protection program, was one of them. I'd begun discussions with Aegis about a potential partnership at the opportunity center, so when they asked me to join them on a visit to Grace's home, I accepted.

Grace lived on the outskirts of Nyimirambo, one of Kigali's oldest and liveliest neighborhoods. The area's chronically jammed streets and sidewalks are lined with an odd mixture of corner stores, clothes shops, funky bars, and betting sites. It is also home to much of the country's Muslim population and a landmark mosque with green and white minarets. Muslims were only a tiny fraction of the population before the genocide, but their influence was mighty. Refusing to participate in the mass killing, a number of imams had given shelter to those fleeing and hiding. They'd looked past their otherness and led with their humanity. This caused significant numbers of Rwandans to convert to Islam after the genocide.

"I became an orphan when I was two years old," Grace explained, as we sat together on the black and gold patterned sofa in her living room. Her mudbrick house, finished with a layer of cement—a gift from the government—seemed a cut above the others in their village. The house and furniture were given to Grace and her daughter, Vanessa. Their case was special: Grace was not a genocide survivor, but Vanessa was.

Grace was ten when they started killing. "The first person they killed was our neighbor and his children. The next morning I saw the bodies. Then they buried them. I saw many children being killed. People who hid Tutsi were killed. My grandmother hid someone in our house, but I don't know what happened to that person."

They had to leave their village when they heard the Inkotanyi (RPF soldiers) were coming. Grace walked with her grandmother and all of the people who were fleeing to Congo.

"I heard screaming beside the road. My grandmother didn't want to stop, but I went to see. A woman was bleeding and dying. A small child was lying on her. It was a baby girl, too small to walk. She was crying."

Although the mother couldn't speak, she made motions to Grace to take the baby. Her grandmother, afraid of being killed, instructed her to leave it. Grace refused. She picked up the baby and put her on her back. She carried her thus as they traveled over the mountain and across the Nyabarongo River. When they finally reached a refugee camp in Goma, she named the baby Vanessa.

"After we walked back to Rwanda, I never returned to school. I had to look after Vanessa, so I started to sell vegetables on the street to make a little money. Because Vanessa was Tutsi, she was not accepted by others. Vanessa kept asking me why people hated her."

When Vanessa was thirteen, Grace told her the difficult truth. "I had decided to be your sister, but I am also your mother. If you understand that, we can live together for a long time."

As a ten-year-old, Grace demonstrated one of the most extraordinary acts of moral courage I had ever heard of. She gave up her own childhood, her own dreams, to raise Vanessa, now a beautiful young woman in her twenties. Grace is married now with two children of her own and another one on the way. She still sells vegetables in the market when she can. Vanessa is in school but continues to struggle with her identity. When asked about her future, she said: "I want to help other miserable children improve their lives."

Leaving their home that afternoon, I wondered how Grace and Vanessa were able to live and function day to day, with their stories, that truth, inside of them. It had to be debilitating. The heroism Grace had shown in picking up a dying stranger's baby and raising her as her own was remarkable in and of itself, but I also marveled at the enormous strength it must have taken to move beyond what had happened, to accept what had occurred with such, well, grace, to own it and still maintain hope for the future.

The pain from my past didn't even register on the scale in comparison, and yet I hadn't truly been able to do what Grace or even Vanessa had done— accept what had occurred, move beyond it. Every now and then, there would be flashbacks, a trigger. And, yes, my own bursts of anger. Once, when my parents were visiting, Sam and Eli were babies then, Dad came running across the street as I was talking to our neighbors. The sight of him running toward me induced such a panic that I stopped, mid-sentence, and held my breath, waiting for the expected blow. It didn't come, of course. I was an adult with my own kids, but, in some ways, I was still that kid.

The women who were sharing their stories, though, were helping me to see things, deal with things differently. Little by little, I could feel myself opening up. Living in Rwanda was more frustrating, perhaps, but also enlightening on another level. It wasn't that these stories were new, but, for some reason, they hadn't fully sunk in. I was a development professional doing my job. Maybe it was a simple matter of the amount of time I had—a year as opposed to weeks—but I felt an unfamiliar closeness to these women.

Grace could have left the baby. She could have picked her up and then abandoned her later when caring for her was too difficult, or given her to another family. Grace was just a child herself, but she showed such audacity, such heart. She wasn't paralyzed over the decision, and she didn't ask for permission. She was focused. She was intentional. She jumped without knowing where she would land. She made a choice and saw it through. And she owned that choice completely.

These recent conversations with Josephine and Euphraise, and now Grace, opened my eyes in a new way, not only to the depths of human suffering, but to the resiliency and the special commonality between women of all types and walks of life. They also showed me the power of choice. The power of choice for women in particular. I came away with new respect for who they were and what they had endured, while at the same time more conscious of some of my own long-repressed family memories, of the choices *I* still needed to make.

I was starting to see that each of us had our own story, even if it was just the one we told ourselves to get through the day.

9

Women in Rwanda

There was another reason that Rwanda had been a fortuitous choice for me at this particular time. The country's women were on the rise. Thanks to President Paul Kagame's leadership on women's rights, the phrase *Abagore ba Kagame* ("the women of Kagame") has become commonplace. His promotion of women, I'd since learned, was inspired by his own mother. When the family escaped to Uganda in 1959, it was his mother who learned how to farm and hunt to keep them from starving. Kagame worked to advance women, as a rebel leader and during the rebuilding that followed the genocide. When asked why he was behind women, he said, "It just made common sense."

Today, women are encouraged to assume leadership roles in politics and business, and they share relatively equal access to health care and education. Yet women also remain thwarted by poverty, patriarchy, and exclusion. Rwanda, therefore, makes for a fascinating case study as a country that has put women at the top of its development agenda.

Before the 1994 genocide, only a handful of women served in national government. Women could not own land nor have bank accounts. Taking a job outside the home was almost unheard of, and educational opportunities were limited. Now, at roughly half the population, women continue to play a vital role in nation building. The Constitution requires a 30 percent quota of women in government, but they have far surpassed that. Rwanda can boast the highest share of women in elected and appointed leadership positions in the world.

Visions 2020 and 2050 and the country's progressive gender policy aim to integrate women throughout government and society. Rwanda complies with UN Security Council Resolution 1325, which provides for women's partici- pation in peace building and the protection of women's rights, and it is one of only fifty-two countries that criminalize marital rape. A police hotline is available to report cases of rape and abuse, and perpetrators receive actual jail sentences. One-stop centers in Rwanda link the police with other ministries to provide coordinated support and services to victims of violence.

Investments in forging a strong legislative framework are starting to pay off. Women are allowed to own land and inherit property and pass on inheri- tance rights to their children. When they legally marry, they can choose to hold assets separate from their spouses.

Girls, in particular, have made measurable gains. Literacy rates for females aged fifteen and over are close to 80 percent, and girls participate in primary and secondary school at higher rates than in most neighboring countries, though secondary completion rates remain low in parts of the country and tertiary education numbers are still in the single digits.

Over the last decade, women have had more access to economic opportu- nities than ever before and are beginning to make inroads into a number of key industries, including hospitality and tourism and the all-important tech- nology sector. More than thirty-eight thousand or 26 percent of businesses are now owned by women.

Is Rwanda a role model for women's and girls' advancement? To a certain extent, it appears to be so. In some respects, though, not yet.

While women are strongly represented in government, men still occupy many of the local leadership positions, and the president retains ultimate authority. Knowledge and enforcement of laws and protections for women, especially in rural areas, are persistent problems. This is often the case for poor and excluded women, who either don't know or are unable to claim their rights. Patriarchy, as well as traditional norms and attitudes, continues to limit women's status in the family and community. "When a woman is tak- ing the front seat, the household is in trouble," goes the old adage.

Rwanda was certainly an interesting and complicated place to try to get back to a sense of being a "woman-in-charge" of her own fate, her own choices. Rwandan women have made such remarkable progress on so many fronts, and yet, being a "good Rwandan" meant women still might have to take a back seat, submit to their husbands, in their homes. Perhaps it was my Western feminist lens talking, but I was finding it difficult to reconcile those conflicting paradigms as I continued to connect with the women around me.

"We have a big legacy to overcome in terms of marginalizing women," said Jean Bosco Murangira, the director for women's economic empowerment at the Ministry of Gender. "Some poor women are benefiting from the programs, but not all. Demand is greater than supply."

"Many women became more vulnerable or traumatized as a result of the genocide and are still struggling," Murangira continued.

Anastasie, a 2009 graduate, admitted to being "in a miserable situation" before the program. "I didn't know my rights or even my responsibility in the family and in the community. I was expecting all family needs from my husband, even my clothes. I did not know that a woman can lead and be protected by law, can generate income."

Labor-force participation rates are high for women in Rwanda, but the majority of those who do work outside the home are still engaged in "vulnerable" employment, meaning they work informally or are self-employed. Much of this work is in agriculture. While women contribute food and small amounts of cash to the household, their income rarely corresponds to the time and effort invested in farming. One of the more successful ag cooperatives led by women—recognized for its quality maize, market focus, and environmental practices—experienced a huge drop in membership because there was no cash to pay members, even though women were putting in a full workday or more during harvest time.

As a result, many working women continue to live in poverty. Like their counterparts in the US and around the world, they also suffer the double burden of work and family. In addition to primary child- and elder-care responsibilities, they still do most of the cooking, cleaning, and other time-consuming household chores. This impacts their ability to engage in paid work, but also their overall empowerment and agency.

I thought of Ange, a graduate in her twenties living just outside of Kigali, in the village of Gisozi. We met the year before when a small group of visitors from the US came to her home. A demure woman with a soft, open face and an easy smile, Ange for me typified the double burden in Rwanda. She was married with two children—she had a new baby girl—and was working and taking care of the household, including a younger sibling.

Hers was one of the stories I had collected myself and brought to Rwanda. I'd asked a staff member to reach out to Ange again to see how she was faring, and she readily agreed to meet. When we had met the first time, we sat together in her sparsely furnished living room; a well-worn sofa filled most of the space. A few plastic chairs were brought in for the extra guests. The room was illuminated by dusky light that filtered in from a tiny barred window high up on the wall of her mud house, aided only by a single bulb overhead. Her husband sat by her side as we talked, either to show his support or to monitor the conversation.

"My parents were killed in the genocide when I was young, seven years old. I became an orphan. I stopped my primary studies," she'd told us in a quiet voice. "I was obliged to 'marry' at twenty-one years old and I became a housewife. After that, I would sit at home waiting for my husband to come back. I was longing to learn a vocational skill, and so I was trained on tailoring sponsored by Compassion International. This was in vain, however, because I could not afford a sewing machine. My husband refused to buy me a machine, pretending that once I had my own income I could undermine him.

"My husband was an electrician and had a low income. Sometimes we had no food. My husband undermined me because I had no input in household needs, and I was mistreated." She'd glanced nervously at her husband when she said this but his expression remained unchanged.

"The local leaders selected me [again] among others and told us that we were to go for vocational skills training. During the program, I was trained on life skills such as health and wellness, sustaining an income, household savings, creating and starting a small business. Every woman received ten dollars per month as sponsorship fund. I used my savings to buy clothes and food.

"After that, I was introduced to Gahaya Links, where I worked on beadmaking. I was given transport fees and earned between 40,000 and 70,000 RWF (between $60 and $90) per month, depending on supplies made. I opened a bank account.

"My savings assisted me to prepare for a legal marriage and to rehabilitate the family's house, which has three rooms. I renovated another five rooms and they are rented out. I receive 50,000 RWF (about $70) per month as rent revenue. This assisted me to buy two cows and two sheep, plus a dog. I also paid school fees for my sister who lives with us."

Like Josephine, Ange's industriousness was striking and how she was thinking about the end game, using what little money she had to finance her rental-property and animal-husbandry businesses that could pay dividends over the long term.

On this second visit, Ange wasn't there when we arrived, though we were expected; she had gone to pray at a local church nearby. Her husband and his brother kept us company as we waited out back. A string of laundry hung along the side of the house, above a row of yellow jerry cans. Behind the house where we sat was a narrow dirt passage lined with tiny animal pens that held Ange's noisy sheep and black cows. An injured dog and its pup lay panting under a small overhang, trying to escape the afternoon heat.

Ange looked frazzled as she rushed to greet us, wearing a bright green and yellow *kitenge*, her head wrapped in a white scarf, the baby tied to her back. Since we last met, Ange said that she had given up her work at Gahaya Links in order to renovate and rent out more houses and focus on her animal-husbandry business. The cows had had a calf and she had six new lambs to sell in the market. She was also making and selling her own jewelry.

Ange spoke of being the one to support her family because her husband spends most of his income on alcohol, which leaves him in a bad state. "Sometimes he mistreats me and I decide to run for safety to my mother and father-in-law who are more caring. They advise him and unite us, but this does not stop his habits."

Ange came across as a woman who had taken ownership of her life, becoming legally married and making investments in her home and businesses. She was right to take pride in that success, to seize her dream of someday being able to buy enough land to start a cattle ranch. But I came away feeling that her situation was still extremely fragile. She was the only one in her family with a job and was supporting several poorer relatives on her income. I also worried about her marriage, given her husband's "mistreatments."

"Men have always been exploiting women, not for the good of the family but for their own good, and it's having a devastating impact on women and children," said Edouard Munyamaliza, executive secretary of the Rwanda Men's Resource Centre in Kigali.

In Rwanda, there is still resistance in families and society to a woman's voice. Too often, a woman's value is determined by the number of children

Ange with her client ledger.

she has. In too many households, domestic violence persists. Financial dependence on husbands as well as cultural barriers prevent women from seeking help and reporting cases of abuse.

Munyamaliza supports a national campaign to mobilize Rwandan men to take action on gender-based violence and inequality. Due to his efforts, and those of others, greater numbers of men are working to end violence against women and promote their full participation in society. The government is also doing its part, spearheading public-awareness campaigns in communities across the country to address the more entrenched norms and restrictions that continue to impede the progress of women and girls. Long-held attitudes and biases are not easily shifted. It requires consistent leadership and the vigilance of those who most want change. It takes time.

Still, a program assessment in Rwanda and Congo, led by global consulting firm KPMG, showed a clear link between women's status in the family and community and their economic independence. It found "significant changes" in male attitudes toward women, decreases in domestic and sexual violence, and improved health and wellness for women and their children. These changes were primarily due to women earning an income.

The government, aid agencies, and the private sector can do even more to propel women, and the economy, forward. Many of the training and incentive programs they offer, though well intentioned, remain out of reach for poor and more excluded women, who continue to lag behind men in terms of access to skills, markets, capital, and technology. To move a large percentage of women into off-farm jobs over the coming years, a stated goal, that will have to change. Global corporations will also have to step up. Despite recruitment efforts and a World Bank report that ranks Rwanda among the top African countries as a place for business, they have been slow to invest. Kate Spade & Company stands out for that reason.

Kate Spade has a history of working with marginalized women in postconflict communities. In 2007, Kate Spade launched an initiative to engage hundreds of women survivors as producers in Bosnia, Kosovo, Afghanistan, and Rwanda. The company later started *on purpose* in rural Masoro, Rwanda, working to set up an independent supplier for its own brands and others. The social enterprise is fully owned by its artisans, virtually all of whom are women.

Also, Marriott Hotels has joined forces with the Akilah Institute—Rwanda's only all-women's college—in a partnership for their flagship hotel in Kigali. Akilah's innovative, competency-based degree programs in information systems, business management and entrepreneurship, and hospitality management emphasize subject matter expertise alongside leadership skills such as critical thinking, collaboration, and communication. Young women graduate with the knowledge, skills, and confidence to launch their careers in high-growth areas of the economy.

There is the peace dividend to consider as well. Women's economic participation not only has the potential to spur long-term growth, but it can also help mitigate future conflicts. If any country can attest to the need for such a dividend, it is Rwanda.

II

The most common way people give up their power is by thinking they don't have any.

—*Alice Walker*

10

Home

Allan met and married Marjorie, Marge as he called her, in June of 1957, seven months after they had been fixed up at her brother's wedding in Portland, Oregon. Because they lived across the country from one another, it was almost like an arranged marriage; they had spent just two weeks together. Petite and pretty with dark, wavy hair and fair skin, Marge weighed a scant ninety-eight pounds when she walked down the aisle. Right after they wed, she moved from Chicago, where she had grown up sheltered by a domineering mother, into Allan's home in Portland. It must have been a difficult transition for her—twenty years old, isolated, and pregnant with a honeymoon baby, in a still unfamiliar part of the country. His parents were less than welcoming.

Allan completed two years of college before enlisting in the air force. After a year of electronics training, he was sent overseas as part of the war effort, to Korea for six months and then Japan for two years. Once his tour of duty was up, he joined the family business, Henry Sherman and Company, first as a shipping clerk and then a traveling salesman. They sold work clothes mostly, heavy boots, thick flannel shirts, and the like. Other than his annual buying trips to the Far East, his days were spent calling on mom-and-pop stores throughout the Pacific Northwest. He did that for forty-two years, even after he took over the company when a series of strokes left his father incapable of managing the business.

While Dad was on the road during the week, Mom was on her own, practically a single mother. With no car and little cash, she was effectively bound to my brother, sister, and me. Money, particularly in the early days, was a constant problem. I could tell Dad worried about it, about having enough to support the family.

For as far back as I could remember, Mom had been emotionally distant—unavailable even when she was present. It was as if she were afraid of getting too attached to us. The hugs were infrequent. So were the "attagirls." I once asked her why she never complimented me.

"I didn't want you to get a big head," she said, matter-of-factly.

She did all of the normal mom stuff—prepared our meals, took us clothes shopping when we needed some. She volunteered once a week at Good Samaritan Hospital, passing out magazines and sundries to patients; once a month she played mahjong or cards with the girls. Her heart didn't seem to be in any of it, though. Her emotions seemed to have gone missing from the motions.

I'm not sure why she chose to wall off her heart. I'd wondered if this had to do with the death of my older brother, David. A full-term baby, he came home right away but was rushed to the hospital three weeks later when his eyes rolled back in his head. He died after a few hours from kidney failure, a complication resulting from a congenital birth defect.

My mom must have been devastated, but we never discussed it. We made an annual pilgrimage to the Jewish cemetery to place a stone on his tiny grave. She was always stoic there, seemingly more attuned to the custom than her grief. Dad never came with us on these visits, as if the loss were hers to bear alone.

Much later, after having my own children, I got a glimmer of what his death must have been like for her. Perhaps she'd never recovered from the loss, as if one could. But her distance was almost certainly also the result of my father's treatment of her.

When Dad was at home, he berated Mom incessantly, belittled her for all her inadequacies. A missing knife, a messy drawer—nothing was too small to escape his notice or condescension. *Stupid.* They were opposites in every way—his hardness to her softness. *Bitch.* Dad was a schoolyard bully and Mom didn't know how to fight. *Cunt.*

Home is where I learned to be afraid, that words can hurt as much as blows. I couldn't stand the pretense, the fact that we were living this lie. And yet, I myself started to lie at an early age. Most of it was normal kid stuff, but there were bigger lies too, crafted to make me seem more daring or glamourous than I actually was. I told friends that I worked as a model, once having been in a children's fashion show and that I had gone skydiving, adopting the story of a roommate who had done so.

I became sullen. I acted out with men. It made me feel powerful somehow, more in control. The Weather Girls' "It's Raining Men" became a personal theme song. My parents used to joke that my name must have been written on hundreds of bathroom walls because the phone didn't stop ringing. But no amount of attention could have filled the void left by our troubled family.

Yet, if I had to choose sides, I chose him. Dad's intensity and severity seemed preferable to Mom's emotional stinginess, her coolness and passivity. Adopting his fiercely critical eye as my own, I believed her to be less capable, less deserving of respect. Rightly or wrongly, I blamed her for being too weak to stand up for herself, for not showing her love.

We called Dad Taz, short for Tasmanian Devil, because of his wicked temper. A plastic miniature of the Looney Tunes character dangled tellingly from his car's rearview mirror. He was a whirl of energy, positive and negative. Hypercompetitive, whether we were out playing catch or running foot races on the beach, Dad's physicality could barely be contained. He was small in stature but larger than life in my eyes. I lived in awe and fear of him.

His judgments were as fast as his temper. He reproached me for being too sensitive, a crybaby, and chubby, comparing my prepubescent body to my short and stocky Grandma Lilly's. My confidence wrecked, I began to wear big, drapey clothes to hide myself beneath their folds. I developed an obsession with "healthy eating," and turned to school sports, soccer and track, and then taught aerobics for years to prove him wrong.

Then there was the annual "birthday spanking" that always arrived first thing in the morning. Every year I would stay in bed as long as possible, pretending to be asleep, to delay the inevitable. I dreaded it, remember bracing myself for each painful slap on the behind, one whack for each year. This continued until I was well into my teens. I tried running away a few times but never managed to get far. The bed of rocks underneath our deck became a frequent hiding place.

One night, when I was around sixteen years old, I was up in my room reading and didn't hear the call for dinner. Late coming down, I offered some kind of snarky apology and sat at the table to eat. My father rose with a menacing look and moved toward me. With his open hand, he struck me so hard across the face that my nose started bleeding. I sat there, stunned. A minute went by, another minute. Blood dripping down my face, my lip swelling. I expected the spankings and kicks, but this caught me off guard. This was the first time he'd hit me like that.

I rushed upstairs to the bathroom and locked the door. For a while I just stood there crying. Then I began to clean myself up, staring in disbelief at my swollen face, the metallic taste of blood on my lips. I heard someone coming up the stairs and froze, my heart pounding, afraid that my father was after me.

I was surprised when it turned out to be my mother. She comforted me, and then, she went back down and confronted my father.

"You went too far this time, Allan," she said, threatening to call child protective services on him. "You need to get help."

It was the only time I saw Mom stand up for any of us, herself included.

The hitting was in some ways better than the silent treatment. It didn't matter what I'd done wrong—a lack of proper deference, a missed curfew or chore—or who was at fault. I'd be deprived of affection and communication, even so much as eye contact. I became invisible to him and thereby the rest of the family, who didn't dare cross him. To prove his point, to prove my unworthiness, he would shower an excess of attention on my brother and sister.

It became a battle of wills, one that I could never win. Left to drown in the stench of my wrongdoing, I was isolated, ignored for days, even weeks at a time. When I couldn't take it anymore, when my humiliation was complete, I would force myself to write my father a letter of apology. Only then would he acknowledge my presence again in the family. Relieved to be back in his good graces, I would secretly hope that the next time my brother or sister would be the target of his hostility.

My older sister Laura was also in his crosshairs. Her shoulder started dislocating around the eighth grade, the result of a wayward javelin throw in PE. The pain was excruciating, but she became adept at popping it back in. This went on for five years—in and out, in and out—though the doctor had recommended surgery. Dad would have none of it—he simply refused to believe it was that bad. When Laura finally went ahead with the surgery instead of taking a summer job after her freshman year in college, he was so angry he refused to speak to her. It didn't matter that, as the surgeon explained post-op, all the tendons had been stripped and her shoulder was hanging by a thread.

But the absolute worst battles were waged between Dad and my brother, Ken. He was the baby in the family by three years, the only son, and clearly my mother's favorite—the boy she had always wanted. Smart and sensitive with dark, curly locks and glasses from the age of five, Kenny was easy to tease and quick to cry. He made for a stark contrast to our father.

Ken started to get into trouble at an early age, opting out of academics and sports despite being a gifted athlete. Dad's yelling at his soccer matches and track meets, his chastisements on the ride home, became unbearable. He was constantly on Ken's case, castigating him as he made orange juice or did his chores. Doing yardwork one Sunday morning, a weekly task for all of us, Ken went too far cutting back some bramble. Seeing this, Dad stormed over and, without a word, punched him. Ken would try to get away, escape to the only room in the house with a door that locked, the yellow bathroom, but Dad would chase him down and force his way in.

Ken and Dad would constantly butt heads in his teens as he tried to fight back, to step in and protect our mother from the onslaught of verbal abuse. "Leave her alone!" he'd shout at him, risking his brutal response. Defending her was easier than standing up for himself; she was innocent, defenseless. He was the bad one, the one who deserved to be hurt, or so he thought.

One evening we were over at our sister's for dinner. She had recently finished design school and was living on her own not far from our house. Equally traumatized but unwilling to engage, Laura was starting to detach herself from the family. Ken had been spending more and more time at her place. He felt safe there. Mom must have been out of town then because it was just the four of us in her apartment. Ken and I were there when Dad arrived from work, already in a frenzied state—something to do with a lost client and the business. He looked terrified. Almost immediately, he started going at it with my brother.

Before we knew it, he had Ken up against the wall, a contorted, sinister look on his face, threatening to choke the life out of him.

My sister and I froze, too stunned to move, then began shouting at him to let go. We didn't know what he was going to do.

And then, Dad's hands relaxed, as though they had made the decision for him. There was nothing anyone could say. My brother and I grabbed our things and left, left Laura there with our dad. I drove us to the nearby parking lot of our orthodontist, and we spent the night in the car. We couldn't think of anywhere else to go. Both of us scared, unwilling to go home.

Even so, I never stopped respecting my father and craving his love. His approval was everything.

11

Straddling

It was the end of October, nearly three months since our arrival, though it felt like we had been there for much longer. There were parts of our new life in Rwanda I had started to love. Waking up to the morning call to prayers, the sweet sound of songbirds outside the bedroom window, the occasional rooster crowing. I loved the warm days and cool nights, our front garden with its red flowering shrubs and single banana tree, the way the kids from the neighborhood and others joined in with us on our morning runs as we trained for our climb up Mount Kilimanjaro.

Eli and I were out on a run one Sunday morning when a woman, clearly on her way to church in a slim fitted skirt and low heels, prayer book in hand, joined us at pace for a good half mile. We high-fived each other as she turned off the road, then continued on our ways. I'd found the level of religiosity here surprising, how people didn't lose faith, given the number of killings that took place in and around churches during the genocide. Several dozen priests and nuns had been implicated, having lured people in with the promise of sanctuary; many of them even took part in the violence. Some had, in fact, turned away from religion altogether while others turned to Islam. Yet religion has proved instrumental to Rwanda's recovery. The country remains predominately Christian and is filled with active churchgoers.

I loved the gap-toothed women. You rarely see them in the States, owing to personal preferences and good orthodontia, but they were everywhere here.

I had a gap myself and felt right at home. Some African tribes considered a gap a mark of beauty, even wisdom. Through travel, I'd come to appreciate the different kinds and standards of beauty for women around the world. In America, thinness was very much the aesthetic ideal. Bethesda was known as one of the country's fittest cities, so there was always a certain pressure to be thin. In Africa and other parts of the world where food was scarce, however, men were more attracted to larger women because it showed they were well fed. Context, I'd learned, was everything.

I loved running with the boys, and the way little kids wished us "good morning" or said "hello" to practice their limited English on us as we ran past. They seemed to open up in a way they wouldn't otherwise. Instead of the typical grunts, quick dodges, or Sam's snarky "I'm living life to the fullest, Mom" refrain, we had actual conversations. Running and hiking with my sons had been great ways to stay connected, particularly to the older ones, as they grew up.

So had travel. The boys were hooked early on it. At six weeks old, they had their first passports. I remember having to cradle each of their tiny heads for the required photograph. By the time they were three, they had each visited three countries and several states. Road trips, train trips, domestic and international jaunts. We did all of it. Travel became as normal and natural for them as it had for Bill and me.

Eli still remembers our trip to New York to see the Broadway production of *Billy Elliott*. Caught in a fierce downpour after the show, we'd laughed at all the discarded umbrellas littering the streets as we ran to a nearby hotel for shelter. For Sam, it was our post–bar mitzvah trip to the Galapagos Islands, just the two of us. We'd prepared for weeks by reading the same books about Darwin and his finches; we swam with the sea lions and got a peek at Lonesome George, the elderly Pinta Island tortoise, the very last of its kind. Bill and Eli had made their own trip to Costa Rica. The benefits of travel went far beyond connection. It was perspective altering in the best sense—people, art, culture, different ways of thinking and being. From our first days as a couple, travel was something we both prioritized and valued.

There were other parts of our life here in Rwanda, little things common to developing nations, that didn't quite work the way they were supposed to. Customer service was one of them. The boys and I had taken to carrying around a deck of cards or a book to pass the time in restaurants as we waited for our food. Yet there were often multitudes of solicitous wait staff on hand who didn't appear to be doing much of anything. We had a similar experience at RwandAir's Customer Care desk when we inquired about an abruptly canceled flight. The staff were all extremely polite and listened to our problem, but none of them were willing to take action. They simply referred us on to others.

Culture was likely a factor. Rwandan social norms value deference to authority. Recent history had shown that. I'd also noticed it in the office. Employees were hesitant to speak up or push back with supervisors, and each other. Even senior-level managers were reluctant to show initiative or make decisions, to put themselves in front. Education could have also played a role. One study showed that almost half of all workers required training in basic communication and problem solving. Given investments in education and the importance of hospitality and tourism to the economy, this will improve over time.

Rwandan driving skills also left serious room for improvement. It was true that many Rwandan drivers were neophytes—a positive sign of the country's growing prosperity and middle class—but they didn't seem to have learned the basic rules of the road. Drivers, cell phone in hand, would often stop in the middle of the road to take a call or greet a friend. To do otherwise would be considered impolite. The driving schools we saw looked like miniature dirt bike courses, with bright orange cones placed around small ovals so that new drivers could practice stopping and turning.

Road rage didn't begin to describe it. Few knew how to merge; packed commuter vans called *matatus* would just pull out into moving traffic. Moto drivers were particularly heedless, weaving in and around cars, driving on the side of the road or in between lanes. Not only did *they* pose a safety risk, but so did many of their passengers, who rode with everything from live and dead chickens to large plates of glass and doorframes or gigantic metal poles.

Riding on a moto was even less safe than driving beside one. Helmets were required for drivers and passengers, but they were perfunctory. None of them were sized, so in an accident your helmet would simply fly off your head, and we saw accidents all over the place. Our American doctor friend told us that 80 percent of the injuries he treats in the emergency room involved motos. Still, motos were ubiquitous as they were the cheapest and quickest way to get across town.

At least in Rwanda, there was a nod to road safety. No such helmet laws existed in South Sudan; they rode three to five passengers to a moto, with mothers holding their infants to the side or wrapped around their backs. I could see anxious American mothers cringing—car seats facing backward, kids on boosters until they topped eighty pounds. Africa was another world in this respect and so many others.

Bill was coming back to Rwanda today just as I was leaving for D.C. We thought we might meet in the airport—and Bill tried to get airport security to make it happen—but we ended up unable to see each other. Disappointed, but frankly, a little relieved that we had to text our hellos instead, I told him where to find the car in the airport parking lot. *Tag, you're it.*

As I was waiting in the Kigali airport's departure lounge for the flight to Washington, the boys were on my mind. The four of us had been together almost nonstop. The time together had been good. They were beginning to understand what my work was about, just as I was starting to realign some of my thinking around family with the reality of living in Rwanda. Instead of the usual pre-departure scuffle, we sat around the long dining table in the living room and played Five Crowns, a rummy-style card game the boys all loved. Kai was mopey and a bit off his game. So was I; leaving somehow felt harder now.

For the first few hours of the plane ride home, I was still mentally with my family. Then somewhere over the Atlantic my thoughts began to shift. Thinking about my inevitable one-on-one with the new CEO made my stomach churn. She had an intensely critical eye that reminded me too much of my father. I knew she wanted to lay the entire South Sudan mess at my doorstep. Perhaps I deserved it, but she had no idea how complicated the situation had become, how little room there was to maneuver in.

When I got home, our house was so quiet it felt eerie. We were at the tail end of powerful Hurricane Sandy, so even outside it was unusually still. I walked from room to room, hearing my own footsteps, trying to re-familiarize myself. It all felt so unnatural, unsettling even, as though I no longer occupied this life at all. I moved around delicately, like an out-of-town guest in my own home.

My days were to be spent at the annual country director's meeting, planning for the organization's future. Nights, I would be on my own, except for a couple of dinners friends were hosting for my upcoming birthday.

On the cusp of turning fifty and at an inflection point workwise, I had to face facts. It seemed unlikely that there would be room for me at headquarters with the CEO now in place and in the process of restructuring. I'd given up my old job as head of global programs to take the one-year assignment in Rwanda. It seemed equally unlikely that, with Bill at the helm of his DC-based firm, the family would consider permanently moving overseas. Professionally speaking, that left me somewhere between two worlds.

There were other jobs of course. I'd halfheartedly thrown my hat into the ring on a couple of searches, more for the sense of options than out of any real desire to leave. I was still passionate about working with women survivors—it was hard to imagine doing anything else. A new job that might involve less travel meant less time with the women, and that was by far the most rewarding aspect of this work. The women kept me grounded, focused on what was most important. Even with all the uncertainty in my personal and professional life right then, it still felt worth it.

Because of the lingering effects of the storm, the venue for the meeting was changed at the last minute to the hotel where all of the country directors were staying. Arriving just after eight, I circled the lobby and greeted my colleagues from headquarters and around the world, many of whom I'd worked with for close to a decade and, like Sweeta, considered friends. It had been my responsibility to organize and lead these meetings for many years. Now, strangely, the tables were turned, and I was a participant in from the field. With the meeting about to begin, everyone filed into the conference room and found seats at one of the round tables.

The CEO welcomed us and spoke of her commitment to ushering in a new phase of development. She emphasized the need for stronger systems and processes, to move decision making closer to the ground, into the hands of the country offices and leadership. We would spend the time together, she said, learning how to better manage for results and building a common framework for our future work.

That all makes sense, I thought. *Maybe this restructuring is going to be a positive thing.*

Later in the day, I was asked to explain how the program's four integrated outcomes—*women are well, women are decision makers, women earn and sustain an income,* and *women have rebuilt social networks and safety nets*—contribute to lasting change for women. I'd not only given birth to those outcomes, I'd lived by them. A rush of nerves hit me as I made my way toward the front of the room for my presentation. After a few minutes, I relaxed into it, using a flip chart to describe the three-pronged methodology: create awareness, promote behavior change, enable action. And when women had access to knowledge and access to resources, it led to lasting change, and ultimately, to women-led change in the community. It felt good, comforting even, to be back in my accustomed role.

That night over dinner at the home of close friends, I tried not to think about work and just bask in their easy warmth. After a nice bottle of merlot and a perfectly grilled steak, they surprised me with a cake and a slinky black dress for my birthday, which they cajoled me into modeling. I returned late to our empty house.

Lounging in bed the next morning, my mind drifted back to Rwanda, to a trip from a few years earlier. It was a scene that I often returned to:

Women from several neighboring villages have gathered as one. They greet me like a long-lost sister, beckoning me out into the sunny fields to dance with them, with fast clapping and song. I hesitate at first, self-conscious and awkward, my American sensibilities keeping me in check. After a few moments of watching from the sidelines, the rhythm begins to course through my body. I can't hold back any longer and rush out to join them in the dancing.

When I raise up my arms to imitate the revered cow for the traditional cow horn dance, they laugh, and I laugh, too, entranced by the steady beat of the African drum, the raw power of the women's voices raised in song. Their spirit embraces me, connects me to the earth and a past that is not my own yet feels just as real, as if I had lived every moment of it myself. Though I don't belong, I am one of them. These women, my sisters.

I thought about Cecilia, one of the women who spoke at the previous year's graduation ceremony. Her husband would actually count the pieces of meat she ate to make sure that she didn't consume more than her perceived worth. "I never had anything and spent my days crying," she said. Her husband beat her when she enrolled in the program, but still she found the courage to attend the training sessions. As she gained confidence and began to understand her rights, she learned that she did not have to keep quiet about the beatings. She finally reported her husband to local leaders, who took action.

Witnessing the strength of women like Cecilia, who could still smile and laugh in spite of her misery, reminded me that we, all women, were made from the same stuff and possessed the same inner core, an internal reservoir that kept us going, longing, striving for more. Cecilia's resiliency and spirit, like that of the other survivors, had been well honed under the most oppressive conditions—conditions that, despite my abusive father, I had never faced, hoped never to face. I was one of the lucky ones: a woman with choices.

Alone in our tranquil house, and more or less on my own timetable—among the few times since having kids—I continued to think about my options. Should I consider not working for a while, taking a real break from the constant work-life juggling, the repeated departures and reentries? What would it be like not to live like this, with one foot out the door, my heart and loyalties divided? Neither fully here or there. Still, it wasn't a serious option. Given my parents' marriage, I never wanted to feel stuck or trapped in my own. *Having* to stay and *choosing* to stay were two entirely different things. Well before Bill arrived on the scene, I made a personal commitment to remain financially independent.

Several women I knew were trying to reenter the workforce after opting out at some stage of motherhood. The transition wasn't proving to be quick or easy. No doubt the employment landscape had changed, but they had changed, too. They were less sure of themselves, had lost some of their mojo. Most of them had had to claw their way back in and up. And it would be even more difficult to find work over fifty, let alone *meaningful* work.

The *Oprah Winfrey Show* once aired a segment on our program in Congo, and a woman viewer sent in $5,000 in cash. Her note said that she had been saving the money for years in case she needed to leave her husband, but after seeing the story, she felt that those women needed it more.

One of my core beliefs is that economic independence brings choices, especially for women—choices on how money is saved and spent, choices around sending and keeping kids, particularly girls, in school, choices when a woman is suffering from violence or abuse in the family. This proved to be the case in every country I've worked in, including the United States.

Amartya Sen, winner of the 1998 Nobel Prize in Economic Sciences, was among the first to tout the benefits of women's economic participation in his seminal work on gender inequality, *Development as Freedom*. The solution to gender disparities, Sen argued, is to increase women's voice and agency. Agency speaks to one's capacity to act or exert decision-making power; simply put, it is the ability to make one's own choices. Education, ownership rights, and employment outside the home are the best means to that end, enabling women to become empowered and independent, to have a life of their own choosing.

At the heart of women's empowerment, posited Naila Kabeer, a social economist who was recently named one of the foremost women in gender economics, is the process by which those who have been denied the ability to make choices gain such an ability. And resources, material and otherwise, are a precondition for that change. Paid work then, even when that work is not necessarily empowering, is essential, and not only for women.

Income-producing women typically reinvest most of their earnings in their families. They have healthier children, with higher immunization rates and greater nutrition. Their daughters tend to stay in school longer, marry later, and have fewer of their own children. In Africa in particular, every year of schooling boosts a women's wages by 10 to 20 percent. Sen concludes that with voice and agency, "women are increasingly seen, by men as well as women, as active agents of change: the dynamic promoters of social transformations that can alter the lives of *both* women and men."

According to economist Ester Boserup, when women are income earners, their status improves in the family and the community, with a ripple effect that extends well beyond those circles. Joyce Banda, Malawi's first female president said, "We believe that . . . if there is income the woman is in control and can provide better health and nutrition and even send the girls to school and will also make decisions about her life; she can make choices to stay or leave an abusive place." A World Bank study across twenty developing countries found that women's ability to engage in paid work is "one of the most visible and game-changing events in the life of modern households and communities." Even informal work and self-employment have been shown to increase women's agency.

I witnessed this over the course of my work many times. I'd met so many women who, despite overwhelming odds against them, had been able to transform their lives through income generation: women who now had running water and electricity in their homes, their own bank accounts, enough food for two or even three meals a day, and health care for themselves and their families, and who made a decent living by local standards and contributed to the decisions that impact their lives.

A woman I met in Congo once described her life this way: "I wake up each day and say a prayer for safety, then sweep the house, wash the dishes, and fetch water at the river—one and a half kilometers from where we live. I use the water to cook for my children a meal if possible, but sometimes they go without food." But later, after she'd received job training and support, she was able to overcome her circumstances. "I now have a business selling soaps, sweets, charcoal, and flour near my home," she proudly shared. Through perseverance, she was able to create an income to support herself and her children.

Tereza, it seemed, was one of those women. Entrepreneurial and resourceful, Tereza was one of the success stories I came with to Rwanda, though we had never met.

"I was the type of woman who just lives in the house," Tereza said as we sat down. We were in a newly converted conference room on the office compound, a space that once held several early-model Singer sewing machines used for vocational training. Seven months pregnant at the time, Tereza wore a short-sleeved green and orange-patterned *kitenge* with a matching headscarf and large gold hoop earrings. An extra piece of the same fabric was loosely tied around her growing belly.

"I depended on my husband for whatever I needed. He wouldn't give me permission to go to the market like other women. Mostly I stayed inside or would go in the garden and plant things, look after the livestock, a few pigs and a cow. After getting crops I could not go to the market to sell them. That was my life."

Tereza was born in the Muhanga District, in the southern part of Rwanda. She was sixteen when she was forced to drop out of school after her father's death, shortly before the genocide. He had paid for her education at a private school, even though the cultural expectation for girls there was to stop going to school after primary school or sixth grade.

Her mother was left to raise her and her three brothers and seven sisters on her own. "It was a difficult time," she said. "My mother was unable to support the family alone and pay school fees for all the eleven children." They had land then, and were able to grow and sell food. Sometimes though, the family went hungry.

After dropping out of school, Tereza "married" a neighbor and had five of her own children, two boys and three girls. They legally married a few years later. She approached her husband about joining the program so she could be with other women, and he accepted the idea. She started in 2011 and was trained in agriculture. She heard testimonials from other women in her area about business, and they encouraged her. You need to look for markets for your products they told her.

"This opened up my mind to think about starting a small business," she said. "During the training I joined with other women to form a group, and we were able to harvest 300 kilograms of beans that we shared. I sold my share and made 20,000 RWF (about $33) which I used to buy piglets, and later sold them at a profit."

Tereza then started several more businesses. She bought and sold cows in the market, managed a small banana plantation and two fishponds, and opened a bar and restaurant in the town center. Her businesses began to turn a profit. She bought land and built a house for her family. They even had enough to purchase a new television set and a generator.

"I am a member in one of the savings cycles with thirty members; each one contributes something per week," she said. She took a loan from her group to expand the bar, which they had had for two years, but her husband took

Tereza holding a photo with her two cows.

the loan money from her and bought a moto. When the moto he bought was stolen from him, Tereza no longer had any capital to repay the loan. She lost the bar and still had to pay back the money.

"Weren't you angry with your husband?" I asked. She thought about it for a few moments, and then said: "I was discouraged but just decided to continue."

Her husband, she thought, needed to have his own work, so she made a connection for him with a brick maker and encouraged him to learn the trade. He is now a casual laborer and earns a little income brickmaking. Tereza also taught him how to read and write by painting a wall black in her house where he could practice his writing with chalk. "Like you would teach a baby," she said with a mischievous smile. Eventually, he was able to pass a written test for his license to ride a moto.

"My neighbors used to say demonic things about me, that I am not peaceful. They were not used to seeing a woman make money, riding a bike or taking a moto to the market. They thought I was using witchcraft to earn money. They stole the fish from my ponds. I silenced them, though, by showing them all the things I am doing."

Following Tereza's example, most of her neighbors started their own small income-generating projects. She gave them banana seeds so they could grow their own plants. After seeing that other young women in her community were idle, she decided to support them by buying them ripe bananas and avocados to sell (in the market). They pay her back at cost and keep the profit for themselves.

Tereza no longer farms fish or sells cows. She has a swamp where she cultivates rice and her bananas. She has hired a few program graduates and others from the community to help her. Every Saturday she goes to the market to sell. Tereza plans to continue in business, to start her bar again and a small food shop, and leave agriculture to her husband.

Two of Tereza's daughters are in private day school, a "school for the rich," she called it, and the other children are in government schools. She wants them to continue their education and do income-generation projects.

"How come you never gave up?" I asked her.

"I don't like asking for anything from people," she said after a pause. "My husband is very happy that I take responsibility for school fees, anything that is needed. All in all, I am the one who supports the whole family."

There were so many things about Tereza that I could identify with: how she disliked asking for help; how committed she was to her own financial independence; how she cleverly helped her husband to find work and her distrustful neighbors to start their own income-generation activities. What most impressed me, though, was how calm and deliberate she'd been when she discovered that her husband had taken her money, that he had undermined her and her dreams. Calm and deliberate. I was striving for that with Bill and the boys.

I thought back to Sen's work on voice and agency, how women are the dynamic promotors of social transformations that can alter the lives of men and women, and how true that was for Tereza, and for so many other women throughout the world. It's why income generation *is* the global game changer, the magic wand, with the potential to erode some of the more systemic challenges that continue to hold women back.

I was in love with this work, with this business of enabling women to become empowered and independent so they could have a life of their own choosing, as Sen had said. Every person, every woman, wherever they were born or lived, deserved that. My mother deserved that.

At the end of the annual meeting, I'd planned to spend a few more days at headquarters catching up on other work. They were rolling out a new grants-management process that was supposed to address many of the historical disconnects between the US and country teams. The complaints ranged from grant tracking and oversight in the field to challenges around budget reconciliations and often confusing communication with/from HQ. Although it had only been a few months, my lens had already shifted with the move.

This HQ-field dynamic had been a constant in my work in international development—the subtext of every conversation, email exchange, and interaction. It wasn't exactly "us versus them," but pretty close, and it played out in a myriad of ways. When something didn't happen how or when it was supposed to—which was often the case—both sides were quick to point fingers.

"You're not being accountable," HQ would say to the field.

"You can't possibly understand our reality," the field would counter.

Our time in Rwanda was teaching me that the truth was a whole lot muddier.

On my last day there, we—the CEO and several colleagues from the regional and program team—spent two long hours dissecting what went down in South Sudan, who was responsible, and how we were going to fix it. She was right to hold me accountable. Everything that had happened, happened on my watch. I wished I had been more vigilant and had verified that everything was as it should have been. I'd failed to comprehend the amount of influence the former staff had with the government, but also this: no matter our intentions and the good we were doing, we were still foreigners, outsiders, and one looks after one's own. People are generally a product of their environment; the local staff, in every country, was no different.

Later, I met with Erin, my coach, and shared what had happened. Her advice: Don't be a victim. "Own what you own," she said, "and let go of the rest." Now, with a little more distance, I knew she was right. Tereza was, too. It was time to start letting go.

Of course that's easier said than done. Work—this work, in particular— had become such an integral part of my life and persona that it was difficult to separate the two. I didn't know who I was, or how to go about answering the standard "What do you do?" query without a cause to back or define me. My sense of achievement was completely tied to my professional status. I was afraid that without work, my self-confidence would plummet, and eventually a part of me would simply disappear. What if work turned out to be the best part, the only thing that I was any good at? What if the boys were, in fact, better off with me as a more virtual parent?

And what about Bill? "How can you become one with your husband if you don't change your name?" an irksome uncle had asked at one of our prenuptial events. It had never been my intention to become one. Married, yes, but separate, independent. One plus one.

In just the few short months since the move to Rwanda, the past had bulldozed its way into the present. My determination to remain separate and independent, I was coming to understand, was more influenced by my parents, individually and together, than I even imagined. The fear of ending up like them had led me to the other extreme. My refusal to be treated as a wife, like my mom, had resulted in Bill becoming less and less like a husband.

I now recognized that the acrimony and withholding I had observed in my parents' relationship—exactly what I sought to avoid—had seeped into my own marriage. That emotional and physical separation, both a cause and an effect, had led to our potentially broken marriage. Maybe things didn't have to be quite so black and white, though? Maybe, if we were both willing to make adjustments, we could find a middle ground.

12

Social Networks

On the long-haul flights back to Kigali, I watched a few movies for the second or third time and tolerated the meal service with a couple of mini bottles of wine. Sleep was impossible, but I closed my eyes and tried to rest, listening to a "Happy Birthday Karen" playlist on my new iPod nano, a gift from my friend Cheryl. I thought a lot about the week in Bethesda. The love and attention from my girlfriends actually surprised me. I'd often felt more like a misfit among the other moms because of the two worlds I inhabited—one filled with peace and prosperity, the other consumed by war and poverty. In one world, women discussed detox diets and their favorite new eateries on the elliptical trainer and worried about where their kids would go to college; in the other, women were commonly treated as slaves in their own homes or used and discarded as weapons of war.

Both places were familiar. Both places were my places, but it was like having a secret identity. The comfort and ease of our lives in Bethesda clashed with the excessive hardships and insecurities in the places I worked. I'd felt embarrassed, guilty at times, about being an extremely fortunate "have" among a vast majority of have-nots. No more so than when those worlds collided, for example, when the country directors—most of them survivors of war themselves—visited our home. That tension had been there for as long as I'd straddled the two worlds.

But that wasn't the only divide. Looking back—throughout school and my career—my closest friends and mentors had all been men. I simply felt more comfortable in their presence, moved easily among them. With men you knew where you stood; there was less pretense, little nuance. With women it could be the opposite. I understood the roots of that preference, could trace it back to my upbringing, to my parents' relationship.

Mom and Dad each had their roles and responsibilities; neither seemed to question that, or their respective fates. Or perhaps it was resignation, a bitter submission to the inevitable. They both did what was expected of them. To do otherwise, to prevail over their templates, the norms of the time, would have taken a lot. Mom never really smoked, but she couldn't resist those free promotional mini packs they would sometimes hand out on the street. She would stash them in an overstuffed kitchen drawer, her drawer, and every now and then I would see her light up, exhaling through puffed out cheeks as if she were blowing a bubble. It was a small act of defiance.

Mom kept an encouraging stack of *Redbook* and *Good Housekeeping* magazines, with the latest advice on how to be a better this or that, under the TV. Watching her flip through those magazines was like catching a glimpse of my future, a future I already knew that I didn't want. She seemed wholly dependent on my father, lacking knowledge or interests beyond the family. Without ambition or a sense of her own potential, it was as though she was partially formed. I was determined to have a bigger life, to become self-sufficient, and in that sufficiency, to have and make my own choices. Though the irony was not lost on me, I continued to discount my mother's voice and contribution, even as I was building a career focused on women's empowerment.

That bigger life meant working and traveling throughout my pregnancy. Though I'd planned to go back to work after having the twins—a decision Bill supported—that first solo trip was unbelievably hard. Wide awake in the predawn hours in my hotel room in Johannesburg, I longed, ached for their soft milky skin, that precious smell of my new babies.

Before and after the birth of our twins, I participated in two Vital Voices Democracy Initiative conferences—in Vienna in 1997 and Reykjavík in 1999—meant to galvanize women's political and economic participation. The women leaders there, many from Russia, the Baltics, and other socialist countries, were surprisingly open about their own personal and professional hardships. They described how the command economy left little room for initiative and how being solely responsible for household work and childcare, the double burden, had had a negative impact on their professional careers.

In Reykjavík, then–First Lady Hillary Clinton gave an impassioned closing address. She captivated and energized the audience with her zeal for women's rights. She captivated me. I returned home eager to learn more, do more for and with women. My chance came four years later with an organization working to better the lives of women survivors of war. It was 2003; Sam and Eli were about to turn five, and Kai was almost two.

Before kids, Bill and I would often go weeks without contact. Travel to the Soviet Union in those days was like a communications black hole. Nothing came in or out. Children changed that (and new technology). Even if I couldn't be there in person, I was determined be there virtually. When the boys were toddlers, Bill would play them a video of me singing their favorite songs: as they grew older, we traded emails or chatted on Skype. I checked in as much as I could. Bill kept me connected to home and family.

It took both of us pretty much working around the clock to manage our reality, with two demanding full-time jobs and three very young kids. We called it "winning ugly," and it was. Household and parenting responsibilities were divvied up based on affinity and proximity as opposed to so-called gender roles. Given my frequent absences and his professional organizing skills, Bill was the one to set up play dates and car pools with the other kids' moms, and even most of our social engagements as a couple. Bills, laundry, academics, and yardwork were mine. Cooking was more naturally Bill's thing.

As I traveled to some of the most challenging areas of the world, the boys were left in Bill's able care, supported by a series of African nannies: Miriam, Marian, Marigold, Mary, and finally Big Sam. The other mothers and Bill's friends and colleagues, would ask him, "Is Karen in or out of the country today?" Or sometimes, "Is your wife ever here?" To me it was always, "Who's watching the kids?"

I got used to the little digs, most of them from other women. I remember running into a friend at the school bus stop. Rarely home in time to meet the bus, I was just happy to be there. As we stood around chatting, waiting for our kids, I mentioned that I had been helping one of my sons with his homework.

"Oh, my kids don't let me help them with homework anymore," she said. "But you're never around, so it must be more of a novelty."

The comment stung. I'm not proud to say that I got in a few of my own digs at "those crazy PTA moms" who channeled their personal and professional ambitions into all-star event planning and peppy school fundraisers.

Women, myself included, were so often their own worst critics, both self-judging and judgmental of other women's choices. Perhaps we were projecting, or deflecting, our own guilt, fears, and insecurities onto other women?

Through my work with survivors, though, I was learning the importance of meeting women where they are, not where you want them to be, or think they should be. Lately there'd been a shift in my thinking beyond the realm of work. Why couldn't I meet my mother where she was, accept her for who she was? Was it right, or fair, to load all of my unmet expectations onto her, to ask her to be more or different for my sake? What about doing the same for other women?

Thanks to Bill's persistence, I was friendly with a couple of other working moms who had been living in Kigali for some time. One was Amy, a spunky, sharp-witted development pro with long blond hair and a sturdy disposition. Amy is American but, other than a few stateside stints, she had spent most of her career living overseas with her Dutch husband, Eric, a trailing spouse, and their daughter Muriel, a classmate of Sam's and Eli's. Amy was in Rwanda leading a multiyear USAID-funded development project. She told me over lunch one day that she was considering a job change but worried that she might be forced to board Muriel due to poor schools or living conditions in another country.

The other mom was Julia, a short and fiery, kick-ass Italian woman who grew up outside of Milan. A decidedly single mom with two sons—the older one a classmate of Kai's—Julia worked for an established international humanitarian aid organization and changed country posts every two to four years. I liked her no-nonsense attitude. She was a woman used to taking charge and getting things done. On her third year in Rwanda, she was in the midst of looking at options for her next country posting.

The three of us got each other instinctively. We saw the world for what it was and what it wasn't. We had made similar choices.

I had tentatively suggested a girls' night out, or a meet-up with the kids. That was enough to break the ice. From then on, we got together most weekends—usually with kids—and both were kind enough to introduce me to some of their friends.

Our lives seemed closer, more interdependent, in Kigali's small expat community. Over several dinners out and in each other's home, I came to know a diverse group of (mostly) expatriates who had elected to live in Rwanda. Julia's was a favorite gathering spot due to her covered porch and big-screen

TV, a nice distraction for the kids while the adults drank wine and talked. She was also an excellent cook and made delicious homemade sauces and pasta, the long strands of noodles dangling from a thin string across her compact kitchen like wet socks on a laundry line.

When one of us needed to travel or work late, we would help each other out with driving or watching the kids. Their support, their friendship, meant even more as a newly solo parent. It was unusual for me—asking for help from other women, asking for help at all. Tereza and I were alike in that way. Overwhelmed at times by the multitude of responsibilities at home and work, I still answered yes to every work and travel assignment, afraid that saying no would be taken as a sign of weakness. After desperately wanting it all, I thought I had to prove that I could handle it all, even if it wasn't true.

With my work and travel, I missed out on some of the early bonding with the other Bethesda moms, forged through play groups and long hours at the playground. Bill was often closer to my girlfriends because he was the one around. When I was home, Cheryl and I would meet up most Fridays for happy hour at one of our favorite neighborhood bars. We both looked forward to it all week, the chance to connect. Cheryl has an infectious, husky laugh and cheery disposition despite her own less-than-idyllic childhood. A mother of three and former executive at Microsoft, one of the few senior women in the competitive, male-dominated tech industry at the time, Cheryl tried to balance work and life there for many years, had even requested some kind of job share, before finally choosing to leave the company and be a stay-at-home mom.

Women have social networks and safety nets. This was the program outcome I least identified with, until we came to Rwanda.

I'd never quite realized how important it is for women, wherever they are, to be able to count on each other, but also what it must mean to a war survivor. When one is isolated and alone, often shamed from war's violations, another woman reaching out to offer words of comfort or a supportive gesture could be a lifeline. The time women spent together in their training groups had proven to be as valuable as the training itself.

That was certainly the case with "Group 48" in the community, Eziobodoinyi in Mgbowo, in Enugu State. Their story was shared by the Nigeria office. One of the women in this group had been married for over twenty years and had five children, two girls and three boys. A hardworking woman, she was the breadwinner for her family. Her husband beat her regularly and spent all his own earnings on alcohol and other women.

A few years back, her husband told her that he was fed up with their marriage and threw her out of their home. Despite this, his relatives pleaded with her to come back. She eventually agreed to return, but not to the village. Instead, her husband's elder brother gave her and her five children a place to live in his house in the city. Not long after that, her husband also left their old mud house and joined them in the city.

Once they were under the same roof again, her husband continued his violent ways. He castigated his wife in public, claiming that her private parts stank, and used that to justify going after other women. On one of the market days, the women from her training group discussed his comments and decided to take action. Thirty women marched over to their house, and when her husband opened the door, they demanded that he explain his degrading statements about his wife. When he couldn't or wouldn't, the women insisted that he needed to pay a fine, which they were there to collect. The fine money would be used to buy soap to wash his wife's private parts so they could be restored to their premarital state, they said.

On hearing this, he tried to run away, but his son quickly caught up with him and dragged him back into town. An aged woman among the group then hit him in a way he could recognize, explaining that his offense was the highest form of insult to all women. They followed him back to his house and waited there until he either paid the fine or packed his things and left for good. As he started to pack his personal belongings, the women couldn't help but hurry him along. In doing so they found several bundles of money he'd hidden in different places. This from a man who did not contribute to feeding his family and beat his wife if there was no meat for dinner.

The women collected the fine from his hidden money and warned him that they would take more drastic action if he continued to beat his wife. The women divided a portion of the money among themselves for their efforts, but delivered the majority of it to the grateful woman as compensation for her dignity.

"One woman can change many things but many women can change everything," was a frequent saying at work. I believed it, had seen the difference it could make when women joined together; the power of the collective. But I knew now that the meaning of this saying hadn't really registered. That was work. This was life, or how I'd been living mine. Change though, on a macro and micro level, in the personal and professional sphere, meant letting others in. *Shag za shagom*, step-by-step, as they say in Russian. The need for women to rely on each other had taken on new resonance in Kigali.

13

Odd Woman Out

I was happy to be back in Rwanda. I missed the boys, of course. But I also missed our new life there. It seemed a little more manageable, a little less complicated than our lives in Bethesda, even as a solo parent. My only hesitation was around Bill. It had been more than two months since we'd seen each other; it felt like a long time. Wary but glad to see his familiar face when we met at the airport, I walked up and gave him a light kiss and embrace before wrapping my arms around each of the boys.

A few days after I got home, Bill threw me a fiftieth birthday party. Upstairs in the bedroom getting ready that night, about to slip into the white sleeveless shift dress I'd just bought at the airport in Brussels—a delirious early morning purchase—I thought about where I was less than a year ago. *Turing fifty in Rwanda. Rwanda. This had to be progress, better than the alternative.*

A small crowd gathered in the kitchen to see the star attraction that evening, the goat, beheaded and skinned elsewhere, thankfully, except for its distinctive black tail. "Why do they leave the tail on?" Bill asked Joie Claire, the head of human resources and admin. "So that it can't be confused with a dog," she replied.

The goat was butchered on our kitchen counter. Eli posted a rather macabre picture of it on Facebook. Bill hired a special goat guy for the occasion. He brought his own charcoal grill and took charge of the butchering and

roasting. Bill had assembled an eclectic and enthusiastic mix of work colleagues—Teddy, the monitoring and evaluation manager, brought along his
beautiful wife—and close acquaintances from previous visits. The head of Gahaya Links was there. Her handicraft company employed about two hundred
program graduates, including Ange at one point. A few newer friends, most
of them ISK parents, came as well. Among them were Amy and Julia.

I was hungry for more connection, and these women were filling me up as
my girlfriends had back home. Bill and I had gotten off to a fine start, too. We
ate breakfast together most mornings, or would meet up on the front patio
for an after-work drink. In the evenings, one of us would bring him a plate of
food upstairs while he caught up with his colleagues in the US.

The adjustment to having Bill back in Rwanda was nevertheless an effort.
During the short week I was away, he had jumped right back into caretaker
mode, serving up made-to-order breakfasts—pancakes, French toast, eggs—
whatever the boys wanted. He was on to the grocery shopping and other
chores as soon as he dropped them off at school. He'd start on dinner once
he was back from the afternoon pick-up. The boys' scopes of work had been
all but forgotten. Even Innocent didn't know what to do with herself. He'd
taken over her job as well.

"Why are you spoiling them?" I uttered, unable to hold back any longer.

"What do you mean? It hardly seems like spoiling them to give them a
decent breakfast," he countered.

"You are, that's what you always do," I protested, aware that I sounded un-
thankful. "I'm trying to teach them to stand on their own," I went on, feeling
compelled to explain myself. "What's going to happen after you leave again?"

From the start, this had been Bill's way of showing love and affection, but
I'd been pushing the boys, and myself, to be more independent these past
months, and this felt like a setback. The four of us had worked hard to get
to this point—me gaining confidence as the primary caregiver and running
the household and the boys taking greater responsibility for their chores and
schoolwork. It was too easy for us to fall back into that space. That couldn't
happen again. It was time to practice the self-sufficiency I'd been preaching
all these years.

But it wasn't only that. It was just so damn comfortable for the boys, for all
of us. Even in Rwanda, with its frequent power outages, unreliable internet,
and restricted water supply, their main worries were around getting decent

grades and fitting in. I didn't want them to suffer. I simply wanted them to learn how to work and fend for themselves, particularly Sam and Eli. And when Bill had to return to the US post-holidays and my work travel picked up after the first of the year, I would need their help. They could easily make their own breakfast or clean up after themselves. They could also arrange their own transport home from school. They had, in fact, been doing all of these things before Bill came back into the picture. They were fully capable young men. Bill understood this in theory, but was loathe to deprive or place extra pressure on the boys.

There was something more, too. I was the one following Bill's lead when I came home from the field, the one who had had to gradually, sometimes awkwardly, reinsert myself into the family dynamic. In a house full of boys, I was forever the odd woman out. We would joke about it, being with women all day and boys all night, but the truth was that feeling like an outsider was hard in your own home. How many other women around the world had felt that way? Fairly or not, I wanted Bill to know what that was like. It was supposed to be his turn to do the commuting, to be the one to adjust, after all.

All the boys, including Bill, looked forward to my time out of the country. It was no secret. The house rules were suspended as soon as my flight took off: it was suddenly fine to eat downstairs in front of the TV and watch endless sports, to live out of the dryer, to run to the mall for the latest gear, tech upgrade, or gadget. Bill aimed to please, mainly through good food and new stuff. He was the "yes" parent.

I was the tough-love, take-it-on-the-chin parent; the "no" parent. The boys were expected to be kind and competent, independent and worldly, good men as well as good global citizens. Violent and exploitative video games were banned from the house. Toy guns and swords were also off limits. While I couldn't stop them from playing at war in other people's homes, I could certainly stop them in mine. I'd seen too many swollen-bellied, shoeless, dirt-smeared kids, all deadly poor, with little chance of improving their lot, to not push my own kids a little harder to recognize what they had been given and take responsibility for their lives. They had to know how privileged they/we were.

Sometimes Bill would try to enforce my kind of discipline, but it was like me trying to cook—it usually ended in disaster, with one or both of us feeling hurt or angry. His efforts just seemed so halfhearted. I couldn't stand his compulsion to satisfy the boys' desires; they had to learn to distinguish between needs and wants. Our co-parenting reflected the ongoing power dynamic in our relationship. My hardness to his softness.

Parenting seemed to come so easy to Bill. A natural caregiver, he was the more likeable and loveable one. For me, parenting has always felt a little less natural, a little more forced.

I was my father's daughter: tightly wound, even crazed sometimes, but more sensitive than I ever let on. Our bruises were on the inside. It was a side of my dad that I didn't see until I went away to college. As Dad called on his customers across the state, every so often he would stop in Eugene, at the university. He would pick me up at my dorm or apartment and take me out to dinner at a favorite local restaurant. There, sitting across the table from him, he would open up about his life, his dreams and regrets. How he loved baseball and wished he could have made a career of it. How his own father—an amateur boxing champion in Portland—taught him how to fight. How he ruled the family with an iron fist and used to whip him with a leather belt. How he always treated him more like an employee than a son. How he never praised him. How he struggled, even at the end, to earn his approval.

"He was a mean son-of-a-bitch," he said one night. I nodded in agreement. *Yes, you were.*

A few days after our fight, once Bill and I remembered how to cohabitate and co-parent, we were more or less back to the status quo—not great, but not so bad either. But now, after coming to Rwanda, I understood more than ever before that "not so bad" was *not* good enough, not for the long haul anyway, though we'd already been at it a good long time. Those same old comfortable patterns had become far less comforting. Even our departure and reentry fights were predictable, so much so that we could have easily finished each other's sentences. I didn't expect fireworks and breathless moments, not after twenty-five years, but I wanted more, closer to great.

Somewhere along the way, we had both grown content with the state of our relationship and had stopped striving for more. I didn't want to be one of those couples that was just biding their time until their kids went off to college, coexisting but with separate lives. I wanted a real marriage, flaws and all. Bill, I thought, wanted the same.

I had begun to see more clearly which of my behaviors were worth changing, not only for the sake of my family but for my own sake. I wasn't quite ready to talk about it, and Bill wasn't pressing. Both of us had our walls, our well-honed defenses. But I could feel my hard candy shell starting to soften, beginning to crack around the edges, especially with the boys. I'd been picking up their favorite banana bread and other things for them on the way home from work. In Rwanda, I was learning that it didn't have to be all or nothing. I could be the "yes" parent, too, and indulge them. Bill noticed it, too, and felt me softening some with him.

14

Debora

Considering the emotional uncertainty that had preoccupied me, the arrival of Global Entrepreneurship Week (GEW) in mid-November was a welcome distraction. GEW is the world's largest celebration of entrepreneurship, engaging millions of people through tens of thousands of activities, with the goal of inspiring entrepreneurs to embrace innovation and creativity in their businesses. Rwanda was marking this annual event for the second time.

Around 40 percent of Rwandans still live below the international poverty line, on less than $1.90 per day, and a subset of those live in extreme poverty, though precise figures are hard to come by. Close to half of those households are headed by women. While the country has taken major steps toward poverty reduction and economic growth, fueled largely by entrepreneurship, economic inequality and unemployment remain a challenge. Driven by a combination of necessity and opportunity, women are the most dynamic entrepreneurs in Rwanda and other developing countries. Starting a business is often the only way to earn a living.

As part of GEW, whose theme this year was "empowering youth and women," the country office sponsored competitions for the top entrepreneurs in four districts across Rwanda. Open to individual entrepreneurs and group enterprises formed by graduates, an average of 450 women in each district competed for cash prizes on levels of business creativity, impact, and innovation. The businesses ranged from hairdressing, bread making, and tailoring to agriculture and food processing and to other kinds of trade and services.

The number of longtime graduates who surfaced for the competition was astounding. Of the fifty thousand women trained since 1997, only 63 percent had attended primary school and 5 percent secondary; nearly a third had had no formal education whatsoever. The majority earned just over thirty cents a day when they started the program. Yet all of them had been able to leverage the training in different ways to transform their lives.

Khadidja Nibabyare was voted top entrepreneur from Kayonza. Selling bananas by the side of the road, Khadidja used to earn about 5,000 Rwandan francs (less than ten dollars) a day. She invested the program's training stipend in her business—making delicious banana pancakes. Seven months in, she had hired five employees and sold her pancakes in three communities, grossing the equivalent of one hundred dollars a day during weekdays and almost double that amount on Saturday and Sunday. Khadidja worked nearly nonstop, like most entrepreneurs across the globe. Though frustrated by sourcing and distribution challenges, she was determined to grow her business.

More important than the cash prize was the recognition and motivation that came with the award. "This competition is important because it makes us visible," Khadidja said. All of the winning entrepreneurs were honored at a national celebration cosponsored by the Ministry of Gender and Family Promotion, UN Women, and a host of other agencies.

"When women are economically empowered, the family is economically empowered," said the Kayonza District's point person on gender who attended the ceremony. With economic and social empowerment comes voice and choice: women gain the confidence, means, and status to advocate for their rights and invest in their families and communities.

Listening to the finalists from the Gasabo District present their businesses made me think about how difficult it must be to bring a business to life, and for these women in particular, given what they were starting with: next to nothing. It took dedication and guts to be an entrepreneur anywhere; to take risks, solve problems, build networks, and learn from failures as well as successes. All of the competing entrepreneurs had done that and more. They'd gone from being among the most disenfranchised people in the country to role models and an inspiration ("positive jealousy" in Kinyarwanda) for women everywhere.

Patricie Mukamazimpaka, the winner from the Gasabo District, used to survive on less than a dollar a day earned doing seasonal work sorting coffee beans. She took a risk by starting an import-export handicrafts business with partners in Kenya, Uganda, and Rwanda. Soon she was handling $500 in transactions per week and had twenty-five employees. In accepting her prize, Patricie urged other women to "have the courage of working for themselves."

Thrilled at the chance to present several of the awards, and to see what the program was accomplishing, I took a mental snapshot of the room to capture the moment. The collective sense of pride among the women there was palpable. This was the kind of long-term impact you strived for but rarely got the chance to see.

There is a Rwandan saying: "One who teaches a woman teaches a household and thus a nation." This was true not only for women in Rwanda but for women everywhere. In Patricie's words: "With a skill everything is possible." Deeply inspired and wearing a big grin, I stepped off of the low platform stage to join my colleagues and the women in some celebratory dancing.

We had our first visitors to Rwanda in November, as well: Bill's sister Marci and her longtime partner, Shelly. Three years his junior, Marci followed Bill out to Santa Barbara, where he went to college. He then visited her in Cameroon when she was in the Peace Corps. When Bill finally settled in DC, Marci did as well. With no children of their own, the aunties had basically adopted the boys. They were their very first babysitters and had been there for every milestone.

The aunties, of course, came bearing gifts. Happy for a distraction from work, and to enjoy Rwanda's stellar ecotourism, we spent their first weekend at Volcanoes National Park. We planned ahead this time and reserved a few rooms at a nearby lodge. With soaring views of the surrounding peaks, each of the rustic cabins on the property came with its own wood-burning fireplace. Hot water bottles were delivered nightly to each guest.

Located about five kilometers from the main park entrance, the lodge catered mostly to hikers—gorilla and golden monkey trekkers—who stayed over to be ready for the early morning start. We were there for the monkeys, as the boys didn't meet the minimum age requirement of fifteen for the gorillas. After having twice seen the spectacular mountain gorillas, the prospect of monkey trekking was less than exciting. But after a short hike into the jungle, we spent a riveting hour watching these playful monkeys wrestle around on the jungle floor, swinging from vine to vine.

While there, however, I started to receive some worrisome text messages from the Bukavu-based country director about growing insecurity in North Kivu. There were reports of heavy gunfire and explosions in and around Goma, where the organization had a field office and small team. The March 23 Movement or M23, a ruthless and violent splinter group from the Congolese army said to be backed by Rwanda, was closing in on the city of Goma, leaving a terrorized population in its wake. Thousands had been forced from their homes. The situation was volatile and threatened to explode. Still in the jungle with everyone, I stood off to the side frantically texting back and forth with the country director.

"What's going on, Mom?" Eli asked.

"Hold on," I said a little too forcefully, still absorbed in our texts. "I need a minute or two. There's something going on in Congo." After seeing me deal with the situation in South Sudan, the boys knew to let me be for the moment. They now understood that these bouts of distraction had nothing to do with a lack of interest in them, but that the job sometimes demanded my full attention. This was another one of those times.

Over the next few days leading up to Thanksgiving, a flood of refugees crossed the newly reopened border into Rwanda to flee the violence. Concerned about the conflict's spillover effect on Bukavu, and about its impact on participants and staff, who were instructed to stay indoors, I continued to monitor the security situation. The program had to be suspended in Goma so as not to expose the staff and women to further risk. Those suspensions happened with some frequency in the countries with protracted conflicts. That was most of them. Three months earlier, the program had been suspended in parts of North Kivu after militants killed a participant.

Women, often the canary in the coalmine in modern warfare, where the vast majority of causalities are women and children, were hard hit by this latest round of fighting. Amid the heavy military presence in the town of Kalehe, in South Kivu, a group of graduates reported that the security issue was paramount. They'd formed a soap-making collective called Nyanguka (Swahili for "raise up"), which had had to stop production due to the fighting. Some cooperative members had experienced looting and violence from soldiers fleeing the hostilities.

The group had been earning an average of $178 per week and used the income to pay school fees for their children and buy clothes and other family necessities. Customers were so satisfied with the product that they'd begun to wait outside Nyanguka's production site as soap was being made. The co-op had recently expanded their successful business to include poultry and goat raising and beekeeping. They'd also brought in eight of the group members' husbands to join the collective.

"Women were not considered, and some local sayings expressed that a baby boy is worth more than a woman," one group member told a colleague, explaining what it had been like before the collective was formed. "All a woman could do was just household activities like fetching water, chopping wood, and cooking food, apart from working in the field and giving birth."

This new wave of violence now threatened Nyanguka's small economic gains, which had liberated them to a certain degree from the dominant cultural practices toward women in the area. Thousands of other women were likely suffering the same fate.

The women were not the only ones to suffer. Dr. Mukwege, the gynecological surgeon who founded Panzi Hospital, had been violently attacked at his home. His two daughters were held at gunpoint by four armed men as they waited for Dr. Mukwege to return. Several shots were fired as he exited his car; he narrowly escaped death, but his security guard, a trusted friend, had been killed. The failed assassination attempt came just weeks after he denounced the conflict and called on those responsible for the hundreds of thousands of rapes, including the government, to be brought to justice.

In a few years' time, Dr. Mukwege would be awarded the Nobel Peace Prize for his life-giving work with rape victims. When asked about the source of his inspiration, Dr. Mukwege said: "My strength comes from women." He now lives under the permanent protection of UN peacekeepers.

Still, with more upstanders like Dr. Mukwege and support for gender equality, women and their families *could* be safer and less vulnerable. It had happened in Rwanda, and it could happen elsewhere, too. It was a matter of will, political and otherwise, to make it so. Societies with greater equality were known to be less violent, less prone to conflict. Absent that, there was sure to be more Congos and South Sudans. One need only look at Syria, Yemen, and Somalia. New armed conflicts were starting all the time. The world seemed to be trending toward the latter.

As dismal as it was, I had to laugh when the country director, a thought-ful, seasoned development pro, sent this email: "Could you please tell all the people all over the world to stop fighting. It's been far too hectic lately."

As the fighting in Congo raged through Thanksgiving Day, I felt a pro-found sense of gratitude for my family and friends. Marci and Shelly joined us for Thanksgiving dinner at the home of our friends Amy and Eric and their daughter, Muriel. Somehow Amy managed to score three turkeys and a goat, and we all made a contribution to the cooking. I'd snagged two expired cans of cream of mushroom soup—an acquaintance who worked for the US government had a pantry full of this kind of stuff courtesy of monthly food pouches—and made a passable green bean casserole. Eli made a delicious apple crisp with imported apples—a dessert that probably cost as much as the goat. Bill whipped up a huge pile of mashed potatoes.

The food and the company were great, but the conflict looming right across the border occupied my mind with what seemed like a never-ending cycle of bloodshed and displacement. What was even the point? It was always one step forward and three steps back—our small gains practically wiped out with each new surge. And the women were left to pick up the pieces, start over. Every. Single. Bloody. Time. They would again have to rebuild life for their families, find food, build new shelters, care for the children. It's what women around the world did best, not because they wanted to but because they had to. They did what had to be done to survive.

I understood the fatigue and cynicism regarding Congo and other pro-tracted conflicts, why the narrative about Africa was often so negative. Rwanda easily stood out for that reason. Most of the conflicts in the region had gone on for two decades or more. And it wasn't only the violence. Ram-pant corruption and mismanagement, poverty, hunger, and disease contin-ued to thwart Africa's prospects. Some days I could barely look at the paper, which I knew would contain yet more news of people whose lives had been devastated.

It would be so much easier to turn away, tune out, and let the warring par-ties have at it.

But then what?

At least we were here, in Rwanda, talking about it, living it, trying to make it a little less wrong. We all gave thanks for the day and raised a glass to our security, abundance, and good fortune.

A hired safari car arrived early the next morning for a planned excursion with Marci and Shelly to Akagera National Park, a game park set in the eastern part of the country. The Belgians established Akagera in 1934, designating about 10 percent of the country as protected lands, less for tourism than as a valuable source of research and ivory. It was so vast that its borders nearly reached the Women's Opportunity Center in Kayonza, more than twenty miles away. Considered one of the seven best parks in Africa at the time, Akagera became a major battleground during the genocide. Almost 60 percent of the animals were lost; many escaped or were killed or eaten by soldiers. Since then, more than half of the park had been given back to the surrounding communities due to intense land pressure from all the returnees. The much smaller game park, set on just over one hundred thousand hectares, was now the main employer in those communities, which shared in the revenue, anti-poaching efforts, and upkeep.

The rolling hills, boggy swamps, and wide-open savannas were teeming with elephants, zebras, giraffes, warthogs, baboons, hippos, Cape buffalo, and a huge assortment of exotic birds. No lions though. The few that remained after the genocide had all been poisoned off by nearby villagers because they were attacking their cows.

On the way back to Kigali, we stopped by the future Women's Opportunity Center. Eager to show off the project, I led everyone on a tour of the muddy construction site. There was much oohing and ahhing at the half-built classroom structures and panoramic views into the valley, but the center was still very much a work in progress. The place looked practically abandoned, even though there should have been workers there that day. Edward, the construction manager, would definitely hear about it.

Bill and the boys knew how frantic I'd been over the CEO transition and then the onslaught of problems in South Sudan. Despite my frequent visits to the construction site, the project was well behind schedule and likely over budget. Congo was still a mess and required constant attention. Back in the car, my mood collapsed. I stared out the window the rest of the way home, watching the now familiar countryside slide past.

A few days later, the real source of my distress dawned on me: the organization, under new leadership, was moving forward without me. My colleagues at headquarters had been less communicative than usual, but what I did hear made it clear that it was time to get serious about moving on. I don't know what I was expecting. That someone would step in and say this had all been a terrible misunderstanding. That they had gotten it wrong, gotten me wrong. That they wanted to make it right.

It wasn't that I couldn't find work again. I wasn't sure I could find *this* kind of work again. A feeling of melancholy once again set in, permeating my interactions at work and home. "Come on, you're Karen Fucking Sherman," Bill said to shake me from my malaise, just as he'd always done. But I couldn't shake it. Moving to Rwanda had been a Band-Aid of sorts but it had finally fallen off, and I realized that the underlying problems that compelled me to leave home, again and again, were still mostly unresolved. What else was I looking for? Validation, some kind of proof that it, everything, hadn't just been about being in the right place at the right time, a fluke or sheer luck. That I deserved to be where I was. That I wasn't a fraud.

How many times had I delivered supposedly inspirational talks to groups of women when *I* was the one sorely in need of inspiration? And what about the mental energy it had taken to maintain the pretense of my "happy" marriage, my "rock star" job, my three "perfect" kids, my so-called balanced life—more and more energy as I had lost faith in these facets of my life and, ultimately, in myself.

Being in Rwanda had started to change me, though. The survivors had influenced me to look harder at myself. There were so many others, so many women, with stories far worse than mine. Pain is, in fact, relative. I wanted for nothing, needed nothing. My family was well, safe and intact. I had always believed that however awful my issues were, my chosen suffering simply didn't rank in the world at large. It was true. And yet there was no way to deny this growing sense of personal failure. Whether I was entitled to those feelings, or there was another way to deal with them, those hard-won lessons in tenacity and courage revealed in the lives of the women around me were finally getting through.

Still, it wasn't enough. Debora, one of the program graduates, had been on my mind. I'd read her story several times over and knew the broad outlines— that she had lost her family in the genocide, that she had been sick for a time but now ran a successful business. The matter-of-fact way she described what had happened to her, though, made me think that there was more there. I wanted to meet her, hear what she had to say.

On the day she agreed to talk, Debora arrived at the office compound wearing a short-sleeved gold, red, and black stripped kitenge; her head was wrapped in the same fabric. A sheer lilac flowered scarf was loosely draped around her neck. A driver drove the two of us and a staff person/interpreter to her workshop in Kicukiro in the suburbs of Kigali, where she made knitted goods for several clients. The workshop lay off a stretch of dirt road next to a few other small businesses.

One of the older graduates, in her fifties, Debora led us into her cramped workspace, which was painted bright turquoise and barely had room for the three vintage knitting machines; one stood broken in the corner. Two other women were working with her that day, but they stopped what they were doing for a few minutes while we stood and talked.

"I heard about your program from our local community leaders. Lucky enough I got enrolled into the program and during that time, I received a monthly training stipend which I used to open a bank account, pay rent for a house and buy food. I saved 3,000 RWF (about $5) every month. I learnt different topics in life skills such as health and wellness, sustaining an income and household savings. There are other skills that I learnt which opened my mind and these included how to start a small business. I was trained in knitting as a vocational track."

Before Debora graduated, a cousin who lived in Europe offered her financial support and bought her a knitting machine, her first one. The machine changed everything.

"I started to work from my home. Many people came to see what I was doing. It was the first knitting machine in the area and it amazed them. I started to make sweaters for school kids. After that, I got an order from Solace Ministries of knitting 450 sweaters and made 1,015,000 RWF, more than one thousand dollars. With the money I earned I bought two more knitting machines and another one was donated."

Debora told us that, at one point, she joined with six other people to rent business premises, since it wasn't easy to do so alone. She also talked about having an account in the Bank of Kigali and receiving a loan, which she was in the process of paying back.

"I have received orders from several schools and individuals, a church, and from Solace's donors in Germany and Netherlands. I have an order of making 230 sweaters for a school. When I have big orders I hire other people to work for me," she said. "I have a signed contract to train others in knitting. So far I have trained four women, twenty-three students, and ten others from Solace."

We left Debora's workshop and drove along the same unpaved road to her home, about twenty minutes away. The neighborhood was brand new, with several houses still under development. Like Grace and Vanessa, her two-bedroom house, and the *kitenge* she was wearing that day, were given to her by the government as reparations. The house came furnished with two plush tan sofas and an armchair, several mattresses, and a simple wood coffee table and hutch, where she was storing a ripe melon; only the television set in the corner, a small carpet, her clothes, and a few plates were hers. A cow also came with the house; it was pregnant and in a tiny shed out back.

Once we were seated, she offered us tea with sugar and lemon. I felt uncomfortable bringing up the genocide with Debora in front of the other women at the workshop, but as we sipped our tea, I asked her if she would tell me what had happened. Debora's face took on a grim, faraway look as she considered where to start, how much she wanted to share.

"My husband died on the eleventh and my children on the twenty-fourth," she began. "I was carrying my small baby on my back and they just lifted him up and cut his neck." Here she paused for a long moment. We sat quietly. "He was one year and two months old," she said finally, her voice barely audible. Though her memories were nearly two decades old, the gruesome images still seemed fresh in her mind.

Debora at home.

"All six of my children died during the genocide," she said, her hands fidgeting with the lace doily from the coffee table as she continued with her story.

"Four died on the spot when they were shot and two died after being thrown in the river in Gikongoro, including the baby. I was slashed on the head. I floated in the water so they would think I was dead. My husband died in the water. I was the only survivor."

Some of the emotional intensity of Debora's words was lost through the filter of an inexperienced interpreter, but her body language conveyed so much. She suddenly appeared smaller, wilted.

"After losing my family, I decided to look for some relatives, but they weren't there. I had no clothes, only the small t-shirt I was wearing. I hid for two weeks with no food or water. I heard people being killed from my hiding place. I decided to go back to where I lived but the houses there were all burned. Everything had been destroyed.

"After the genocide I shifted to Murambi in the French military zone commonly known as "Zone Turquoise." The French started killing people there, putting people into sacks full of nails, two to three people a day. Children disappeared; bodies were thrown into the forest. I saw it with my own eyes.

"I remember one young man who was crying. He said 'you have killed my brother, my only brother.' They told him 'if you continue crying we will also kill you.'

"In 1996 I moved to Kigali with 80,000 RWF (about $130) that I had received as reparation for losing family properties during the genocide. I started a charcoal business. After making some money, I started running a café at Migina, Remera and taking care of three orphans, paying their school fees. I fell sick and after being hospitalized for a long time, my business collapsed. I got discouraged but decided to start selling milk and pancakes, to survive."

It was only when Debora started to talk about the program that she broke into a big, buck-toothed smile.

"When I was young I used actual sticks to knit hats and shawls. I was inspired to see other women knitting and felt like I wanted to do it. I have learnt a lot, including having self-esteem. I appreciate the special way they connect participants with their 'sisters' abroad. This gives hopeless women, poor and vulnerable like me, to hope for a bright future.

"I formed a group called 'Fear Not You're Not Alone' in 2012. Everyone in the group lost all their family in the genocide. Six people started the group;

there are fifty-six of us now, men and women. Many are still traumatized. We meet once a month. Our aim is to be together. On the seventeenth of May every year we give speeches and go to memorials to remember our families.

"I've embraced what has happened to me, these big changes in my life. I didn't have anything before. Now I have something to do. . . . I have people who care for me, like the family I lost. It makes me not feel lonely."

I tried to hold back the tears as Debora was sharing her story, but they spilled down my face anyway. She was a woman who had truly lost everything—her husband, her children, her home, her livelihood—and had had her dignity stripped away by atrocities on a scale most of us cannot even imagine. Yet she was still hoping for a bright future, still embracing life. All this time, I thought I'd been doing that, embracing life, embracing my choices. My usual hard-driving, get-it-done self never really stopped to think about it. But my efforts so far paled in comparison to Debora's. She had clearly owned her past while I'd tried to distance myself, literally, from mine, from those hurtful memories, to pretend to be above or beyond them. Well I wasn't. It was just more shit, more pretense, and it was weighing me down.

Living in Rwanda had stripped away my protective layers, exposed them to the light. Buried there was a deep, unhealed wound from my girlhood, from growing up in a family where I didn't feel loved and protected, in a home where it didn't feel safe. *Stupid. Bitch. Cunt.* That was my victim loop, the soiled underpinning of everything that came after. I couldn't see my way over or around it. I couldn't let go.

To rebuild my life as these survivors had done, as Debora had done, I would have to deconstruct it first, go back to that foundation.

15

Women Leaders

It was early December, a few weeks before our climb up Mount Kilimanjaro, the highest peak on the continent, the tallest freestanding one in the world. The mountain loomed in my imagination like an African holy grail even before we left home. It started as a conversation with a colleague, both of us athletic, nearing fifty, and interested in the physical challenge. But now, with everything that had happened, it had become something more. Something elemental.

Once we had made the decision to spend a year in Rwanda, Kili had become a beacon for the entire family. All of us were in decent shape. For months now, the boys and I had been training at elevation, as Kigali stands four thousand feet above sea level. Weekends were spent running or boot hiking one of the many hills around the city. Bill had also worked out like crazy back home. Labeled the "weak link" by Eli, he had returned to Kigali ten pounds lighter and fitter than he'd been in years.

The bigger question was around mental toughness. We selected a route that would help us acclimatize, but wasn't the easiest nor most direct way up the mountain. I'd never been much of a camper, much less a high-altitude one. Almost everything about the climb fell well outside my comfort zone. But I needed that: to be completely out of my element. I had something to prove now, for myself more than anything.

Before Kili, though, I had to go back to South Sudan, my third trip to the country. After the recent extraction from Rumbek, it was quickly becoming one of my least favorite places. The world's newest nation, and arguably its most fragile, South Sudan as a whole lays claim to some of the worst human development indicators—maternal mortality, school-completion rates, child marriage, you name it—the legacy of entrenched conflict and entrenched cultural practices. Together they made for a deadly combination for women in particular. A woman in South Sudan is more likely to die in childbirth than to finish primary school. School fees, early marriage, and family decisions are cited for the high incidence of girls dropping out.

The burden of hardship falls on South Sudanese women in other ways as well. They represent the majority of those living below the poverty line and have little access to economic opportunities that could better their lives. Women are not allowed to own land, or any animal bigger than a goat, and they still make up the largest source of unpaid domestic labor. When women do work outside the home, they are more likely to be informally employed, earning lower wages and in positions with greater job insecurity.

When the country formally gained its independence in July 2011, the South Sudanese people were ecstatic, celebrating on packed streets and town squares across the country. Hopes were high that it would finally bring an end to the fighting and usher in a new era of peace and prosperity.

It didn't. At the time of my visit in 2012, the country was less than two years old and virtually bankrupt. The government was in a standoff with Sudan over oil revenue, security, and other issues, and well on the way to becoming yet another failed state. It would only be another year before tribal politics and infighting, and the reckless egos of inexperienced, greedy leaders, would plunge the country back into civil war. Millions would be displaced, and as many would be on the brink of starvation, the government's oil riches being spent on arms instead of grain. Numberless women inside and outside of UN protection camps would be raped.

In this moment, I was grateful that Bill was in Rwanda to look after the boys while I spent the week in Juba, the capital, with the country director. The purpose of the trip was to raise money and support for the program's relaunch in Yei, the new base in South Sudan, one that almost didn't happen. The leadership team had intensely debated whether or not to continue work- ing in the country—given the persistent insecurity, high operating costs, and management challenges in Rumbek. I'd fought hard for it, making my case in memos and on calls with the team, more from my heart than my head. South

Sudanese women critically needed training and support. If we abandoned these women, who else would step in? As far as I knew, this was one of the few programs for women there.

Yei was selected after a feasibility study that considered several other sites. Situated 150 kilometers southwest of the capital, near the Congo and Uganda borders, Central Equatoria's fertile land and consistent rainfall represented a promising opportunity for women to earn an income through agriculture and related businesses, as the majority of households depended on crop farming or animal husbandry for food as well as income. The state's prime location at a market crossroad between Uganda, Yambio, and Juba was ideal for women to sell their products.

The goal was to enroll three hundred participants by early in the next year. Setting up the program in a different part of the country was almost like starting over. It required an entirely new staff and infrastructure, everything from laptops and modems to basic office furniture to phone lines and a large generator for the frequent power outages. All but the phone lines would have to be procured outside of Yei, likely in Juba or the US. Politics was important. Good relations with the government, particularly the local government, would be critical. They could identify the most underserved communities and open doors, as well as ameliorate any cultural disconnects, with village leaders. If they found us uncooperative, unable, or unwilling to meet their needs and the needs of their constituents—ideally one and the same—they could just as easily shut us down.

The governor asked us to submit a formal letter explaining what had happened in Rumbek—people seemed to know anyway—and our intentions for Yei. Without his blessing, an official stamp on government letterhead, and written approval from the RRC and the commissioner of Yei County, nothing could move forward. Written agreements with the local authorities and relevant line ministries would follow, though no amount of paperwork could conceal the government's dysfunction. We also needed money, at least half a million dollars from one or several of the international donor agencies with offices in Juba, to enroll around a thousand women in year two. More money meant more women could be trained.

I was staying at the Ambassador Resort Hotel. The "resort" part seemed to refer to the hotel's proximity to the Nile River, not to any sort of parklike setting. Right across from the hotel was a makeshift camp for the internally displaced, a smoky, urban slum built with and around large piles of garbage. To the camp's right was an untended graveyard, denoted with a handmade "No Parking at Graveyard" sign, and across from this stood a slaughterhouse.

Juba was an oil-rich town that ran on generators. Instead of waking to the sound of songbirds, I woke to the machine's steady drone right outside my hotel window. As I left the hotel for a meeting one afternoon, hundreds of cattle were being herded down the street on their way to slaughter. The acrid smell of blood lingered in the air, causing vultures to circle overhead.

Garbage was everywhere, despite the signs posted on street corners enjoining residents to "Keep Juba Clean and Green." With no pickup service and no dump, the trash was left burning in small fires along the side of the road. The stench given off made you gag. The stomach-turning smell was magnified by the omnipresent heat and haze.

Foreigners lived in guarded and gated compounds, cloistered away from Juba's mess and crime. One perky woman from the United States Agency for International Development likened their compound to "summer camp." I wondered what she would think of pristine Kigali when I heard this. The entire city resembled their compound.

International nongovernmental organizations (INGOs)—there were more than two hundred of them working in South Sudan—had been somewhat discredited for spending huge sums of money with very little impact. On the other hand, a senior US government official had shared in casual conversation that INGOs were the only ones able to deliver services. The government was so corrupt, and had such a deplorable work ethic that almost nothing got done. Fridays were dead, for instance, as officials retreated to their weekend homes in Kenya and Uganda, which they reached via their own helicopters.

No one, from the president on down, had any direct experience. No governance. No training. No accountability. No one was equipped to run the country. As Hillary Clinton said, one day you are a rebel and the next you are running a country. That was South Sudan in a nutshell.

The Chinese had built almost everything in South Sudan, from paved roads and schools to low-cost housing and commercial farms, as they had in Rwanda and Congo. Beyond an interest in oil and new markets, they were looking to export workers, because there were too few jobs at home, and import food for the same reason, according to an investment facilitator for Central Equatoria's state government. In exploiting Africa's resources and opportunities, the Chinese had been remarkably smart. The United States less so. US investments on the continent were nowhere to be seen, other than on the development-aid front, and there they gave so little in comparison with the need that it barely made a dent.

Our days were jam-packed with meeting after meeting with local officials and US government representatives, including the ambassador, and a variety of international donor agencies. Most nights were spent holed up in my hotel room troubleshooting issues in the other field offices, namely Congo, or on calls with headquarters hashing out start-up and contingency plans for the new program in Yei, a program I would only have time to get off the ground before the end of my one-year assignment. But I couldn't dwell on that.

One of the big lessons from Rumbek was that, when push came to shove, the organization didn't have protection at the national level, meaning Juba. Our fate was in the hands of mostly self-serving local officials. What we needed was a "roof" as they used to say in Russia. Mobsters there provided this protection, for a price of course. In South Sudan, that roof would hope-fully be the minister of gender for Central Equatoria-Juba, the Honorable Mary Apai Ayiga.

It took days to secure a meeting with the minister. With the meeting finally confirmed the night before, the country director and I arrived early and were directed to her waiting room, where a village drama—a local soap opera—was on television. I sat riveted to the screen even though I couldn't understand a word of it until she was ready to see us. Ushered into her office, we found the minister seated behind a large dark wooden desk.

Proper formalities observed, we got down to business. We explained who we were and what we were planning to do, expressing our desire to work closely with the ministry, given its role in driving policies and programs for women in South Sudan. She emphasized the importance of building the capacity of women in her country to engage in productive work, of doing more than training for training's sake. She wanted to see results. We agreed to formalize our relationship in a written agreement as a next step; the details could be hashed out at a later date. The meeting was over in less than fifteen minutes. Despite what I'd said about South Sudan, the women, as usual, knew how to get things done.

The next morning, I was on my way to the airport to catch my flight back to Kigali, ready to be going home. Gazing out the car window, I saw tall, lean men in dark business suits, their faces scarred with their distinctive tribal marks, and policemen in uniforms casually holding hands as they walked down the street. The scene was deeply familiar and foreign at the same time. I realized then, with a sudden pang of regret, how Africa would only be our home for another six months; that I might never be coming back. It triggered on onslaught of gloomy thoughts.

A policeman signaling the driver to pull over forced my attention back to the present. It wouldn't be the first time my car had been stopped for no good reason. The ubiquitous police roadblocks in Nigeria, where every few kilometers a tree branch or other obstruction was laid across the road and you had to pay to pass, and the Tanzanian policeman who flagged down my driver and said, "Brother, I didn't have any breakfast today . . . ," came to mind. But no, this officer wasn't looking for a bribe but to hitch a ride. He hopped in the back of the car and we continued on our way.

Back in Kigali the next day, on some weekend errands with the boys, I picked up a copy of the *New Times*, the Rwandan English-language newspaper, and stared in disbelief at the full-page cover photo of Aloisea Inyumba, Rwanda's minister of gender, announcing her death. How could this extraordinary woman be gone? Known simply as Inyumba, she above others was instrumental in the government's promotion of gender equality. From 1994 to 1999, she served as the country's first minister of gender and social affairs and returned to the position again from 2011 until her passing. A friend of the organization for almost fifteen years, Inyumba served as a member of the advisory board and laid the first stone at the groundbreaking ceremony for the Women's Opportunity Center.

I had come to know and admire Inyumba over many visits to Rwanda. The last born in a family of six children, after her father was killed during the 1963–1964 massacres in Rwanda, she was raised by her mother in a refugee camp in southern Uganda before going to a university and then joining Rwanda's liberation movement.

Inyumba was a powerful force in the fight to end the genocide against the Tutsis and in the recovery and reconciliation process that followed. Under her leadership, the ministry established a nationwide women's network to resolve family and property disputes resulting from the genocide and the policy framework that led to the adoption of substantial numbers of genocide orphans within the country.

I had last seen her a year earlier at a dinner hosted for a visiting delegation. The restaurant was crowded and noisy, and Inyumba arrived late, looking haggard and spent, but determined to make an appearance. Seated beside her at the long table, we talked quietly while she ate a few bites. Then she asked for a car to take her home. She wanted to say goodnight to her children.

An acting minister was in place by the time we moved to Rwanda. Inyumba was reportedly out of the country on an extended work mission, but there were unconfirmed rumors that she was ill. The entire nation grieved the loss of a woman many believe could have been president one day. President Kagame described Inyumba as "a selfless leader" when he eulogized her at Parliament, where she lay in state. He recounted her tireless work throughout her illness, her refusal to care for herself and rest until he finally ordered her to do so. She was forty-eight years old.

Under a huge lighted tent erected next to her home, a memorial service was held in her honor. The tent and newly paved entrance road were made ready with astounding speed due to the expected crowd. The country director, Antonina, and I arrived a little early and managed to grab a couple of seats. She was the one who had kindly led me to the sports complex to get Sam after his shoulder injury. Talking quietly with Antonina as the other mourners streamed in, I was struck by her resemblance to Inyumba, in both appearance and demeanor. A former senior banking executive, Antonina was soft-spoken like Inyumba but was no pushover. As women leaders, it wasn't easy to navigate being gentle and forceful at the same time. Both did it remarkably well.

The space filled quickly, well beyond capacity, yet people kept on coming. Government leaders, colleagues, friends, and well-wishers all came to pay their respects to the fallen leader. Some of the mourners wore t-shirts emblazoned with her likeness. The first lady of Rwanda, Jeannette Kagame, also came and stayed. A strong and committed leader in her own right, Mrs. Kagame headed the Imbuto Foundation, which created opportunities for girls' education and empowerment.

The place, the whole mood, had the look and feel of a Christian revival meeting—or how I'd imagined one—deeply spiritual, at once somber and upbeat. Gospel singers and many others sang Inyumba's praises over the four-hour service; early video footage was shown on a big screen, and a special song was written and performed live for the occasion.

The details of Inyumba's life and contributions were narrated in tribute after tribute: how she was the one who led the charge for members of the diaspora to come back after the genocide to help the country rebuild. How she worked to assist widows and victims of violence, to place orphans into homes and families. How committed she was to placing women on an equal footing with men. Inyumba was described as a humble and devoted Christian, a party loyalist, and an uncommon patriot. I knew her to be a kind and thoughtful woman, a globalist, and an unflagging advocate for women's rights.

The day after the memorial service, her funeral was held at the Christian Life Assemblies Church. Condolence messages from political leaders and admirers around the world were read aloud. The following story was shared in the Order of Service:

> One day, as minister of social affairs, she handed over an orphan to its new mother. Overwhelmed by the thought that perhaps it might have been this woman who had been involved in the murder of the child's parents—and with no other option but to cede the child—Inyumba turned her face away from the cameras and wept.

Surrounded by close to a thousand weeping mourners, I too wept openly. She belonged to all of us, whether Rwandan or not. The courage and conviction she gave to a nation, she also gave to each of us. Inyumba had not gone down quietly, had fought for what she believed in until the very end. Her work. Her family. Her country. Women. Inyumba's indomitable spirit and inspiration were sure to remain with me for years to come.

Still thinking about Inyumba, I debated whether or not to go to the staff holiday party. Everyone was excited about it, and the party-planning task force was hard at work organizing every detail of this daylong celebration. I was in no mood to feign enthusiasm for a party, not now, not after Inyumba's passing and with everything going on at work. And then . . . I changed my mind. My colleagues here had embraced and included me as one of their own. It felt wrong, disrespectful, not to give them the same courtesy. Showing up was part of the job, part of being a professional.

We took an antiquated, sixties-era bus to Lake Muhaze Beach Resort, about an hour's ride east of the city, with lots of singing and praying on the way. The weather was fine, so the party kicked off outdoors with a series of fun relay games on a grassy spot near the lake. Then everyone moved inside for a late lunch. Someone had brought along a boom box, so we danced to hip-hop music as we polished off several trays of goat brochette. Clemence, the income generation manager, was a sharp Kenyan woman with an even sharper sense of humor. She had us all laughing at her jokes about former Ugandan dictator Idi Amin's ignorance and poor literacy skills. Who knew Clemence was that funny.

Antonina appeared to be comfortable and confident in her new role, and the staff all seemed to respect her, which was important, particularly here. The team, like the country, needed a strong leader to continue moving past the genocide. For as long as I'd been coming to Rwanda, there'd been an undercurrent of ethnic discord in the office, a mirror of the divisions that led to the genocide. Even though I lacked language skills, it was clear to me that it rose above the usual workplace politics. Everyone seemed to know who was who, who was where, and who'd done what to whom.

But this team led by Antonina seemed to have things well in hand. I'd watched her in meetings and quiet conversations deftly encourage the staff to lay aside past grievances for the sake of the work. It was an excellent message, one that resonated more personally now as I tried to come to terms with my own past: how in some ways I was still allowing it to control my life instead of taking charge of it. I admired Antonina's finesse.

Toward the end of the party, a young staffer serving as master of ceremonies called Antonina and me up to the front of the room. Though we'd both been there for months now, we were still the newest staff members and thus bestowed with a welcoming gift of a hand bouquet of red roses. Those flowers, the gesture, caught me by surprise and I choked back tears.

Back at the house, I placed the bouquet on a table in the living room, thinking about the staff. The roses stayed there until they withered away. The day, the party, was a good morale boost. Those connections to staff, and the women, meant more than anything. I needed to try and stay positive, to focus on the strength of those relationships and my convictions, instead of on what was being lost. That, and more of Antonina's finesse.

16

Top of the Continent

At home, the topic of conversation shifted to our climb up Mount Kilimanjaro the following week. It would be a serious adventure over the boys' winter break, but I was hoping for more. What exactly that meant—more insight or certainty, more of a sense of what came next—was hard to pinpoint. But Kili, for whatever reason, had become integral to figuring out my attempt at reinvention.

We planned to ease into the climb with two days of safari in Tanzania, at Tarangire National Park. Other than our post-Thanksgiving visit to Akagera, we'd been on safari once before—in Kenya, when the boys were much younger. They all still remembered it, not for the animals as much as for our visit to a Maasai village near the Mara. Mary, the village chief's second wife, showed us around the compound, then invited us into her grass-thatched mud hut, a dim, cool room lined with narrow wood benches. She described how her tribespeople lived and worked, how they drank cow's blood mixed with milk for strength and nourishment, and revered cattle as a source of life and wealth.

"Now can I tell you about my world?" asked then-five-year-old Kai, his shock of white-blond hair all the more conspicuous here. He described our dog Max, how we lived in a house and shopped for food in a store, how broccoli was his favorite food. That visit to Kenya was the first time the boys understood that there was more to the world than the microcosm of America they inhabited. That it was okay, even interesting, to interact with people who looked and lived differently from them. They've never forgotten it. After several months in Rwanda, their eyes were open a little wider now.

Tanzania was home to some of the best places for safari. Our knowledgeable guide wound us around Tarangire's ruggedly beautiful plains, offering insights about its flora and fauna. The safari jeep was happily full with the five of us in the back, jostling each other for a prime view through the tall grasses and brush. Our guide, an animated storyteller, told us about the all-purpose "sausage tree" with its sausage-like pods used to make beer, treat malaria, and induce abortion. A few minutes later he pointed to the gorgeous baobab trees that can live for thousands of years, their ancient root-like limbs sweeping the sky. The curvy dirt road was jarring at times but worth it for the chance to observe the rich diversity of wildlife in its own habitat.

Toward the end of the first day, we stumbled upon a group of female lions. I was captivated watching them hunt in small groups, patiently surrounding their prey, while their cubs observed from a safe distance—the animal kingdom's version of engaged parenting. The boys' kept up a steady stream of crude jokes after they spotted the water buck, the dik-dik, and the dung beetle, which produced fits of adolescent laughter. It was harder to joke about the baboons. Parked at one of the designated picnic spots, we got out of the jeep to eat our boxed lunches. Suddenly one of the more aggressive baboons was on us, snatching a banana and part of a sandwich right off the picnic table. We packed up quickly and finished eating in the car.

We spent the night at a place called the River Camp, set on the banks of the Tarangire. Managed by a Zimbabwean couple who had set up the stunning Nyungwe Lodge in Rwanda's Nyungwe National Park, they were relaxed, professional hosts. The river was bone dry now due to the season, and with no gates or hard boundaries, we could see well into the game park. Guards from the local Maasai tribe kept watch due to the nearness of the animals. A tall, spear-wielding warrior draped in beads and a red cloth, a *Shuka*, escorted us along the darkened path to our safari tent after dinner. The next morning after breakfast, Kai spotted twelve enormous elephants and excitedly called us over. We stood watching them enjoy their breakfast right beside our tent, in awe, for several minutes. It felt good to be together, to be sharing this experience as a family.

Our safari guide drove us to Arusha later that day, to the Moivaro Lodge, where we would spend the night. Set on a working coffee plantation below imposing Mount Meru, Tanzania's second highest mountain, the lodge itself had the look and feel of a country inn, cozy and inviting. We spent most of the afternoon on the covered veranda, snacking and checking emails, then walked the footpaths around the expansive grounds. The property was huge, forty acres, dense with leafy tropical trees and plants and lush, color-soaked patches of lilies, bougainvillea, and hibiscus, and farther along, row upon row of coffee plants.

That evening we began making final preparations for Mount Kilimanjaro. On the veranda, our trek organizers gave us a detailed briefing on what it would take to summit the tallest peak in Africa. A Kilimanjaro climb is a serious undertaking. Acute mountain sickness and other health issues are common, they said. It was critical that we drink plenty of water—three liters a day at a minimum. They walked us through other health and safety tips and double-checked all of our gear.

Though we had plenty of new stuff from our REI purchases over the summer, and would have had more if it were up to Bill, we had rented some additional items we would need at the higher elevations—thick insulated jackets, sleeping bags for extreme weather, and walking poles. As we listened to all of their instructions, we finally realized that this was not going to be a walk in the park. On the way back to our cottage to get packed and ready, I thought that maybe I'd underestimated the challenge ahead, especially for the boys.

Eli in particular was getting pretty anxious about the climb. That morning, he confessed, he had thrown up after breakfast, overcome by nerves.

"Mom, I don't know if I can make it all the way to the top," he said, after some hesitation.

"It's okay, bud," I replied, trying to reassure him. "I don't know that any of us can make it."

I told him that it didn't matter whether any of us summited, that it was much more about the physical and mental challenge. A soothing thing to say, but I wasn't sure I believed it. The climb's significance had only grown in my mind over the months in Rwanda. So much so that I could hardly fathom what it would mean to not summit.

As we were packing, I suddenly remembered what day it was. December 20, our twenty-fifth wedding anniversary. Both of us had forgotten it. We decided to head back down to the main lodge for a quick drink to mark the day. *How could a quarter century have passed so quickly?* I thought, sitting across the table from Bill in the homey bar. But here we were, still together after all these years. Bill's time back in Rwanda now matched the time he'd been away. In those two months, we both had made more of an effort to get back on track, but I still felt something between us. We weren't so much fighting—although that happened—as stalled. We were a great team when it came to the boys and practical matters, but the most passionate moments between us came out as bursts of hostility. I felt shifts had occurred, were occurring within me. But I didn't, or wasn't yet able to process the adjustments Bill was making.

I wondered if Bill felt as though he had something to prove on that mountain, too. If he did, it probably had a lot to do with Eli's comment about Bill being the weak link. I said as much over the years, faulted him again and again for being too soft, too weak, for being too much like my mother. It's difficult for a man, or a marriage, to recover from that. The deeper conversation about us, what we would do, was left unspoken.

Kilimanjaro rises out of the Rift Valley in northern Tanzania, just below the equator, near the border with Kenya. Members of the Chuga tribe populate the villages surrounding the mountain, growing coffee and vegetables and raising livestock—all fed from streams and springs that swell from seasonal rains and Kilimanjaro's melting snows. Mount Kilimanjaro was formed by three volcanic eruptions over the past million years; the last eruption, 350,000 years ago, left behind a large crater at the peak where ice fields and glaciers survive.

We met our local climb team near the Shira trailhead at the base of Mount Kilimanjaro: Stratton, our lead guide, and two assistant guides, Naiman and David, both members of the Maasai tribe. They were all of medium build, strong, and fit. Stratton had grown up in the foothills of Kili, where his eighty-eight-year-old father tended four hundred coffee plants and a dozen sheep. Many porters would join us later, lugging our food, belongings, even a toilet tent, from campsite to campsite. Collectively, our team had spent decades on the mountain, first as porters and then working their way up to guide. In a place with meager job prospects, they took every trek they could get, which meant dozens of punishing trips up the mountain each season.

Our route was Shira Seven, considered one of the best nontechnical routes but also one of the most strenuous because of the frequent altitude changes across the mountain's southern slopes. The first two days were not too arduous. We walked and talked—an easy camaraderie among our family as we got to know our guides. Each of them was the father of adolescent boys. Sam and Eli had paired off and were becoming good hiking buddies; Kai was the man of the hour with his invented alter ego, Captain Sky, a man who craved nothing more than a Subway deli sandwich. He kept us all laughing with his spot-on impersonations and steady repertoire of "Yo mama so fat" jokes. It was just as I had envisioned it.

Day three was a hard acclimatization day. We ascended four hundred meters (1,300 feet) over five hours, up to the summit of Shira Cathedral, a large rock spur on the edge of the Shira Plateau, and then down another hundred meters to our campsite, Shira Two Bivouac. The morning had been clear and beautiful; we took in our first full view of the mountain as we ate breakfast outside the mess tent. Clouds set in around midday, followed by an unseasonably icy rain. Freezing cold and damp by the time we reached camp, we huddled for warmth in the mess tent, drinking cup after cup of hot tea until dinnertime. The boys were ravenous. I had to laugh at myself, at my fixation with healthy eating. Our day started with steaming vats of soupy porridge, stacks of fried white bread, hard-boiled eggs, and sausages. They, or I should say *we*, consumed all of it.

High-altitude sleeping was fitful, punctuated with serious high-altitude farting, the sound of which echoed across our three tents over the long, bone-chilling night. Kai was my tent mate and Bill and Eli were together; both had wanted a reassuring parent nearby. Sam was in a tent by himself. We were drinking water nonstop to try and stay hydrated. Kai kept a large, empty water bottle next to his sleeping bag to pee into. The rest of us were too embarrassed to do the same. We kept our headlamps close in case we couldn't hold it any longer. The guys could go right outside the tent, but I had to pick my way across the dark, lunar landscape to the semi-enclosed toilet tent a hundred or so feet away, clutching my one and only dry roll of toilet paper, which I kept ziplocked deep inside my daypack.

"Washy, washy," said David, rousing us the next morning. He set down a large plastic tub of warm water and a bar of soap in front of the tent, then returned a few minutes later with steaming mugs of instant coffee for me and Bill and hot chocolate for the boys. A thin layer of ice had formed around the tent's zippered threshold overnight. It felt just as icy inside. All my clothes were cold, wet, and dirty—but I'd stopped caring days ago. I knew I looked and smelled terrible. I hadn't taken off my hat, and barely managed to change clothes or brush my teeth, never mind the makeup and face creams I had foolishly packed.

Day five was a killer, with a grueling hike along lava ridges beneath the glaciers, and up and down multiple rock walls. As we hiked above the tree line, bare to the elements, we were doused by intermittent sleet and snow for several hours. I regretted having nixed the extra rain ponchos and backpack covers as unnecessary. Bill, who'd pushed for more gear, gave me a nice "I told you so."

Bill was in fine shape, chatting with the guides about politics, development, and parenthood as he hiked. The combination of Diamox pills (to prevent altitude sickness) and intense training seemed to do the trick. Maybe it was the days-old beard or the sweaty, soiled gear, but his new physical prowess was kind of sexy. The boys were upbeat, cocky even, unfazed by the challenging climb or weather. By the time we reached camp, I was nauseated and had a massive headache. Stratton thought it was a touch of altitude sickness and pulled out his first-aid kit, which was loaded with Panadol. I swallowed a couple of pills and could only pick at dinner before excusing myself and heading back to the tent.

What's wrong with me? I thought as I zipped myself inside. Apart from the altitude sickness, I couldn't shake these feelings of inadequacy and self-doubt that arose during the long hours of trekking. I became convinced that I lacked the stamina to make it to the top. I was supposed to be the tough one—the woman who could do one-armed pushups with relative ease, who once dreamed of sprinting in the Olympics. But the weak link, it turned out, wasn't Bill at all. It was me. *Come on, Karen, you've got this,* I muttered as motivation.

Day six, Christmas Day, dawned piercing cold with endless blue skies. The tropical rain forest at the lower elevations had become a desert-like landscape as we got closer to the top. We started out fine with a dramatic descent into the Great Barranco Valley. There we caught our first glimpse of the famous giant lobelias—statuesque, distinctive, cactus-like plants that resemble huge upside-down pineapples, like the land before time.

As we rested on a bluff, nibbling hard crackers, Stratton's cell phone rang, and he moved away to take the call. We were still talking about his amazing reception on the mountain when he came back to us, close to tears. It was his wife with the news that their oldest son had been accepted into the college-preparatory high school. It meant that his son would have a future, the opportunity to build a life beyond the trails of Kili. We all cheered.

Lunch was followed by a near-vertical ascent on exposed volcanic rock. As I clung to the rocks for balance, adrenaline swept through me; I was afraid to look down. The effort to summit this smaller peak was almost too much. My body had practically never failed me. Maybe this time, though, this was my limit? How much harder would it be to scale Uhuru Peak? I pushed the thought from my mind, refusing to go there. *Focus, Karen. Focus.*

At dinner that night, our guides placed a small plastic Christmas tree and a box of white wine on the table. The boys were all starving, as usual, chatting away, exhilarated by the day's hike and to be closing in on the summit. Bill was exuberant as well. Watching them gulp down their heaping bowls of warm stew made me even more nauseous. Done in by the day's exertion, I managed a few sips of wine and bites of bread before offering a weak goodnight and returning to the tent. I fell into a deep sleep.

I woke up a few hours later, confused and disoriented. It took me several moments to remember where I was. Lying there fully clothed in the tapered mummy bag, struggling to catch my breath in the frigid air, now wide awake, I felt all of my lingering insecurities come into focus. This mountain, my family, my marriage, my work, my ambitions, all of them had become one comingled mess. How did it get this bad?

For as long as I could remember I'd been fighting myself: to suppress my own rage, to overcome my own stinginess, my tendency to be critical and withholding, particularly with those I care for the most. I'd tried to manage my fear of rejection, my deep-seated need for approval, by being above reproach. But when my marriage and my work—the dual foundations of my life—began giving way beneath me, that illusion went with them. Everything I'd learned from my parents came spilling out in ways that I seemed to have no control over.

My childhood protective armor had been with me for so long, covering hurt and vulnerability with a veneer of distinction. I dumped boyfriends before they could dump me. I married a nice man, a good man, who didn't scare me, who wouldn't push me back or away, as my father had. Someone I could comfortably manage while keeping at arm's length. Professionally, I would overwhelm colleagues and supervisors with competence. *Yes, I can. Yes, I will. Yes to more.*

I will not be found lacking.
I will not be my mother.
I will earn my father's praise at last.
Win my mother's love at last.
Mom and Dad will be proud, both would love me, because I was just that good.

And it all worked, worked well in fact, for a while. But now I could see that the armor that had protected me, served me so well in the past, was a barrier to my future.

I'd walled off my heart, just like my mother, without even realizing it. Both of us had done so to mask our true fragility, our fear. I longed for closeness but was afraid of getting too close, of becoming too attached to Bill, even the boys. It was only a matter of time before all my "sorries" and "regrets" were no longer enough, before I actually hurt them, fundamentally, as I had been hurt myself. Afraid that if Bill knew the whole of it, the real me, knew how damaged I was, he would leave first.

Instead, I threw myself into important work, and was good at it. Passionate, committed, hardworking. I allowed work to define me, divert me from the problems in my marriage, in my family. I had the best, most noble of excuses: helping women war survivors. They needed me. But in truth, I needed them. They were, in much greater measure, bolstering me.

I dismissed the good in both my parents, especially my mom. The bologna and ketchup sandwiches she made just for me when she thought I liked them; the Valentine's Day sweeties she remembered every year, even when I was out on my own; her little nickname for me that I pretended to be annoyed by but secretly loved; and her silly made-up songs that I later sang to my own children.

Then there were the summer horseback rides and raging driftwood bonfires beside the chilly ocean on Neskowin beach on the Oregon coast. Mornings there, my father would dispatch us to the village store to buy a newspaper, and he'd throw in a little extra for penny candy. Game nights at the coliseum to watch the Portland Trail Blazers during the best "Dr. Jack" years, when we won the title.

I glanced over at Kai, sleeping peacefully next to me, mummified against the shivering cold. He was trying so hard to be strong, to keep up with his brothers, but he was still my baby. Bill and Eli were probably sound asleep as well in the next tent over. Then there was Sammy: stubborn, deliberate, so intent on being independent, in a tent by himself. We were alike in many ways. He was even less comfortable asking for help, showing his soft side, but on the inside he was such a big-hearted, decent boy.

Complicated, scary at times, this was the life, the work, I had chosen. And I loved it, every sad, beautiful, ridiculously overstretched bit of it. I had to set things right.

But now just a day away, that summit was looming, larger than life. One thing I knew: I have always been tenacious enough. Like a dog with a bone, there was no way I was letting go of this one. I was going to summit that fucking mountain, even if I had to crawl my way up.

III

Above all, be the heroine of your life, not the victim.

—*Nora Ephron*

17

Pain into Power

I was still processing what happened during those final, tortuous hours of our Kilimanjaro climb, as we ushered in the New Year. It was impossible to articulate my feelings then. What's more, Bill's return to the US was imminent. He would be gone for almost three months this time, our longest separation yet. The separations in Rwanda were proving to be more difficult than I had expected, though we had yet to openly resolve anything between us.

Before Bill left for the United States, I had to go there myself for a job interview I'd lined up. My anxiety was definitely growing around what would come next. This job wasn't a perfect fit, but still, it was time to get out there again, to think about the future. My plan was to slip into the country for about forty-eight hours and be back in Rwanda before anyone noticed. Bill called the office to let them know I was too sick to make it in. "She's probably contagious," he explained to dissuade visitors. It felt naughty, like I was cheating on them.

Once again, Bill and I literally passed in the airport, not meeting, as he returned to Bethesda and I arrived back in Kigali. It was *Tag, you're it* all over again. The story of our lives.

Going back to single parenting after weeks of family togetherness was harder now. Bill spoiled us as usual, willingly attending to all of the driving, shopping, and cooking; it was what he did best. Our opposite parenting styles were the source of many an argument, but the more time I spent with the

boys, the less I felt the need to counterbalance Bill's inclination for caretaking. Until Rwanda, I didn't fully appreciate what great kids they are: kind,
intelligent, funny, aware. They were discerning, too. I trusted them more to
manage our sometimes competing influences, to take what they needed from
each of us and leave the rest.

Like them, I'd also fallen back into a comfortable state of dependency,
not even bothering to carry money when Bill was around. It troubled me,
but I was starting to wonder if it was it so wrong to enjoy being taken care
of in certain ways. Perhaps this was, in fact, Bill's way of giving me room to
express my softer side, and I only had to allow myself to express it. Didn't I
want that? Did that make me a hypocrite in the eyes of other feminists? Did
that even matter?

Feminism, I knew, was not a monolith. It differed from country to country, woman to woman. Context, again, was everything. Even the word struck
a negative chord in Rwanda, a decidedly pro-female country, at least the
American brand of it. There were times when I had to remind myself to meet
the women I worked with where they were, not where I wanted them to be, or
think they should be. Why couldn't I give myself that same leeway?

When we first came to Rwanda, being on my own with the boys felt like
the most important thing. Now, I could see how thoroughly I relied on Bill,
not only for his caretaking but deep down, at a gut level, when it mattered.
There, at home, in our favorite pair of green chairs by the corner window,
we'd poured out our hopes, fears, and frustrations to each other, year after
year after year. Work crises, parent crises, boy crises. When Sam had a febrile
seizure when he was just weeks old, Bill raced through the city streets to
Children's Hospital while I held tiny Sam in my arms, my face pressed up to
his mouth to make sure he was still breathing. We both sat with a pit in our
stomach on opening night of Eli's turn as the tap dancing, cartwheeling tin
man in the school's fourth-grade production of *The Wizard of Oz*. He nailed
it. Upon the wonderful, unexpected arrival of Kai a year after we'd moved
into our new house, our planned library/office was happily converted into a
baby's room. We'd argued over politics and social change strategies in those
chairs, organized countless trips. We made plans for the future, for our future.

"You're just like your father!" Bill would sometimes shout at me angrily in
the heat of a fight. "You're just like *your* father!" I'd shout back, even louder.
And we were. Our fathers. And our mothers, too. They were the same, like

their own fathers and mothers. But perhaps we could be more than a mirror of our respective family templates? In spite of the hard times, the mean times, the times when we relentlessly pushed each other's buttons, knowing how to inflict the most damage, I couldn't help but like him, admire him. At the start of this latest period apart, I was beginning to realize how much I'd taken Bill's kind and generous heart for granted, just how much I stood to lose.

When we returned to Kigali after Kili, Innocent, our sometimes cook, shopper, and nanny, failed to show up for work. We called and texted to no avail. The woman did not want to be found. With several must-do trips coming up, the thought of having no one for backup threw me into a panic. I needed help, someone who could be there for the boys.

Before Bill returned to the States, he did some quick work and found us Paula, one of the African Bagel Company's former job trainees. Paula was twenty-two years old, though she appeared much younger. Her slight, child-sized frame was likely due to chronic poverty and malnutrition. Working for us was Paula's first job. She came to work in the same tiny pair of blue jeans but with different plaited or combed-out hairdos each week. She lived with her mother, two aunties, and their five kids in a house without electricity near Kicukiro. Her father and older sister had died during the genocide, when the family scattered in pairs for safety. Paula and her mother survived in the bush for weeks until the country was liberated, and it was safe to return to the city. She began calling me "Momon" and was soon sitting down to dinner with us most nights.

Paula spoke limited English but was anxious to please and was used to feeding a crowd. She prepared heaping bowls of pasta and rice, often accompanied by french fries, during her first week. It was likely her training at ABC, where she learned to make bagels by the hundreds, but also the standard belly-filling, multi-starch diet of most Rwandans. Beyond a lack of food (and land to grow it on), poor nutrition was one of the main contributing factors to persistent malnutrition in the country. A nutrition specialist from UNICEF described farmers eager to exchange their wholesome eggs for a loaf of white bread. With a subsistence-based economy came a subsistence mentality, which meant people would take what they could get when they could get it.

Rushing to the office one morning, I left Paula a shopping list on the kitchen counter, placing a star by only those items to be purchased that week—fruits and veggies, brown rice and bread, milk, some protein—along with money for a week's worth of shopping. When I returned home, however, it was clear that she had ignored all the starred items and bought as big a quantity of anything on the list that she came across first, until she ran out of money. She spent the entire 50,000 RWF in one shot, then borrowed another 5,000 RWF from Sam and hit Kai up for some cash as well. We still had none of the staples we needed, but were flush with several kilos of brown sugar and three pineapples.

"What were you thinking?" I demanded, incredulous, regretting the words as soon as they were out of my mouth. Paula looked mortified, afraid that her new, desperately needed job was on the line.

"Sorry, Momon," she mumbled.

What was wrong with me, picking a fight with someone who would never dream of pushing back? It was like crushing a butterfly. I suspected that Paula, like the participants in the program, must be living day to day, hand to mouth. She was another woman with too few choices.

I gave Paula a quick hug to assure her that she, and her job, were safe.

Given her poor English, and my nonexistent Kinyarwanda, I asked ABC to facilitate our communications a few times. They shared our food preferences with her, and even invited her back for extra cooking classes. She told them to tell me how much she needed the job, and that she was willing to work hard and open to learning.

Over the weeks and months, we got better at communicating. One evening when I was out, the boys let Paula know she could leave early as they rushed out the door to meet up with friends. A couple of hours later, I received a text message from Paula urging me to come home. She needed transport money, the equivalent of about two dollars. She had been sitting alone in the house all that time, unsure of what to do. Though Paula received a monthly salary and daily transport money, it turned out that she kept none of the earnings for herself—everything was going to support her extended family. These moments helped us to understand her better.

Paula grew to love the boys, but she was especially sweet on Kai. "How was your day, Kai?" she'd ask eagerly when he arrived home from school, welcoming him with a special treat—homemade chips and guacamole or mini-doughnuts—she'd prepared just for him. The affection was mutual. Kai would often chop vegetables or fetch things out of the pantry for her as she made dinner, or he would ask to help with the dishes. And Paula would be out front cheering Kai on during his one-on-one soccer matches with Joseph. "Oh, so nice," she gushed whenever he scored a goal.

A couple of years later, Paula became pregnant and had a baby boy of her own. She named him Kai.

The kids were back in school after the long winter break, and I reimmersed myself in work, more clearheaded after Kili. Work was going to be even more demanding over the next few months with the program relaunch in Yei, South Sudan, and construction on the Women's Opportunity Center nearing its final stages, though it was nowhere near ready for the planned June opening. On any given day, several workers failed to show up or were underperforming. Frustrated to not be further along, Bruce and I upped the pressure on the contractor by switching to a new payment schedule based on completed milestones, to be verified during weekly site visits to Kayonza, just over an hour's drive east from Kigali.

The boys and I gradually settled back into our routine—school, work, soccer, homework and chores, theirs and mine—though Bill's absence was keenly felt. Lonely, desperate for adult conversation, I was missing our built-in social life as a couple. We were talking more often now, with a longer video call on the weekends so that he could see the boys. He was in good spirits, back working with the trek organizers from Kili to plan a trip to South Africa over the boys' spring break.

In the meantime, Sam, Eli, and I were back to doing our regular morning runs on the weekend. Sam was the big motivator. When the boys and I first started running together, I was the one coaxing them along, but lately, they were the ones pushing me. They had seen me at my most vulnerable; I had been completely exposed on Kili. "You've got this, Mom," Sam would say on some of the steepest parts of our runs, jogging in place until my fifty-year-old body caught up.

Kai and I had become good weekend playmates as the older boys increasingly spent time away with their friends. "What's the plan for the day?" he would ask, ready for a new adventure. Usually we'd head to a favorite lunch spot or one of the nearby hotel pools for a swim. I loved the one-on-one time with him. I knew I hadn't always been there for the boys, but it felt important to try to remedy that now, to make up for those absences.

Watching Kai splash around in the deep end of Umubano's pool from a patio chair nearby, I mused about what our day would look like if we were in Bethesda on a mid-winter Saturday. The streets would be slick with a few patches of ice or dirty snow. I'd be up early, before six, making coffee; as it brewed, I would dash outside to grab the *New York Times* from the front lawn, scanning the headlines for the latest outbreaks or upticks of violence. There might be a fire in the fireplace once everyone else got up, and later, omelets and chocolate-chip pancakes; breakfast was Bill's specialty. He had talked about starting a bed and breakfast when we retired. Sam and I would take a run if the roads weren't too icy. Sunday nights were steak night. Those images of our family routines often soothed me while I was away.

I always did this, longed for home when I was in the field and wanted to be in the field when I was home. Now that we were here, I found myself yearning for the other, for those small yet necessary things that brought comfort and a sense of place. *I am capable of contentment*, I thought. In straddling the two worlds, however, that feeling has been more short-lived, elusive. Unsettled is more like it.

That weekend in Kigali, there was a James Bond film festival on TV, and they were showing all of the films in order. Lying there on our uncomfortable banana-leaf sofa, feeling unproductive but disinclined to move, I started tracking Bonds for some reason, to follow the character's progress over time. The early Connery Bonds are these macho, hard-drinking womanizers. The later Craig Bonds, in line with the times and evolving gender roles, are more sensitive and monogamous. Part of me preferred the emotionally accessible Bond, but there *was* something compelling about the Bond who knows just what he wants and goes after it.

I could take a lesson or two from these testosterone-ridden guys. Hell, most women could, I thought. We rarely feel deserving even though we are. There'd been plenty of instances when I'd held myself back or imposed certain constraints. I can't, I shouldn't, I'm not supposed to. . . .

I can't . . . try for another CEO role.

I shouldn't . . . worry about what others, and particularly other women, think of me.

I'm not supposed to . . . need a man.

That little voice inside my head was so often there, telling me that I wasn't good enough, smart enough, thin enough, mom enough.

Those self-imposed limits applied to more material things, too. The huge breadth of choices in the US had been overwhelming at times, usually after a few weeks in the field. Returning to a place of unlimited access and opportunity for those with means—where virtually anything could be had, upgraded, or procured in bulk—was a shock to the system. I remembered my wide-eyed colleagues from the Soviet Union as they took in the dizzying array of choices on grocery store shelves and restaurant menus on their first visit to the United States. The sight of Walmart literally left them dumbstruck.

Gosudarstvenny Universalny Magazin, or GUM, running the length of Red Square, was Moscow's only department store at the time: a misnomer, as most of the kiosks in the mall-like structure carried exactly the same item. Depending on the day, it might be a bottle of shampoo or cheap plastic toy. Waiting in line was a full-time profession. People stood in line for hours, or if they could, hired a professional line holder, in order to buy the one item that happened to be available on that day—a roll of toilet paper or a bag of strawberries. Whatever it was.

Once I was accosted by a woman at the St. Petersburg airport who demanded I hand over my lipstick. On a visit to a local synagogue, another woman cornered me in the bathroom for a pen. Hotel soaps and toiletries were standard gifts from foreign visitors. The scarcity of consumer products induced such a profound sense of longing among a population deprived and desperate for choice.

Over the years, I'd chosen to narrow my choices in small ways. I generally avoided buffets, bulk purchases, and shopping online. But the big choices—the life choices—around when and whom to marry, whether to pursue my education, to have children and/or to work, were the ones I truly valued. Those were mine, thankfully, by virtue of being born in a place and time where women are allowed to make those kinds of choices for themselves.

Maybe I needed to refine my thinking around the very concept of choice. To think of it as more rare and precious. With that lens, I could consciously decide to change course, become unstuck, or choose a different path, in the same way that so many women survivors of war have *chosen* to turn their pain into power. I'd seen this happen again and again in women like Debora, Euphraise, and Tereza. Not only in Rwanda but around the world.

I could see now that the paralysis I felt at this point in my life, my struggles with my identity as a wife and mother, were in fact things that I could change, if I chose to do so. I don't know why, but I hadn't comprehended before how this concept of turning pain into power could apply to me, to all women, no matter their circumstances.

The gift of choice had been in my hands all along.

18

Yei

It was February now, and like an athlete gearing up for a big game, I was trying to psych myself up for another trip to South Sudan. Leaving felt even harder this time after so much time with the boys. The ten-day trip was the longest since we'd been in Rwanda, and Paula, as sweet as she was, was not ready to handle things on her own. A young woman Julia knew was coming to support her so that Paula could go home at night. Julia, bless her, was taking Kai camping for the weekend and Amy, thankfully, was driving them all to school and hosting movie night at her home. Knowing that Amy and Julia had my back made it easier to go.

I'd become adept now at managing my own pre-departures, making sure Paula had enough money for groceries, the boys' homework assignments were underway, and the electricity was paid so the power wouldn't go out. Since the boys needed access to large amounts of cash, I ferried home several stacks of Rwandan francs in my computer bag and hid them under a pile of clothes in the back of the closet. Sam, with his superior math skills, was designated as the banker in my absence.

Sadly, I would be a world away in Yei on Valentine's Day and would miss sending Eli off on a date with his first girlfriend, Muriel, Amy's daughter. Eli and I were out on one of our morning runs in the neighborhood when he told me he wanted to learn how to French kiss. Without thinking, I told him to cut a hole in an orange and practice on that. "Mom, that's weird. Stop," he said, feigning disgust. But I think he listened and I was glad he felt close enough to me to ask.

Our relationship hadn't been the easiest. Eli's deep sensitivity, the way he wore his heart on his sleeve, reminded me so much of myself at that age that, at times, it was difficult to watch. He was often the first kid to grumble, "It's not fair," the one to go after attention, even negative. But this kind of intimacy was new, and good. Maybe he was growing up; maybe we both were. That boy had such an innate sweetness about him. To see him becoming his own person gave me such pleasure. That Sunday afternoon, we went shopping at Kigali City Tower and bought Muriel a cool pendant necklace at a boutique called Mille Collines. *She better be nice to him,* I thought. *At least nicer than I was to boys at that age.*

In the bedroom packing to leave later that night, it finally hit me that being an engaged parent was more than obsessing over the boys' grades or what they ate or watched on television. That was actually the easy stuff, the surface stuff. It was more about the in-betweens: Eli's first kiss and Kai's soccer matches with Joseph on the front lawn, sharing our days around the dinner table. So many of those everyday moments I'd already missed. I'm not sure why I didn't get that before. Perhaps I had been overcompensating for my absences, for a deep-rooted insecurity that I wasn't enough for them. But really, it was all about showing up, about paying attention to the little stuff even when the biggest stuff, the rest of the messed-up world, was screaming for attention.

On the late-night plane ride to Nairobi, I concentrated on switching gears, from mom working to working mom. All my faculties would be needed in South Sudan, which had to be one of the most difficult development environments. Arriving well before dawn, I managed to doze for an hour or so on the hard floor of the Nairobi airport ahead of my next flight to Juba.

Landing at Juba International Airport instantly put me on alert. Military helicopters, aid-agency aircraft, and a few commercial planes were scattered on the ground around the terminal; it was hot and chaotic inside the airport as well, the perfect definition of a free-for-all. I had developed no fondness for the country since the last visit. Yei, the new program base, would likely be just as challenging as Rumbek.

The only ways in and out of Yei were twice-weekly commercial flights via Eagle Air from Entebbe, but only when the weather was fine (it was too difficult to take off or land during the rainy season). There were also a few less predictable UN flights, but seats were very hard to come by. There was also an interminable stretch of dirt road connecting Juba to Yei, which was how I was traveling via a hired car and driver.

Despite Juba's usual road congestion, it didn't take us long to clear the city. Then everything seemed to slow down. Little was moving as we made our way in the scorching midday sun. What would have been less than a two-hour drive in Rwanda took more than double the time because of the rough terrain. The driver had to swerve like a slalom skier to avoid large ditches and potholes. Herds of cows and goats quietly grazed on the side of the road while a handful of vehicles, some ferrying soldiers, others daily commuters, rumbled past.

Small groupings of grass and mud huts dotted the rural landscape. White markers denoted areas previously cleared of landmines. Most of the villagers had sought some kind of shelter from the oppressive heat. Men gathered under traditional *tukuls*, playing cards or drinking tea. Yet the women were out working, with infants tightly swaddled around their backs, balancing heavy loads of firewood, produce, or water on their heads to prepare the evening meal.

The vegetation grew dense as we approached Yei, located in the Greenbelt Zone in Central Equatoria, with some areas positively lush. With a population of nearly 172,000 and few, if any, organizations providing programs or services for women there, Yei held real potential to impact the lives of women, their families, and communities.

The war between the Sudanese government and the Sudanese People's Movement/Army (SPLM/A) reached Yei in the mid-1980s, and for most of the next decade, the Sudanese government controlled Yei. In 1997, the SPLM/A retook Yei and turned the city into a center for humanitarian relief operations. Yei then saw an influx of soldiers and their families, internally displaced persons, Congolese refugees, economic migrants, and those fleeing the Lord's Resistance Army, a vicious guerilla group led by fugitive Joseph Kony.

War all but decimated the local infrastructure and economy. Today, almost half of the population lives below the poverty line, with an average income of roughly ten dollars per month. Women in Yei, like the rest of the country, bear the brunt of the challenges: households headed by females represent a significant percentage of the urban and rural poor. Customary laws and discriminatory cultural practices, from land access and ownership to inheritance rights, combined with household food production and crushing domestic responsibilities, serve to limit women's participation in the formal economy.

Women also account for the majority of those in Central Equatoria who are unable to read or write. And health and education metrics for women and girls there are among the lowest in the world. The maternal mortality rate is just below the national average at 1,867 deaths per 100,000 live births. Only 37 percent of girls are enrolled in primary school, according to a 2011 UNICEF report on education in South Sudan, and the percentages are worse for school completion.

Around 6:00 p.m., the driver turned onto a packed dirt road leading to the Episcopal Church of South Sudan's gated compound, where I was staying. It was supposed to be one of the safest, cleanest places in Yei Town, which seemed almost sleepy compared to Rumbek, though hostilities were simmering below the surface. In a few short years, Yei would become a hotbed of horrific ethnic violence, with the UN warning of the potential for genocide there. But in early 2013, before it descended into chaos again, Yei was mostly peaceful.

My dormitory-like room was one of the best on the compound, with a private bathroom and phone booth–like shower stall, which didn't turn out to be much of a perk. Hot water was in very short supply. So was electricity. The management turned off the power every night between 11:00 p.m. and 7:00 a.m., so the room became a virtual sweat lodge when that one stand fan stopped running. The clicks and hums of unfamiliar animals sent me to sleep, but several times a night I woke up drenched and befuddled, surrounded by a mosquito net and wondering where I was, where the boys were. I tried to coax myself back into slumber, squinting to read in the darkness with a headlamp.

On my way to the dining hall each morning, I had to dodge several wild dogs that were roaming around the compound. Breakfast was served cafeteria-style by women church members who lived onsite: homemade chunks of white bread with berry jam from a tin can, hard-boiled eggs, finger-sized bananas, Nescafé, and tea. The guesthouse offered three meals a day, plus sodas and water, but two seemed plenty—it was too hot to eat much anyway.

As we passed the Yei River, on my way to meet with the leaders of a loose coalition of women's groups, it was teeming with life. Bathing children shared a narrow stream of murky water with a few cars and motorcycles also being washed. Some women from the nearby village were attempting to scrub a week's worth of dirty laundry. The surrounding bushes were covered with newly washed clothes laid to dry beneath the beating sun. Water, particularly in a place like South Sudan, was as precious as electricity.

The women leaders arrived at the meeting place in Mugwo Payam wearing a vibrant mix of ankle-length skirts and head coverings. Plastic patio chairs had been arranged under a free-standing lean-to made with wooden poles and a corrugated tin roof as protection against the sun. Talking with these thoughtful, serious women, I learned that most were war widows who had struggled to survive on the paltriest of means and raise children on their own. Almost all of them had been victims of domestic or sexual violence. They were women who so easily could have given up or focused on their own immediate needs, yet they devoted time and energy to helping other women in their community. Out of necessity, they had formed their own social networks, supporting each other with hut building, farming, and child care.

"Tell me about the economic situation for women here," I said.

Meeting with women leaders in Yei.

"We have no money for medicine," said Patrice, "and have to buy our own things like bandages if we go to the hospital."

"Women end up selling the clothes on their bodies to buy medicine for the sick child," added Marie.

"No one thinks about the women," said Susan, who grew up in Uganda and spoke passable English. She used to teach tailoring and agriculture to other women until the supplies ran out. "We have no more seeds to plant," she said. "We used to save, but now it's too hard."

Susan was a natural leader, poised and intelligent with a quiet strength. She would have been a successful businesswoman in almost any other context. Yet circumstances limited her choices—all of their choices. War and conflict, yes, but that was only part of it. War and conflict were to some extent indiscriminate; they afflicted men and women, boys and girls. But women and girls also had gender inequality to contend with, from the very time they were born. Customary laws and adverse cultural practices with regard to marriage, education, work, even sex, effectively rendered women like Susan voiceless. Choiceless. They also placed women and their families at heightened risk of destitution.

Many of the women had begun to make and sell a local brew to earn a little cash, which was contributing to widespread alcoholism—among men and women—as well as exceptionally high levels of violence. In a vicious cycle, men would steal money from their wives to buy the liquor, drink themselves blind, then go home and beat their wives or stop on the way to rape other women. Without money, the women could not afford to pay school fees for their children, particularly their daughters, denying them an education and a pathway to a better life. The women were eager to break the cycle, but to do so they would need another means of earning an income.

The stories of women taking the brunt of violence in their families and communities appalled me, yet I tried to remain dispassionate, businesslike, as if I were a journalist sent there to document such abuse. The distance made it easier to stomach. The violence was in some ways a reflection of the war-torn areas where we worked, but also of the more systemic problem. One in three women worldwide were survivors. One out of every three women! It touched women everywhere.

Yet there were also examples of men who stood up and behind their wives, sisters, and daughters, who supported their progress each step of the way.

One man refused to allow his wife to join the program, thinking it would turn her against him. But when he heard what the women were learning from others in his village, he came himself and asked us to train her.

On the drive back to the church compound, I thought about how to better engage men as advocates and allies for women. If more men took up the mantle of women's rights, and shared those messages with their families, their sons might develop more consciousness, more compassion for their mothers and sisters, perhaps their future girlfriends and wives. Though it was difficult for men as well as women to step outside the bounds of a culture that favored male dominance and freedom from the earliest age, with time, others in the community might see that there was a different way to think about and behave with women. Working with men, I'd learned, was just as important as working with women.

With the needs of the future program participants still on my mind, I grabbed my things at the church compound and quickly switched cars so that we could be on the road to Juba before dark, when it wouldn't be safe. I was ready to be going home but dreading the five-hour car ride on the Yei-Juba road. I also had one more critical meeting, with the commissioner of Yei River County.

The commissioner was on his way back from Juba that same day. I'd been trying to meet him ever since I arrived, but his return kept getting delayed. We ended up planning a roadside rendezvous—the only way not to miss each other as he was coming and I was going.

Commissioner Juma held a lot of sway in Yei. The powerful position was similar to a mayor, and at age thirty-five, Juma was one of the country's youngest commissioners. He earned the post after serving as the successful campaign manager to the minister of gender for South Sudan, a post senior to the gender minister for Central Equatoria-Juba. Juma's approval and support could make all the difference.

We drove to a pre-designated spot in Lainya County and parked there to wait for the commissioner. Young boys stood by the side of the road selling inland coconuts, which looked like small pumpkins with orange pulp inside. When he arrived several minutes later, we got out of our cars and shook hands, then got back in our cars and drove to a little market nearby where the meeting took place. His entourage included his pretty wife and young son, as well as a few armed guards and other assorted officials. His wife looked bored and sat at a small table off to the side sipping a Red Bull. I made a point of shaking her hand and tried to catch her eye to engage her in the conversation. We discussed an array of issues for the next hour, including priority communities for the program and his aversion to food aid because it builds dependency. "You need to manage expectations among my people, to sensitize them properly so they know this program is not a handout," Juma said.

Smart, ambitions, and committed to helping women in his county to improve their lives, he was an anomaly among South Sudan's leaders. He promised his full support for the program in Yei and made a personal call to his former boss, the minister, to facilitate our meeting in Juba. I openly shared our problems in Rumbek. "Yes, I've worked in Lakes State," he empathized. "I also found it hostile, very difficult to work there."

Already I liked this man.

After the privation of South Sudan, the relative ease and predictability of life in Rwanda was both a relief and maddening; there was no earthly reason for women to suffer so much in that country. But now, the car wasn't working. Or the plumbing. Or the internet. My place of rest and sanctuary was buried under a mountain of problems that needed fixing, and a mountain of clutter. The boys had made a wreck of the house and seemed oblivious to the mess.

Without thinking, I swept my arm across the table, scattering their accumulated piles of crap onto the floor.

"Pick all this shit up," I shouted.

"What the hell, Mom," Eli responded in disbelief. "What's wrong with you?"

"You guys are total pigs. I should not have to come home to this!" I yelled.

Couldn't the boys think about someone other than themselves for once? They were thoughtless and spoiled. Of course, they had no idea what I had just seen and heard in South Sudan. How could they?

South Sudan was like a parallel universe where nothing made sense, a place where young and innocent boys—boys just like them—could become lost boys, walking for weeks on end through the unforgiving wilderness, starving and afraid of being eaten by lions. Or what about the lost girls for that matter, generations of them? They'd been overlooked by history yet suffered just as much, maybe more, than the boys.

Then Bill called. He sounded ridiculously cheery, sharing details about his daily workouts at the health club and plans for weekend ski trips to Utah and California. He, too, seemed thoughtless and spoiled. "Tell me about real things!" I yelled into the phone. I don't know if I was more bothered by his seemingly petty preoccupations or by just how well he seemed to be coping without me.

Remember to breathe, I told myself, trying to recover. I thought about those women in Yei—women who had almost nothing, who would consider the problems of my life a fairytale and was overcome by a deep sense of shame. There was no excuse for my behavior.

"I'm sorry, guys," I said, suddenly deflated. "I'm under a lot of stress right now. I promise to do better."

If I wanted to continue this kind of work, then I needed to do a better job of reconciling my worlds.

Later that evening, I remembered what had happened in Yei that had upset me, aside from the situation there. It was the phone call, the one with the CEO on Valentine's Day. We were supposed to talk on Skype but the connection was so poor at the compound that she ended up calling my cell phone instead. The call was brief and staticky, but to the point. My one-year contract, she had said, would not be renewed.

I'd been expecting it of course. I'd been upset, even depressed about it for months already. So was I shocked? No. A little. I don't know why.

My first instinct had been to push back, to tell her it was a mistake, how much I loved the work and mission and was willing to do for the women. I thought back to Antonina's finesse with the staff, how calm and deliberate Tereza had been when she learned her husband had stolen her loan money to buy a moto. Channeling both of them in that moment, I fought the urge and said . . . nothing.

I thanked her for letting me know.

19

Women's Day

Certain now that I'd be leaving the organization, I was determined to manage my departure with as much integrity as possible. Besides, there was little time to wallow. Sam and Eli were about to leave for Nairobi where they were participating in the East African Model United Nations' Conference, part of a twelve-student delegation from ISK. They had been preparing for months, honing their diplomacy skills in mock debates, drafting resolutions they would present in their respective committees: Eli as ambassador to Samoa, Sam as a delegate from Albania. More than a thousand students from Rwanda, Kenya, Tanzania, Uganda, Democratic Republic of Congo, Ethiopia, and South Africa would attend the conference.

I'd already bought a new suit for Sam and waited for hours to pick it up at the tailor's. I still had to get them some cash at the bank and remind them to bring their yellow immunization cards. Meanwhile there was another trip to South Sudan to prepare for in early March. Because South Sudan didn't have an embassy in Rwanda, I'd had to FedEx my passport and visa application to Kenya before each visit and hope for the best. Then there was the cash: clean, unmarked one hundred dollar bills with a post-2006 series date. Otherwise the local banks and foreign exchange bureaus might refuse to take them.

The night before the boys left for Kenya, my friends from Maryland, Cheryl and Patty, arrived for a weeklong visit. It was the first trip to Africa for both of them. On the fence about the trip for weeks, Patty finally decided to come along after convincing her husband, and herself, that it was okay to leave her four-year-old twins. Bill helped put together an itinerary that included a mix of outdoor adventure and edu-tourism where they could learn about the genocide.

In between their sightseeing and my work, we relaxed at home, enjoying the fine weather on the patio and the white wine they'd brought from the States. It felt good to get out of my own head for a while, to let go and have fun. We ate junk food and indulged in some honest husband talk; we might have mentioned our kids a few times, too. Cheryl had loaded a couple of first-run movies onto her computer, so we watched those and still managed to hit most of our standby restaurants. Kai relished all the attention as an only child for the week.

Standing around the kitchen with our coffee one morning, I shared the news that my contract had not been renewed and that the job I'd interviewed for in DC wasn't going to happen. I was embarrassed, and more than a little dejected. "This is actually a good thing, Karen," said Cheryl, giving it her best, most positive spin. "I think you're going to enjoy the rare experience of downtime." Patty and I even talked about starting a business together in Bethesda, one that would showcase women's artisan products from around the world as well as from home.

Their next-to-last night, we joined a few friends for a girls' night out at one of our favorite spots. More than anything, Patty and Cheryl's willingness to leave their busy lives and their families to come to Rwanda filled me with gratitude. That night around the table, I toasted the women in my life and, maybe for the first time, felt just like one of the girls.

Patty and Cheryl's visit came to an end as Sam and Eli returned from Kenya. Then it was time for me to leave again for South Sudan. Kai was unhappy about me leaving again so soon. "How long is a week?" he asked. I showed him on the calendar so he could see for himself. "It's hard for me too, Kai-ku," I said, wrapping my arms around him. "You have no idea how much I miss you when I'm gone. But I'll be back soon."

Coverage at home was still a challenge. At the last minute, Kai's teacher's fiancé agreed to stay at the house. He was a substitute teacher at ISK, so the boys knew him, although they found it weird to have a teacher staying with them. There weren't a lot of options, though, and I could impose on Amy and Julia only so much. And forget about other mothers. Even in Rwanda I felt judgment from moms who didn't work outside the home. Of course they would never say so outright. It was more of an "Oh, you're not coming?" here, a snide look there. Why did women do that to other women? I'd been guilty of that, too, in the past but was more aware of it now, and it bothered me.

It always took so much effort to get the boys organized and myself out of the country, even with Bill there to help. My travel bag was a constant fixture in our bedroom—a reminder that the next trip would soon be here. Bill would be returning to Rwanda after this next work trip. Knowing full well the challenges of reentry, I was already starting to feel anxious, for both of us. With all of that time and distance, a fight seemed inevitable. Over the nearly three months of Bill being gone, the boys and I had recreated our own version of family life. Our systems were once again set and working for us. While I missed Bill and was feeling more positive about our relationship, the "us" part still worried me. If our marriage was to survive, we would have to face our issues head on.

At least this time I was flying in and out of Yei and would avoid the long, bone-jarring drive from Juba. "Are you a Christian?" asked Eagle Air's lone employee as I collected my ticket at their office in the Entebbe airport. It wasn't the first time this question had come up in Africa. "Sorry, I'm not," I replied, a little sheepishly. He looked disappointed. Was this how it was in Uganda? My knowledge of the country was limited to anecdotes about Idi Amin, the so-called Butcher of Uganda chronicled in *The Last King of Scotland*, and to vague memories of the Israeli hostage crisis. That and Clemence's funny jokes about the former dictator.

The church compound in Yei was extra quiet this time, with only a few other guests who appeared in the dining hall at mealtimes. My first few days were spent orienting the new staff, but after hours, I was on my own. The loneliness was as familiar as a dear friend. I'd grown accustomed to it, to the long periods away, even if those reentries were still hard to manage. What moms often craved most was time to themselves, and I'd felt that, too. But more often it was just this intense feeling of aloneness, of being alone. Reading and exercise had been ready escape valves, staving off the pangs of separation and dislocation. Running outdoors was not always possible, mostly for safety or cultural reasons. Sometimes there was a long-forgotten treadmill or elliptical trainer tucked away in a tiny unused room at a hotel or guest house, but not always.

I remember that first trip to Rumbek, before there was a South Sudan. A former colleague called it "the bush of the bush." The town was made up of a handful of dilapidated buildings; the airport's departure gate was a large shade tree next to the short red-dirt runway. Almost everyone survived on humanitarian aid during the country's protracted war. The culture of dependency was deeply ingrained, in the government and its people. My initial UN security briefing included a stern warning about all the poisonous snakes in the area. "The good news is that their bites are only fatal 30 percent of the time," offered the pleasant official. Snakes, evidently, don't use all their venom at once as it leaves them defenseless.

Despite the warning, a colleague and I had taken to running along the dusty roads every day, a route that took us past several compounds of thatched-roof mud huts. One morning a man said to us in perfect English, "Why are you running?" And then, "Who are you running from?"

The next morning as we ran past, he looked at his watch and said, "You're late today."

Unfortunately, I hadn't managed to establish a run route in Yei or spot a worn-out piece of exercise equipment. After three days there without any kind of physical release, I was a mass of pent-up energy, building like a volcano on the verge of eruption. Work was the only answer, and there was plenty of it.

Early the following morning, a few colleagues and I set off on a site visit to Lasu Payam, one of the neediest communities in Yei River County according to Commissioner Juma, who had directed us there. The area hadn't always been so needy. The Equatorias were once considered the breadbasket of South Sudan. This *payam* in particular used to grow traditional cash crops like maize, cassava, and sorghum for the county, the whole country even, but was now food insecure. The road there was barely navigable during the dry season, much worse than the Juba-Yei road. The Americans and Japanese were supposedly building a new one, but who knew how long that would take. In the meantime, Lasu Payam was disconnected from Yei and the outside world during the long rainy season when the road was impassable. Signs for abandoned or defunct aid projects littered the countryside. Projects like these often shut down once the donor funds dried up.

There was a refugee camp situated about eight miles from South Sudan's border with Congo. Some 8,600 Congolese had lived for six or more years in the camp—an ocean of white tents containing the precious and portable remains of so many lives destroyed elsewhere. All had initially fled the Lord's Resistance Army. Although the border had been peaceful for some time, most of the refugees had chosen to stay in South Sudan, supported by the UN refugee agency and other aid organizations that continued to fund and provide services at the camp. As a result, the refugees, almost five thousand of them women and girls between the ages of fifteen and fifty-nine, lived relatively better than many locals. Their ready access to food, medical care, and training was an ongoing source of tension with the surrounding community. But the aid would eventually run out, and these women needed skills to survive when that happened.

When we arrived at the camp, we were directed to the admin office for a meeting with camp officials and community leaders. Addressing the group through an interpreter, I described the twelve-month program and inquired about theirs. The payam's chairlady for women's issues didn't hesitate. "Life and vocational skills are desperately needed," she said.

"What kind of vocational skills?" I asked.

"Bread-making would be good. Duck farming and soap-making also. Women need to earn an income," she said.

We continued to discuss an array of challenges in the camp, among them illiteracy, alcoholism, and widespread gender-based violence. In a plea for support, the chairlady asked us to provide empowerment and leadership training. "Women are human beings, too," she said.

On the way back to town, my colleagues and I debriefed one another on the meeting, talking over the chairlady's plea, and her "Women are human beings, too" remark. Dehumanization was what allowed women to be raped with impunity, abused in their homes, and commoditized on the marriage market, I pointed out. This led to a discussion around local marriage customs and how women and girls were bought and sold in negotiations between families, essentially as a business transaction. The "price" was largely determined by the woman's height, age, and beauty. Her preferences regarding whom and when to marry were rarely taken into account.

"When a man believes he has bought his wife, there is an implicit sense of ownership," I said. "She belongs to him like any other piece of property that he can do with as he pleases."

It made me think of Sophie, one of the graduates from Rumbek, whose parents "sold" her to a husband without her consent. She was tall and lean with short, cropped hair and a stern face. She and her first husband had had two children, both of whom died. Their relationship changed after that as her husband believed she was the one who had killed them. He then fell sick and, with no proper medical treatment available, he also died. Sophie was all alone and destitute.

After his death, Sophie moved to Wau, a city in northwestern South Sudan where her parents lived. She walked about 211 kilometers (131 miles) for seven days to get there. When she arrived in Wau, she met a Catholic priest who provided her shelter and clothes. Later, she could not recall the year, the current president of South Sudan, Salva Kiir Mayardit, came with his soldiers to her area, and one of them asked her parents to give her to him. Her parents felt they could not refuse, perhaps because he was a soldier or because he offered the family cattle they needed to survive. They gave Sophie to the soldier without consulting her. "I got married to the man," she said without emotion, "and had six children with him, four boys and two girls."

"The bride price system exacerbates the fundamental disparities that exist between men and women," I said, aware that I might be missing some of the social, cultural, and economic nuances around the issue in South Sudan. "It's why men feel entitled to 'manage' their wives through violence and abuse." Being an outsider and an American woman gave me a measure of freedom not afforded to South Sudanese women. It gave me a voice, and I used it. "If it were up to me, I'd do away with dowries and payments altogether—take money and property completely out of the marriage equation." My colleagues didn't disagree. They told me how difficult it would be to try and change such an entrenched practice.

The next day was International Women's Day, our first in Yei, just two months after the program was established. More inclusive than Mother's Day, its distinctly American counterpart, Women's Day has evolved into a global celebration of and for women. It began in the early 1900s as a means to build support for the women's suffrage movement and has since become an important platform to highlight female achievements, denounce violence against women, and advocate for greater gender equality.

Hundreds of women from several local organizations were congregating in Mugwo Payam's main market square when the staff and I arrived for the planned Women's Day march. The atmosphere was celebratory, like a neighborhood parade on Independence Day. A police marching band in full-dress uniform—a jumble of red, blue, and yellow trimmed with gold—led the assembled group down a lonely strip of dirt road. The staff and I marched to their beat under a new Women for Women International banner made for the occasion. The women and girls who marched beside us looked smart and proud in their custom t-shirts, colorful uniforms and *kangas*, their homemade placards and banners lifted high into the air in support of women's rights. A handful of men and children joined in the marching; others on the sidelines cheered us on.

We followed the band back toward the main square, where a large crowd was gathering. An unrelenting sun beat down on the group of marchers. My arms grew tired, shaky, trying to hold up that banner. I was parched and desperate for a bottle of water, my sweaty legs covered in red road dust up to my

International Women's Day in Yei.

knees. But for some reason, none of it seemed to matter; I just felt happy. The enthusiasm of the women, the crowd was contagious, invigorating.

This is where I belong today, I thought, unexpectedly beaming. Marching with the women. Proud of myself for being where I was, who I was, proud that we still had a program in South Sudan.

There was something important, vital even, that I'd lost in my quest for a reinvention. Something that had been there all along, though I'd been too wounded, too stubborn to see it. I too was an upstander: the kind of person who sees wrong and acts. The job didn't define me. The job was incidental. This, here, was me. The same person who collected canned foods for the hungry in her little red wagon, who once led a boycott of Nestlé for pushing expensive baby formula in the developing world.

I would never have expected to find joy in South Sudan, of all places, but there it was.

Finally reaching the main square, we were greeted with ululations from women, men and children who had come there from the surrounding villages.

Karen marching.

The square was packed. The local chiefs and elders, government officials, and visiting dignitaries were all seated on chairs in a semicircle around an open, shaded space in the center of the market. I joined them there. So began a long series of speeches, including my own, emphasizing the need for greater access and opportunity for women and girls in education, employment, and health care. The reigning Ms. Yei, in a tight-fitting red dress and gold stiletto heels, gave an impassioned speech about girls' education.

A couple of dramatic reenactments showed women clearing mines. Another was a rape and restitution scene that resembled other village theater programs used mainly in illiterate communities to promote behavioral change. At least on that one day, women and men were united by a shared commitment to gender equality, a belief that when women are educated and able to earn an income, families and communities benefit—whole societies benefit.

"It's too bad every day can't be women's day," I lamented to a colleague.

Listening to the remaining speakers, my thoughts turned to the other women marchers that day, women who had so little and yet so much to offer. Though they had been victimized by war and violence, had their prospects dimmed by nearly impossible barriers, they were willing to stand up and voice their resistance to a culture that continued to demean them, even when the price of that resistance was high. They refused to think or act like victims. They were the ultimate survivors, willing to put it all on the line to forge a better life for themselves and their children.

I wondered about my mother. Had she done that, sacrificed her own happiness and fulfillment, her own dreams, so that her children could have a better life, so that I could have a better life? Her lack of confidence, her weak sense of agency, had been linked to her financial dependence, but also to what society teaches us about women. She couldn't just leave my dad. What would she do? Would she take her children with her? I wondered, given the same set of circumstances, if I would have stayed, too?

She told me once that she was too young when she got married. She and my dad didn't know each other well. They didn't know any better. "I had to put up with a lot of nasty stuff," she said, "but where could I go with three children and no money of my own? I couldn't go home to my mother." Euphraise, one of the program graduates, had said virtually the same thing, about having no means to care for her children by herself. "There really was no choice," Mom had said finally.

Was she another survivor?

On the way back to Yei Town, exhausted but exhilarated, I yelped at the sight of a large black mamba on the road. It had to be close to eight feet long! It's the most dangerous and widely feared snake on a continent in which twenty thousand people die annually from snakebites. The black mamba is capable of devouring a goat or small child whole; two drops of its venom can kill a human in less than thirty minutes.

Normally I'm terrified of snakes. But on this particular day, I wanted a closer look. "Can you back up?" I asked the driver.

An incredulous look passed over the faces of my colleagues, some of whom had shared their own frightening encounters with deadly snakes. But because I was a guest of the country they indulged me. Mambas have an uncanny ability to propel themselves up and into cars, so we closed all our windows before backing up. For some reason I needed to look that awful snake in the face, to confront this longstanding fear of mine head-on. After a few tense, watchful minutes, we drove to the closest village to warn them that the venomous snake was nearby.

I learned later that snakes are often viewed as symbols of transformation and healing, mainly because of their ability to shed their skins. It was this casting-off that allowed for continued growth and renewal. I took this as a sign of better things to come.

Back in Kigali, I hugged all the boys hard. They were no worse for wear. Turns out that Kai's teacher's fiancé was not only a fine babysitter but an excellent chemistry tutor, which Sam and Eli both needed. I was still buzzing about the Women's Day celebration, but they only had ears for the snake. "How big was it really, Mom?" Kai wanted to know. "Can it actually jump through a car window?" Sam asked skeptically.

A few days later, I celebrated International Women's Day again at the home of the deputy chief of mission at the US Embassy. Smart and savvy with an impressive twenty-year career in the US Foreign Service, she had handpicked the guest list of around seventeen, which included a mix of professional American and Rwandan women, a number of them senior officials in the Rwandan government.

Mingling with the other guests over wine and hors d'oeuvres under a large party tent in her yard, I felt privileged to be among so many exceptional women, one of the fringe benefits of a career in international development. The contrasting women's day celebrations, from Yei to Kigali, made me smile. This could easily have been a dinner party in Bethesda. As we made our way to one of three round tables to eat, our host, an accomplished single mother of a four-year-old, asked us to consider two questions over the course of the evening: "What are you proudest of, and what are you most afraid of?" Whenever we felt inspired, she said, we should just stand up and answer the questions.

While we drank and ate and got to know one another around the table, one woman would casually rise to answer the questions, then another and another. Instead of the usual perfunctory responses, standard dinner-party fare, their answers were thoughtful and surprisingly intimate.

Many of the Rwandan women were proud to have achieved such a high place in their government, to be working for "their president" and "their country." Several had fled from the violence with their families and grew up in refugee camps in Kenya or Uganda. They were among the hundreds of thousands of members of the diaspora who returned post-genocide to rebuild the country. There was genuine pride in Rwanda's accomplishments, especially in terms of gender equality. Others were proud to have both a thriving career and family.

A number of the American women, most working for the US Embassy, were proud to have landed their "dream job" in Africa, having made the choice to live and work abroad, often sacrificing time with personal relationships and extended family. Some women were afraid they might never find their life partners. Others with children expressed fears for their safety and future success. A few of the Rwandans said they had no fears because they were "with God," and felt a deeply rooted connection to their Christian faith. One brave woman expressed a profound fear that the country would return to genocide.

It struck me that the women in the room there had even more in common than we knew—a connection beyond surviving genocide for the Rwandans or the work and life challenges and the external barriers known to most women. There was something that lived inside each of us, something acknowledged and harnessed that had propelled each of us forward. Call it resilience, a steadfast belief in self, audacity, a willingness or ability to make tough, seemingly impossible choices when it mattered. Euphraise, Josephine, Tereza, Debora, and Grace all had it; the women marchers in South Sudan did, too.

These women, and so many of the survivors I worked with, each in her own way, had been able to build or rebuild their lives one step, one small change, or in some cases, one brick at a time. Though outside forces may have shaped and even oppressed them, they'd held onto their dreams, forged their own paths, taken risks, and led change in their families, communities, and countries. They had fully embraced their choices. In that moment, I vowed to fully embrace mine.

When I stood up, I shared first my pride in my work to advance women around the world, and also in my three children, for having so willingly taken up their new lives in Rwanda. I had hoped to set an example of a woman out in the world doing good work, to be someone my sons could be proud of.

What was I most afraid of? "I will never be able to find work as meaningful as this again," I said, vocalizing it for the first time.

20

Yvette

There was one woman I had been meaning to see since we first came to Rwanda but hadn't found time for yet. It was our Rwandan "sister," Yvette. She was one of twelve women Bill and I had sponsored through Women for Women over the years. Alongside the training, letters between the sisters are also exchanged, both for emotional support and a deeper sense of connection. I'd traded a few letters with our sisters in different countries but had never met one. The boys wanted to meet her, too.

After school and a morning site visit to the Women's Opportunity Center, we picked up the boys and drove to Yvette's home in the Kigali suburb of Kicukiro, about twenty minutes from the city. Yvette came out of her mud hut when we pulled up and extended her wrist to each of us, a deferential form of Rwandan greeting. She was wearing a faded piece of fabric tied at her waist and a purple t-shirt with the words "Long Beach Island" in loopy white lettering across the front.

Yvette was a single mother of three boys. Never legally married, Yvette's "husband" had left her and the boys two years before; she hadn't seen or heard from him since. Her family lived in a small village a couple of hours away, but she couldn't afford to visit. It had been two years since she'd seen them.

Then she introduced us to each of her sons, aged eight, six, and three, although they appeared much younger and smaller, likely from inadequate nutrition. Her smile seemed forced; she probably had no idea what she was supposed to do or say to a "rich" American sponsor and her sons. I could see the ravages of poverty weighing on her. Halfway through the yearlong program, she told us through a colleague who was interpreting that she liked the lessons where she was learning her numbers and basic math, and was just about to select a vocational skill, maybe hairdressing. Hair braiding was a job she could do in the neighborhood and still keep an eye on her kids.

She currently earned some cash buying and reselling tomatoes and bananas in the market, but it wasn't enough to support her family. She had been spending the training stipend, the equivalent of about ten dollars a month, on rent and food for her kids, none of whom were in school.

"Where does everyone sleep?" Eli asked once we were inside. Yvette pointed to the back of the darkened hut where some grass mats were laid out on the cool mud floor. He also wanted to know why her boys don't go to school. "No money for school fees," she said.

It was heartbreaking. Yvette might not have had much of a chance at a better life, but neither would her boys without an education. She was the gateway to the future for her family. No money, no choice. Yvette was doing the best she could with next to nothing. Mother to mother, woman to woman, I felt deeply for her.

We lingered a little, then left her with a small care package of tea, candy, and cookies for the kids, though it seemed totally frivolous in comparison to the need. I rarely gave out cash to program participants, believing that to teach a woman to fish was of greater value, but in this case I made an exception. Nudging Yvette over to the side, I handed her the equivalent of thirty dollars—everything in my wallet—hoping that she might invest it in a new business. It was a reasonable thought for someone in my position, who didn't have to worry about her kids going hungry. But how was Yvette supposed to think about the future when her kids were crying for food? When she was hungry.

There had been many well-meaning people over the years who had suggested that we dictate how women spend their stipends, implying that poor women are either incapable of choosing for themselves or of making the right choices. But if we make that decision for them, it defeats the purpose, which is for women to have the freedom of choice, perhaps for the very first time in their lives.

Yvette and her boys with Eli, Sam, and Kai.

We were all quiet on the ride home, lost in our own thoughts. I wondered whether Yvette would be able to use anything from the training to make a tangible difference in her life. I wasn't so sure. For all the success stories, all the survivors who had "made it," there were just as many, maybe more, who hadn't. The legacy of war, poverty, abuse, culture, or whatever it was that was holding them back, was too great. There were still women whom no one had reached and those who, in spite of the helping hand, had been unable to lift themselves up.

"Her whole house is as big as my room," Eli commented, as we passed several more groupings of huts identical to Yvette's. Despite being in the country for eight months, the boys hadn't really seen this side of Rwanda up close. It was easy to miss or dismiss it in the heart of Kigali, with its big cars and fancy homes inhabited by expat families and Rwanda's elite, with all the trappings of a prosperous, developed nation. Much of the dire poverty had been forced into the outskirts, swept clean from the country's immaculate and modern center.

In many ways, the city resembled our own bubble in Bethesda. Just twenty minutes away, girls as young as eleven are the victims of child sex trafficking, sold an average of five times a night, seven days a week. The face of extreme poverty in the Washington metropolitan area, across the entire country, is most often the face of a woman or girl. How often had I missed or dismissed the underbelly right on my own doorstep?

I made a note to ask the staff to keep checking on Yvette, to make sure that she selected a good vocational skill, to make sure she didn't give up.

"Are we going to see Yvette and her boys again?" Kai asked, concern in his voice.

"I don't think so, bud," I replied. "But there are women like her everywhere," I said after a moment. "You just have to look."

Kai's comment about Yvette and her kids was touching and sweet. After all our experiences in Rwanda, I believed the boys would look—look twice, look past the impressive facades, the beautiful homes and landscapes—and see what was around and beyond them; see the underside that exists everywhere. They *had* taken in the country's harshness and its beauty; they *had* listened and learned the value and importance of compassion. They were starting to ask questions like *how* and *why*. I hoped they were becoming the kind of individuals who would not stand by, that they would grow into those good men and good global citizens, no matter where they landed or what they did in their personal and professional lives. Rwanda had opened their eyes, and their hearts.

21

Reentry

Bill was coming back to Rwanda in less than a week. It had been a long time to be apart—three months—maybe too long. Back home, a whole season had passed; the pale pink cherry blossoms around the Tidal Basin were almost in peak bloom. My anxiety about his return woke me up even earlier than usual. Careful not to disturb Kai, who was sleeping in my bed again after Bill left, I crept out of the dark room and down to the kitchen to make some coffee before tackling my inbox.

Sitting in front of my laptop, seeing but not seeing all of the unread messages, I wondered whether the distance had been good for our relationship, whether the long absences had shifted anything in our marriage. It seemed as though it had. We were more open with each other, more connected since Kili. We appreciated each other more, too. But we'd been down that road many times, only to fall back into the same patterns, the same disappointments. This time had to be different. We had to be different. Or we would finally have to accept that it wasn't going to happen and deal with the consequences.

If Bill was just as uneasy, he didn't let on. No, he would lead with his usual gregarious self. He couldn't help it—it's who he is.

Being in Rwanda *had* softened me, though, softened my feelings for Bill and our marriage. He had been my touchstone, my anchor, for as far back as I could remember. He supported and respected my work, had never once asked me not to go. And he'd always been there for the boys, giving up his time and routine to accommodate my life choices, including this year in Rwanda, even with his own demanding career. Some husbands had not only failed to support their wives, they'd worked against them. I understood that more clearly now.

I was softer with the boys, too. Though they were still expected to be independent and responsible, I now found myself doing some of the extras that Bill used to do—extra spending money, spontaneous trips to the mall, relaxed curfew on occasion. Maybe it was silly, but expressing my affection for the boys in these little ways made me happy, and they had responded; they were more at ease and lighthearted with me. It occurred to me that I had often been too focused on the negative. Those boys were actually everything, more, than I could have ever wished for them to be. After years of comings and goings, I felt rather possessive of them and our new level of togetherness, relished having them all to myself.

That morning on the way to school, they laid down the law—no public kisses anymore. Maybe, if they were feeling charitable, they would allow a peck well in advance of the school drop-off point. How and when did this even happen? My negotiation skills, normally reserved for recalcitrant colleagues, African kings, and husbands, were not well suited to negotiating affection with a tween and two teenage boys. At least they still allowed hugs and kisses in private, especially Kai.

The boys were all growing up, but Kai had probably changed the most. He'd become a surprisingly strong contender in the daily fight over who got to ride shotgun. Strong willed and scrappy, he loved to mix it up with his brothers. After he pestered me for months, we had finally taken our first run together on the weekend, a few miles down to the Kigali golf course and back. He not only kept up but finished strong, sprinting home at the end. Even though his brothers and I had been running for months now, I kept thinking it would be too hard or hilly for Kai. I'd underestimated him. I would try not to make that mistake again.

The day of Bill's arrival, I couldn't focus during a lengthy budget meeting out at the Women's Opportunity Center. Later, in an awkward two-hour session with the new head of global programs—my old job—who was just getting up to speed, I couldn't stop myself from picturing our reunion.

It was early evening when the four of us met Bill just outside the baggage claim, greeting him in turns with warm hugs and bubbly chatter. It was crowded there, so we left quickly and drove straight to Sola Luna, one of our standby restaurants that was on the way home. We ordered some red wine and pizzas and talked about his business and how our friends were faring back in Bethesda. Sam and Eli gushed about their trip to Kenya for Model UN. Sam told us one of the coolest parts was meeting in the same place as the "real" delegates and how he had stayed up half the night trying to merge resolutions from Croatia and Swaziland on the same topic as his: helping people with disabilities. Eli had us all laughing as he described his first taste of ox testicles at Carnivore, a Nairobi eatery famous for exotic meat. "It was repulsive. They were soft and mushy, like gefilte fish. What a terrible combination."

However, the more animated Bill became, the more my hackles began to rise. Tennis. Football. Ski trips. The latest features of the iPhone. It was the same superficial boy talk, and the boys, my boys, were soaking it up. Our tight new bond seemed to be dissipating before my eyes, and I found myself competing for their attention. I knew it was petty, but I couldn't help feeling jealous. After all we'd been through, how could *I* be the interloper, the odd woman out again?

The small talk devolved into a shouting match.

"Can you just stop talking for once and listen!" I vented.

"What is your problem?" he retorted. "Why are you so angry? I just got here."

"That's my point. You just got here!"

The boys were sitting there, heads down, silently eating their pizzas as they listened to this play out; their short-lived joy at seeing their dad suddenly overshadowed by our fight. Even as it was happening I could see how uncomfortable they were. How many times had I felt the same way as I watched my parents go at it? I had to stop the cycle.

But somehow this fight was different. I didn't back down, but Bill didn't shut down either, as had happened so often in the past when things got too heated. Yes, we were fighting, but it felt like progress. I liked his new spiritedness. It seemed as though the time apart from us had also been good for Bill. He had found his voice.

The next morning, Bill and I went back to *umuganda*, the community service day, for the first time since our arrival. It felt good to be able to participate again, and to do it together. As ever, we were our best selves when we were doing for others—still activists but less in debt, we often joked. It was one of the main things that had brought us, kept us, together. We did the usual weed whacking with machetes and then helped rebuild a woman's home that had been damaged by the recent heavy rains. Her house was only a few short blocks from ours, yet we had never passed by there before. Bill and I worked as a team, ferrying heavy sacks of mud for the new bricks. After we had finished, one woman handed us a bar of soap and another poured a tub of water over our mud-caked hands to wash up.

Walking back to our house, we chatted about the warm welcome by our neighbors this time, wondering what had changed. It could be we were a little less earnest, a little more accessible now, or that they had seen us around the neighborhood. Side-by-side yet worlds apart. This was the other side of Rwanda.

I was reminded how blind we could be, even given our work, how something right in front of you can be so easily missed or dismissed. Maybe it was time now to adjust my lens when it came to Bill. Maybe both of us had to use a different lens now when it came to each other.

As Bill and I got used to each other again, we were invited to the second night of Passover at the deputy chief of mission's home, where I'd celebrated International Women's Day. We were five plus one with Julia's son, who was staying with us for a few days while she was away on a work trip. There were about twenty-five guests, from several different countries and embassies. The Seder was cohosted by USAID's mission director in Rwanda. With fresh-picked vegetables from his garden, he prepared a number of exceptional dishes from the North African Sephardic tradition that were new to us: a spicy Moroccan chickpea dish and a flavorful rice with nuts and raisins. Still learning to cook but enjoying it more, I asked him for the recipe for his spinach soufflé.

Every year at Passover, we retell the story of the Israelite's journey out of Egypt, from slavery into freedom, so the lessons are passed down through each generation. In so doing, we remember not only our ancestors' suffering but those who continue to be oppressed and enslaved. The Seder took on special meaning for us this year in Rwanda, where every April they remember nearly one million Tutsi who were victims of the genocide. Commemoration week is also about retelling the story. It begins April 7 with a solemn ceremony at the Kigali Genocide Memorial, where hundreds gather to hear speeches and the testimonies of survivors. The mourning continues over the hundred days of the genocide, with activities in districts and villages across the country, concluding on July 4, Rwandan Liberation Day.

During this period, it is not uncommon for perpetrators to show where the corpses of victims from 1994 that had not been identified are hidden, and for new hate crimes to occur. Reconciliation, I was learning, was a process fraught with pain, disappointment, and uncertainty. There would be progress and setbacks, some of them devastating. It took a certain kind of mental fortitude, not to forget the past, but to loosen its grip on the present, to invest anew.

Remembrance brought hope that our loved ones, our ancestors, did not die in vain, that "never again" could, at long last, mean "never again," that we'd learned enough from our collective mistakes, that there was a better, more peaceful future in store. Hope was why, after all these years, I was still trying to repair the world, to make it a better place. Tikkun Olam.

At every Seder I make sure to remember the women—those who are still suffering and oppressed, unable to rise above their circumstances. Women without voice and choice, women who may have lost hope. I thought about our sister Yvette, who was still struggling and seemed all but resigned to her fate, and also about the two program participants in Nigeria who had died earlier that day in community violence. Countless women around the world, too many—whether in Maryland or South Sudan—were living lives of quiet desperation. *Wherever you are, wherever you live, it isn't too late.*

On the drive home it occurred to me that, however unwittingly, I'd been drawing a kind of invisible line between myself and those women survivors, that I was still holding myself apart, even above, those other women. The "that's not me" refrain was silent but insistent, part of my long-practiced veneer of distinction. And yet when it came down to it, weren't we, in our essence, more alike than not? I wouldn't dare compare my small traumas to theirs, but I, too, was still trying to rise above the past, still climbing my own mountain.

My mind drifted back to summit day on Mount Kilimanjaro. The day had started with a relatively easy four-hour trek to our final campsite at Barafu (elevation: 15,200 feet). It was snowing when we arrived, the air so thin that walking the short incline to the mess tent induced bouts of wheezing. We were woken at eleven that night to gear up for the final ascent toward Uhuru Peak. The air temperature was close to zero as we set off just after midnight.

We walked with headlamps, though a nearly full moon emerged from the light cloud cover to brighten our path. Other than some fleeting views of Kili, the hazy moonlit vistas were our first glimpses of the daunting challenge ahead. To reach the peak by sunrise, we would have to ascend nearly four thousand feet in six to seven hours.

A few hours into the trek, Kai began to complain of nausea and a head-ache. One of the assistant guides, David, coaxed Kai along to about seventeen thousand feet; they had bonded over multiple days on the mountain. After Kai threw up, he finally called a halt. Up until that point Kai had been able to manage the acclimation hikes, but this was the final climb to the summit. There were no more roundabouts, just a merciless path up and up.

When Kai collapsed onto a nearby rock, pale and shaky, David spoke to us candidly about oxygen deprivation and the stamina of children. Kai put up a token protest, but even he realized after a few moments that he couldn't go on.

Few words were spoken, and those mostly by the guides, who still had the breath to spare. This was common, they assured us, especially with the young ones like Kai. No convincing was needed. Bill and I agreed that Kai should return to base camp with David and a porter we'd brought along to serve as an extra guide. I considered going down with Kai as I glanced up at the mountain, and felt myself in the grasp of its stark and majestic beauty. But in that moment, with my mind and body so completely focused on summiting, something felt at stake. I needed to summit.

I gave Kai a bundled-up hug through our down jackets and watched him for a minute or two as he turned back, then I trudged on, the freezing wind slicing through the bandanna covering my nose and mouth, wondering if I'd made the right decision. I could already hear the questions, the judgments, from the other mothers, the "good mothers," in my head. How could I aban-don my eleven-year-old son at seventeen thousand feet? What kind of mother leaves a child behind to pursue her own quest?

The selfish kind who chooses her own dreams and desires above her children's, one could chastise. But was there a version of motherhood that was just as loving, just as worthy, where my dreams and desires were on par with my children's, not in spite of my role as a mother, but in service of it? I wondered briefly as we climbed if perhaps the altitude was affecting my own judgment, if I was capable of making a simple life-or-death decision. Or if I'd put all that on the shoulders of our guides and was concerned only with my own ability to keep going.

On the other hand, this was no *Sophie's Choice*. We trusted our guides and put our fates in their capable hands. They were the professionals. We had prepared for the possibility of one or two of us not making it by bringing along an extra guide. When the time came, it was for them to decide whether we, any of us, were able to push on. That intensity had communicated itself to the others, even Kai. He would not have wanted me, or Bill, to turn back with him. I had to go on, and so I did.

Sam and Eli moved more quickly than Bill and me, and with Naiman they began the severe switchbacks toward Stella Point. We could no longer see them up ahead. I hiked on, so drained and depleted I could barely put one foot in front of the other, my legs as heavy as anchors. I lost track, focused on calibrating my steps, my exertion, to match Stratton's slow but steady pace. He sang or hummed quietly to himself as he climbed. I listened intently to the soft Swahili chant, trying to maintain my concentration on his footsteps, on the song, on the rocky path.

The sun rose just below the crater rim. The reds, yellows, and oranges made for an incredible sight, illuminating how far Bill and I had come, how close we were to our goal. We seemed well above the clouds, almost level with the sun.

I had a breakthrough then. This so-called year of living dangerously—the family shake-up, the impetuous move to Rwanda—was more like my year of living un-dangerously, about finding, or redefining, my place as a mother and wife, my place in the family unit. Less separate but still independent. An attempt to create, to invent, a new normal.

Maybe there was some kind of hybrid option, not exactly a stay-at-home mom but a stay-closer-to-home mom, at least for the next few years while those beautiful boys were still with me. Regardless of what happened with this work, or any job, it could never be as it once was. I was starting to wrap my head around that, to be okay with that.

Individuals changed all the time, adapted to different circumstances. The survivors I'd met had done that. Why not couples, or families? Bill and I had both evolved during our quarter century together. Had we evolved more independently than we had as a couple? Or was that even the right question?

Bill, Stratton, and I reached Stella Point just as Sam, Eli, and Naiman were getting ready to leave for the final, hour-long trek to the summit. Small groups of hikers were scattered around the rocky, snow-dusted terrain, resting and snacking. We exchanged short hugs, high fives, and fist bumps with the boys, and then they were on their way, determined to push on. Exhausted, we rested for a few minutes, sipped warm tea, and ate a few squares of chocolate, all we could stomach, before heading to the summit ourselves.

It was flatter along the rim; a deep crater was off to the right, a gigantic glacier off to the left. The effect was surreal, like walking on the moon. A long, slow hour later, Bill and I finally reached the green and yellow sign at the summit: "CONGRATUATIONS! YOU ARE NOW AT UHURU PEAK. 5895 M. TANZANIA. AFRICA'S HIGHEST POINT. WORLD'S HIGHEST FREESTANDING MOUNTAIN. WORLD HERITAGE SITE."

We stood on the peak for several minutes, silent, breathless, taking it in. United by the magnitude of our shared accomplishment. We had made it. I had given the mountain just about everything I had. We both had.

As we waited our turn for the requisite photo beside the summit sign, it dawned on me how much I had underestimated Bill: physically for sure, but in other ways, too. He had tackled every challenge on the trek, including the summit, with aplomb. Even after twenty-five years of marriage, the man was still capable of a few surprises. He set a great example for the boys as well. My good and strong men.

Perhaps it was the altitude or fatigue, but a surge of hope had coursed through me. I felt lightheaded, practically giddy with relief and optimism: about summiting, about Bill, about my own uncertain future. In that moment, that invincible moment, it all seemed bright and possible.

There is no lingering on Kili: too high, too cold, too little air. After a few quick photos, we began the very long downward slog back to base camp. Snow and sleet pelted our skin as we descended. It turned out to be surprisingly hard—harder in some ways than the ascent. Going too fast had not been a problem on the way up. Every step was *pole, pole* ("slowly, slowly" in Swahili). On the way down, though, my legs were so wobbly I could hardly stand. Still, the mountain seemed to be driving us forward. The snow and ice made the steep decline even more treacherous. Having had multiple shoulder dislocations, if I fell and it came out again, I would have no way to force it back in. Stratton offered me his arm and firmly escorted me all the way down the mountain. He, all of the guides, had earned our trust and deep respect.

Ten hours after we'd last seen him, Kai was there, waiting for us at base camp. "Kai-ku," I sang out and rushed up to give him a big squeeze, and he squeezed me back. He was in good humor, back to his usual self. He'd passed the time in the warm cook's tent, drinking hot chocolate and practicing his Swahili. He was mad, too—not at us for abandoning him, but at himself for not gutting it out. He made us promise to return in a couple of years, when he was "bigger," to give the summit another try.

Too tired to join the others for a late lunch, I collapsed in our tent. It took some convincing to rouse me for another four-hour hike down to the last campsite, but the enticing lower elevation and the prospect of sleeping on flat ground ultimately won out.

We awoke at 12,200 feet on day eight and walked another five hours through torrential rains down to the park entrance, where we were picked up, soaked to the skin. On the two-hour drive back to Arusha, we began to peel off our wet, stinky layers, our worn boots and socks, and stopped at a market along the way for large beers and sodas and several bags of chips, all of us thrilled to be drier and on flat ground.

Back at the Moivaro Lodge we were ready to celebrate. After exhausting our hot water supply with five oh-so-needed showers, we went down to the bar and spent a couple of hours gorging ourselves on big, juicy hamburgers, french fries, and pizza, toasting each other. Kai, his disappointment forgotten, happily joined in. Sam and Eli were jubilant, boasting to the other guests about their feats on the big mountain. Climbing, then summiting side by side, they had learned to trust each other, not only as twins and brothers but as real friends.

I was proud of myself for sticking it out. It would have been so easy to give up, given how awful I felt. I was prouder still of the boys. It was my dream to climb a big mountain, but they made it theirs as well. Whatever else happened, I finally understood that my family, all of them, had my back.

That night, in a real bed, I enjoyed my best sleep in months.

Still in the car on the way home from the Seder, I could see how the optimism I felt on the mountain was bearing out. Reconciliation, in all its forms, *was* a process fraught with pain, disappointment, and uncertainty. I understood that in a more personal way now, with my parents, with Bill. There had been progress, no question, but there had also been, and probably would continue to be, setbacks. And that was okay. It was real. Resilience would, in fact, carry me onward, as it had for other survivors.

22

Spring Awakening

We landed at dusk in Cape Town, the launch point for our family vacation in South Africa, and made our way to the Victorian-style guesthouse off Kloof Street where we were staying, near tons of cool shops, bars, and restaurants. Well dark by the time we arrived, the three-story bed and breakfast was warm and homey, like a private residence; a good place to try to reconnect with Bill after months apart. We'd taken two rooms on the second floor: one for the boys and another for Bill and me. After dropping off our bags, we walked up the street to a restaurant and had a late dinner on their lamp-heated patio. The boys all tried ostrich, a South African specialty.

We woke early to breathtaking views of Table Mountain, the sunlit backdrop for our neighborhood. The mammoth flat-topped peak towered over the city; we planned to climb up steep Platteklip Gorge in a few days' time. After a leisurely breakfast, we meandered our way down to the Victoria & Alfred Waterfront, following the winding streets and alleys. We stopped to browse at a few upscale boutiques, all pricey, and a Lindt candy store, which the boys all knew—these duty-free chocolates were a frequent purchase between flights. They were in heaven, sampling then buying a bunch of goodies.

Cape Town was like one giant candy store, all very urban and "first-world"—Africa on an entirely new scale. Kigali looked downright provincial by comparison. Both had clean, well-tended streets and gardens, but Cape Town was much more spacious and grander, glamorous even. We walked around wide-eyed and salivating, eagerly devouring its sights.

We took a long stroll through the Company Gardens, adjacent to the South African Parliament, in a historic area of the city, taking turns reading from the guidebook about the country's history, which the boys were all studying in school. The weather was perfect: early fall but warm as summer; the fragrant roses in late bloom. As we followed the manicured pathways around the different gardens, Sam wandered off on his own, taking close-up pictures of exotic flowers that caught his eye.

The waterfront was packed with a bustling mix of tourists and locals. The atmosphere was festival-like: street performers and musicians, trendy outdoor cafés, touristy shops and stands serving up the area's delicacies. We took a turn on an oversized Ferris wheel, which afforded expansive, 360-degree views of the city and ocean, then enjoyed a late afternoon seafood lunch at the Harbor House on the wharf.

It was hard to imagine how different Cape Town must have looked during apartheid, when blacks were relegated to grim townships on the periphery brutally controlled by the police, cleansed from the white-only center. The city was designed to enforce otherness.

In May of 1994, while Rwanda was in the midst of its bloody upheaval, South Africa, half a continent away, was inaugurating its first democratically elected president, former political prisoner Nelson Mandela. Rwanda's restorative justice practices, including the Gacaca courts, which tried nearly two million cases of genocide crimes, loosely resembled South Africa's own truth and reconciliation process. Both were designed to "mend the wounds of the past" in these racially and ethnically divided countries. Through radically different routes, both countries had arrived at similarly modern points. Both now appeared integrated in most respects.

I protested against the injustices of apartheid in college, but not until we were in South Africa did I begin to understand what it all meant. The faces we saw in the shops, cafés, and restaurants were predominantly white. Service people were almost exclusively black. Today, Nelson Mandela's name and image are omnipresent, a constant reminder of how far the country has come, but also of the remaining divide.

On a drizzly day, we took the forty-minute ferry ride to Robben Island, joining a group of more than one hundred. Once on the island, we split into smaller groups and boarded buses for the tour. Deemed a "place of banishment" for undesirables until its designation as a museum in 1997, the island was a leper colony from 1846 to 1931 and then a World War II base; in 1961 it became a maximum security prison for South Africa's top political prisoners and other convicts. It was here that Nelson Mandela was incarcerated for eighteen of his twenty-seven years in jail. We saw Mandela's tiny cell and the courtyard where he planted a small garden. His handwritten biography had been buried there for safekeeping.

"It's so stupid," Eli vented. "He [Mandela] didn't do anything wrong. He was put in jail because he stood up for what he believed. People are afraid of people who think differently from them."

"If a white person did what he did, he would definitely get less time in jail," Kai chimed in. "That's segregation."

"I think you mean discrimination, hon," I corrected.

"Same thing. They both have an 'ation' at the end," he countered.

I loved how fired up the boys were about this massive injustice. I'd noticed that same flicker of compassion in Kai when he learned that Joseph didn't have a real bed, and in Eli after our visit with Yvette and her sons. That flicker seemed stronger now toward the end of our year in Rwanda.

Our guide was a former political prisoner, jailed on the island for more than a decade for unspecified crimes against the state. He spoke of the drudgery and humiliation of daily prison life. Inmates would rise at 5:30 a.m. and clean up their cells. After a quick breakfast, usually corn porridge, they were forced to mine lime in the quarry or collect sea kelp eight hours a day. He patiently answered the boys' questions, explaining how the racial divisions on the outside were reproduced inside the prison walls. Whites got the best food, clothing, and other necessities; Asians and other "coloreds" got second best; black Africans got the worst.

We walked into several of the prison cells, each one with a picture, quote, or personal story capturing a particular aspect of prison life; a few held personal artifacts that had been left behind or donated by a former inmate. In one of the cells, a man imprisoned for several years described how his lonely wife, who had two children with him, met another man and had two more children. When he was finally released from prison, he reclaimed his wife and raised all four children as his own. He refused to blame his wife, saying, "She didn't put me in prison."

In his autobiography, *Long Walk to Freedom*, Mandela never seemed to lose dignity or heart during his long years of captivity. Instead he conquered loneliness and depression by continuing the fight for justice and equal rights on the inside, choosing to view most of his white warders as victims of an unjust system, like himself, rather than oppressors. Mandela wasn't always so sage, according to longtime friend Archbishop Desmond Tutu. He described him as "aggressive and angry" when he first went to prison and suggested it was his suffering that had ennobled him. A humble man and the most courageous of upstanders, Mandela epitomized the best of humanity. Grace, the one who'd picked up the Tutsi baby without a thought or care for her own safety, flashed through my mind then. She, too, epitomized the best of humanity.

Leaving Cape Town, the five of us piled into the rented right-hand-drive microvan and headed south toward the Cape of Good Hope, slowly making our way to wine country. We stopped for a brisk walk along the beach at Hout Bay, a posh residential area close to Cape Town that was popular with weekenders, then on through Table Mountain National Park, a scenic route with coastal views of rugged mountains and plunging cliffs jutting into the sea. After another stop at Boulders Beach to see the African penguin colony—known as the jackass penguins because of their donkey-like bray, which the boys all loved—we lunched at a seaside eatery and then traveled north along the Garden Route to the quaint town of Franschhoek, passing townships and slums where many residents still lived in corrugated metal houses.

Bill and I decided to leave the kids at our villa one afternoon and take a mini-tour of wineries by ourselves, the first date we had had in months. Warmed by the wine and the heat from the winery's blazing fire, it hit me then just how little time we had actually carved out for each other—not just since Kigali, but over many years.

With my in-and-out travel, it seemed like the right decision, the only decision, to prioritize time with the boys. But how often had I listened to those airplane instructions about putting your own oxygen mask on first? The relationship had needed as much care and feeding as the kids but suffered as a neglected child would. It was no surprise that we had grown apart. The distance felt cumulative.

I had given my all to work and family—or I thought I had. Unlike most of the women whose lives I'd worked to improve, I was a woman with seemingly endless choices. But here at the end of the continent, I found myself walking around uncertainly with a man who had been with me for half of my life. I could, if I chose, walk away, start over again. Or I could lay down my armor and open my heart to him. Everything I'd learned this year made me realize that I could decide right then, with Bill sitting beside me, his face flushed by the fire, to forgive the things I held against him, and to hope that he would do the same for me.

I could let myself be loved.

I was the one who had left him. I had kept on leaving. But Bill had left, too. He had matched my distance with his own, replacing emotional and physical intimacy with the comfort and stability of routine. Our marriage had dissolved into an abyss of planning, coordination, and family logistics, the result of a long, drawn-out period of withholding and inattention on both our parts.

When I walked out on him four years earlier, we had been living apart in our own house for almost a year. I slept upstairs with the boys, while Bill was in the basement. By staying in the same house, we were able to keep up appearances without having to confront the shame and difficulty of separation.

Alone in my sterile corporate apartment, the clock hands never seemed to move. The absence of noise and color, the sweet chaos of family life, left me feeling numb, empty. I was lonelier than I had ever been the field. Weekends were ridiculous, holed up in a one-bedroom high-rise when the boys were practically right down the street, eating chocolate-chip pancakes, playing on Xbox or hoops on the driveway. The whole thing was miserable.

I wandered around the streets of Bethesda, passing restaurants as if window shopping. The prospect of eating solo was just too depressing. I missed Bill, missed his calm and reassuring familiarity, our togetherness. I saw a few friends, the ones we had told. They gently spoke of other single friends and the possibility of online dating. But it was way too early and awkward.

The plan was for each of us to alternate and take a couple of nights in the house with the kids. I began looking for excuses to go home, even on my "away" nights. "Just coming to check on the boys," I would tell Bill.

One evening after Bill returned from a business trip to California, he told me about a woman he'd met at the poolside bar of an ocean front hotel there, and he offered details about their rendezvous. He had to prove to himself, and to me, that I was wrong about him, he'd said. It was what he needed. I was shocked. At the same time, part of me was impressed—it was a bold move, so bold it was almost bizarre.

It was the jolt our relationship needed. We began trying to find our way back to the marriage. After a few months, I moved back into the house, and we started to live together, sharing first a roof, and then a bed. The boys, the importance of keeping the family intact, brought me home, or so I thought. But it was as much, or more, for Bill. He made me a better woman, a better human. He was one of the good ones.

Then work started to unravel, and I lost my way again. There had been so many distractions. But, here in Africa, perhaps for the first time in our lives together, I finally felt confident that my conclusion would always be the same: I loved Bill.

After our winery tour, we came back to the villa, sent the boys out to explore, and for the first time in months, maybe even years, took our time with each other. Later, when they returned, we set off on our own quiet walk around the neighboring vineyards, holding hands.

That night, we took the kids out to dinner at one of the best restaurants in town, trading glances, little smiles, across the table.

Hog Hollow was our last and perhaps most spectacular destination in South Africa. Overlooking the Tsitsikamma Mountain Range, each of our rooms at the lodge there was like a mini loft apartment, complete with a flat screen TV for the boys and a lovely bathtub for Bill and me. The trip organizers must have told them it was our anniversary because they kept leaving us little gifts and bottles of wine, even baking us a cake. And maybe it was an anniversary of sorts, a milestone worthy of celebration.

I realized that I had made my choice, had actually made it twenty-five years ago, though it took our year in Rwanda to finally see it, to understand and embrace it. Having to stay and choosing to stay *were* two entirely different things. I was staying. Bill and I had reached a better place together, and I wanted to stay there.

23

Ladies' Choice

After our time together in South Africa, the prospect of another trip to South Sudan was weighing on me. My time with the organization was almost up, though I hadn't said a word about it to my colleagues. It felt disingenuous not to tell them, but a new country director was just starting in South Sudan, and the opportunity center was about to open; the work simply outranked news of my departure. At least with Bill back in Rwanda, coverage for the boys was no longer a problem. We were all in good hands.

Waiting for the flight to Nairobi to take off, I pictured the boys getting ready for a Saturday morning soccer game, or on their way to the African Bagel Company for those Saturday-only doughnuts—and I thought about all the time I'd be spending alone. Once we were on the way, though, I remembered how inspired and reenergized I became working with women survivors. Their lessons had become my lessons.

Reviewing my notes on the flight, I recalled the small group of women leaders from Yei, the ones who had taken it upon themselves to help other women in their community despite their own fierce struggles, who considered women's and girls' education their top priority. "Don't you find it depressing to work with survivors?" people would often ask. At times, yes, but for the most part, it was gratifying and humbling, a vivid reminder of the hardships and humiliations that so many women endure on a daily basis, of the fortuities of birth and life. The choices we make and the ones we don't.

Surely Grandma Lilly could have been killed in one of Ukraine's anti-Jewish pogroms if she had never boarded that steamship to New York with her mother. And I could have just as surely been a Ukrainian countrywoman, an émigré myself, or not been born at all.

One has to believe, even foolishly, in the essential goodness and rightness of humanity to do this work and that change is possible in the most difficult and unlikely of places, despite mountains of evidence to the contrary. Cynicism and pessimism are luxuries, my friend Mukesh Kapila says, only for those who come and go, not who stay and do. He knew this better than most. As a medical doctor and the UN's humanitarian coordinator in Sudan at the time, Mukesh was the one who "blew the whistle" on the genocide in Darfur after learning about the ethnically targeted violence, including mass rape, being inflicted on the people there. He was a prince among upstanders.

Also, it's hard not to be optimistic when you meet a woman like Mary, a mother of six girls, only four of whom lived. When we met on a trip to Rumbek a few years earlier, she appeared older and frailer than the usual participants, though her age was impossible to pinpoint. Nonetheless, she stood with verve before her women's group to practice her numbers.

Married just before the start of the war between North and South Sudan, Mary suffered without food, clothes, or a place to sleep. Her husband became ill and was unable to care for the family. They lived off of lulu fruits and wild vegetables Mary managed to collect in the bush during short breaks in the fighting. Sadly, there were no medical facilities to provide proper treatment for her husband, and he died. As a widow, Mary was forced by soldiers to carry weapons long distances and to cook for them. She did whatever she had to do to keep her children alive.

Her life changed for the better after the war. As a result of the life-skills and business training she received, Mary started a small business selling groundnut paste and lulu oil. She learned to write and count, how to save, and used some of the money to pay school fees for her children, two of whom were in high school.

Mary was still on my mind when I landed in Juba and met up with the new country director for South Sudan. Then we traveled by hired car to Yei on the same mind- and body-numbing road as before, making small talk along the way, getting to know one another. I gave her a brief overview of the program and staff, and shared what had happened in Rumbek. A Nigerian by birth, she had spent years living and working in South Sudan so was well acquainted with its challenges. Mostly, I sat staring out the window at the moving landscape and let my mind wander.

It was mango season in Yei. After weeks of heavy downpours, the ripe, delicious fruit was falling off the trees, providing a ready source of food and income. Groups of women gathered the windfall fruit to eat and sell in the marketplace or roadside, but much of it was left to rot on the ground, its abundance wasted. Mangoes saturated the market for this one month and helped to fill the bellies of many undernourished villagers.

In nearby Payawa Boma, one thousand women turned up at our first recruitment session. There was only enough funding to enroll one hundred of them. The same thing happened in the village of Longamere Boma, where more than five hundred women vied for another one hundred slots. Chiefs in each village helped select the women most in need of assistance, but in reality, all of them were desperate for training and support.

The life-skills training began right away for the enrolled women. One of the first sessions was on the value of women's work, in which the trainer asked the women to describe what they did each day so that she could make a list on white flip-chart paper: one side for the women, the other side for the men. The women's list spilled onto another page while the men's was only a few lines. In a group with generally low literacy skills, the list made a strong visual impact. Most said they worked from early morning until late at night, while the men spent significant amounts of time on leisure, playing cards, or boozing. It was the women who were responsible for all the household chores and expenses, including food and school fees for their children. If the wife was unable to produce children, especially boys, or was considered lazy or just plain old, the husband was entitled to find himself another, often younger, wife or several of them, as long as he could afford the bride price. On a previous visit, a woman had described how her husband stole the bicycle he had given her to use as payment for his second wife. Her village pressured the man until he finally gave the bicycle back.

At another site, one woman who wasn't enrolled sat at the window for the entire two-hour introductory session, hungry to learn what she could. Local chiefs also stopped by to give opening remarks. I sat quietly in the back of the room until I, too, was called upon to speak. After introducing myself and welcoming the group, I told them about their sisters in other war-torn countries

around the world, women just like them who were in the same yearlong program. "You are not alone," I said. "We are here to help." And then: "Would
any of you be willing to share your story?" I asked, my eyes sweeping the
room. A few of the women tentatively raised their hands. With a little more
prompting, the women stood up in turns, patiently waiting for the translator
to convey their words as I scribbled down notes.

Betty Sandy Moses, age thirty-two, was one of the new participants. "I
was supposed to be in class," she said softly, "but war stopped me." Betty
was forced to quit school in fifth grade. With two children of her own now,
she was intent on learning about business so she could send them to school
and give them the education that she missed. Joyce Jamba was a widow
whose husband died early. Left to raise eight children on her own, Joyce
earned a little money here and there, enough to cover school fees, uniforms,
and supplies for only four, or half, of her children. She still had dreams of
her own education; she was interested in the trainings on health and stress
management. There was another Betty, a widow with five children, who was
HIV positive. The issue is a particularly daunting one for women across sub-
Saharan Africa, who represent two out of three new infections. Many never
get tested, either because of stigma or a lack of access to health facilities. Four
of Betty's children were fine, but one was infected. Her illness meant that she
was unable to pay their school fees.

"Do you have any questions for me?" I asked, scanning the room again.
"Who is your family?" one woman wanted to know. I told them about my
husband and three boys and how we had recently moved to Rwanda from
the United States. "Why do you want to help us?" asked another. It wasn't the
first time this question had come up. "Because we believe in you and want you
to have an opportunity to improve your life, and help your children to have
a better life," I said. It was a response I had honed over the years, but there
was so much more to say. I wished I could tell them everything, explain how
complex my feelings were on this topic, but I knew this wasn't the time or
place. I saw a few of the women nod their heads post-translation, apparently
satisfied with my response.

The women were excited to receive their ID cards, each one with their
picture and the name of a sponsor-sister in the United States that they could
write to (or could have help writing to if they were illiterate). Seeing their im-

age for the first time, many couldn't take their eyes off of their photograph. Joseph had done the same when he first saw a picture of himself. The women were then split up into groups of twenty-five for future training sessions.

A number of them expressed hope that the program would serve as the primary and secondary schooling they never received. Women in particular had missed out on a formal education, for many reasons: constant war and displacement; the dominance of Islamic ideology under the formerly united Sudan that eschewed female empowerment and discouraged efforts to educate women; and traditional norms and values regarding girls' education, seen more as a benefit to the prospective husband's family and thus unworthy of the investment.

These women, like so many others I had come to know over the years, had been silenced by an almost innate sense of insufficiency but were, like all women, strong, smart, and courageous. Before Women for Women, I'd never looked deeply at the issues surrounding women's agency—the circumstances that expand and limit our respective choices; the trade-offs that come with any decision. The sheer range of choices we have as women in the developed world compared to our developing-world sisters, where even the most basic choices—what to wear, when to eat, with whom they can leave their homes, let alone bigger choices around education, marriage, children, work—seem beyond reach.

Through these survivors, I was able to see women's unique roles and contributions in a new light, to see my father's abuse for what it was: a pattern evident again and again in the women I met around the world. The uncomfortable, sad truth of its pervasiveness was in some ways liberating. Through them, I was finally able to comprehend my mother's missing voice, her lack of choice.

These survivors showed me the true meaning of compassion, how it could be turned inward as well as outward, and what it means to be victimized without being a victim. I realized victimhood wasn't necessarily a destiny but a state of mind. How I chose to think about and react to my past, my actions going forward, were entirely up to me. Almost every woman has had to overcome something—maybe abuse or discrimination; lack of schooling, resources, or opportunity; or immobilizing fear or self-doubt. In that sense, in one way or another, we are all survivors.

That evening, the lonely little Episcopal guesthouse in Yei seemed even more dismal than before. I looked out of my thickly barred windows and saw the same wild dogs, the same women cleaning the compound, the same block of dormitory-like rooms across the way. But right outside my window was also the most perfect mango tree, dripping with luscious fruit, so ripe and sweet that I could eat them whole—like an apple—and did, every day.

Back in Rwanda, my reentry with Bill and the boys was unexpectedly calm and seamless. My evenings in Yei had been spent alone in my room at the church compound, reading and writing, missing the guys. I felt as committed as ever to the work, but my passion had shifted now. By the end of the trip, I was ready to go home in a way I had not been for many years.

The boys raved about the birthday party they'd had for Paula while I was gone. The celebration was complete with a chocolate birthday cake topped with strawberries and candles, and Joseph had joined in on the fun. When the boys pressed him to share his birthday, he insisted to Paula, who was interpreting, that he didn't know when he was born or how old he was. He told them he'd never had a birthday party in his life. None of them knew what to say.

The Women's Opportunity Center now became my sole focus at work. To complete the construction on time would require a massive, all-hands-on-deck effort. There was less than six weeks until the grand opening. In six weeks, our time here would be over. During those first few months in Kigali, everything was so new and slow and raw. But now, life had picked up speed and seemed to be whizzing by. I wasn't at all sure I could get everything done. Or that I was ready to leave Rwanda.

The center still looked very much the construction site. Piles of rubble and heavy equipment sat fixed and unmoving next to several partially finished buildings. Not only were we running out of time and money, we were also facing an acute shortage of workers, who were protesting repeated late payments by refusing to come to the site. "Maybe if we agree to pay them every day," said Edward, the construction manager, his voice betraying his uncertainty. "At least we can try."

On weekly walk-throughs with Edward and Bruce, we debated paint colors, tiling, and kitchen shelves as we moved around the site. Stopping in front of each structure, I would call out the items on the punch list, a whopping ten

pages long, of everything that remained to be done, and make encouraging
notes in the margins of the new estimated completion dates:

"Door and window frames?"

"Ninety-three percent installed."

"Dorm and ceiling painting?

"About sixty percent."

"Pointing the bricks?"

"Eighty-five percent, give or take . . ."

"Water and plumbing?"

"Close to fifty percent."

"You're kidding, right?"

"No, we can't keep the guy onsite long enough to finish the job."

"That's ridiculous. We have to have running water for the opening. What's
it going to take to get him back here?"

"I don't know. He's a busy man. I will call him again. Maybe he will come
tomorrow."

Edward had clearly lost interest in the project. It had dragged on for too
long, and there was nothing left in it for him, or his firm, which desperately
needed some new paying clients. We had already lost three whole weeks on a
disagreement over budget. With lawyers—his and ours—we dissected every
bank statement, invoice payment, and change order in an attempt to reconcile our numbers and how much remained to be paid. We were in the right,
but it didn't matter.

Edward said he had to make a trip to Kenya, just for a few days to take
care of some business. He would return as soon as he could. It was the worst
possible time for him to go, but we both knew that I had virtually nothing left
for leverage. Without him pushing the workers, I couldn't see how we were
going to complete the job in time.

At least we could count on Angelique, a graduate in her early forties chosen
to lead the cooperative that made by hand more than five hundred thousand
clay bricks used in constructing the center. Tall and lean with close-cropped hair
and a chiseled jawline, Angelique was a woman who rarely spoke unless spoken
to, and rarely smiled. A widow and former farmer who had lost two of her four
children, she once described her life as full of "a lot of miseries and helplessness."

Angelique, who lived within walking distance of the center in the Kayonza
District, learned about the program through her neighbors and was selected

Angelique, head of the Brickmaking Cooperative.

to participate. "Luckily enough I was among the women who were chosen to have brickmaking training as vocational skill training during three months," she said. After graduation, Angelique was picked to lead the women's brickmaking cooperative. She believed her self-confidence and income-generation skills won her the selection.

The brickmaking process itself had its challenges. The women had to dig the clay, mix it, mold it into bricks, dry the bricks, assemble the kiln, and then lay the bricks. It required skilled labor, typically of men, ready access to raw materials, and a place to dry the bricks before being fired, which was problematic in the rainy season. Angelique, with support from the Sharon Davis Design team, oversaw all of it. Together they set up an effective new brickmaking operation: a separate pit to mix the bricks, a level table to form them on and tents to dry them under. The organization's symbol, a woman's head and outstretched arms, was crafted into every single brick. "The best bricks I've seen in East Africa," declared Edward.

Angelique now seemed utterly transformed from the time we had first met several years earlier. Then she had been painfully shy, a person you'd hardly notice. "I was a poor widow in the community with no plan for the future," she told me. Now you could feel her presence. She carried herself like a woman in charge of her own destiny.

Hand selected to participate in Goldman Sachs's entrepreneurship program, Angelique had used her savings to buy a local breed cow for dairy production and to expand into agriculture. She was able to pay family expenses and send her daughter to boarding school, which made her extremely proud.

Angelique had joined a village savings club with thirty other women who took turns investing in one another's businesses. "I have gained the great power of decision making," she shared, beaming. Despite some problems early on, Angelique and her fellow co-op members had mastered the new brickmaking technique. They were now cranking out the bricks as fast as we could put them up.

On the weekend, we stopped by ISK's spring fair, where we watched assorted parents and teachers drop into the dunk tank happily manned by Amy, then we caravanned with Julia and her sons to a rustic, lakeside house she shared with two other families on the banks of Lake Muhazi, less than an hour's drive east of Kigali. The village of mud brick houses lay just off the main road, up a steep, red-dirt hill, surrounded by encroaching jungle. Despite its ambition to serve as a major tourist destination for water sports and weekend getaways, the area seemed underdeveloped and desperately poor.

We arrived late Saturday afternoon and took advantage of the remaining daylight to put up the mosquito nets, set out some well-used patio furniture, and unpack all the food we'd brought from Kigali. Like the surrounding community, the dilapidated house had no running water or electricity. It consisted of two small bedrooms, a tiny, unusable sink with a few wood-plank shelves that served as a kitchen, and adequate storage space for two old, rickety canoes. The bathroom was rendered useless without a bucket of water.

It was quiet beside the long and narrow lake, as clear and smooth as a sheet of glass. We had left our computers and e-devices at home, so were all nicely unplugged for a change. Julia had set up a tightrope of sorts between two trees. While the boys took turns walking along the thin line, the three of us talked and relaxed over a good bottle of cabernet we'd brought back from South Africa.

Watching the boys get on, steady themselves, walk a few steps, fall off, get back on and try again, I thought about my own flailing efforts to find balance. It had been all too fleeting, too precarious, for the most part. Life lived on the head of a pin, as Bill liked to say. One tiny step from utter chaos. Striving for some kind of work and life balance, I'd learned, required constant vigilance, as much vigilance as it had taken to fight my wiring. At best, it meant continuous, even daily, trade-offs. "You can have anything you want, you just can't have everything you want," as my friend David Baum often said.

Right then I felt nothing but gratitude for the life we had—the whole crazy, ugly, joyful mess of it.

Just before dark, we hung lanterns along the patio as the local caretaker, who doubled as a grill master, slow roasted large quantities of meat for us. As we moved our lawn chairs out by the water's edge to better capture the fading light, a feeling of peace and contentment enveloped me. Ready, finally, to let the past go.

I thought about my parents, and about the beauty of forgiveness. Forgiveness is the greatest lesson I've learned from working with women survivors of war, from the work in Rwanda. Forgiveness is the only way to heal ourselves and be free from the past, Archbishop Tutu has said. If a woman can find it in her heart to forgive the perpetrator who slaughtered her child, her children, during the genocide, who am I not to forgive?

It was time—well past—to forgive each of my parents for their shortcomings, and to learn to forgive myself for my own. I needed to do it for them, but even more so, for me; for *my* family. It was the only way to move on, the only way for my own partially formed self to heal, to become more whole. It wasn't as easy or simple as that, I knew, but what if it was? Forgiveness, like victimhood, was also a state of mind, a choice.

The stars came out as evening encroached. The world seemed at once vast and small from our vantage point beside the lake, with nothing to obstruct our view. We lingered there for a few more minutes then slowly made our way back to the patio, where we devoured our feast under a brilliant sky.

Bill and I rose early Sunday morning, Mother's Day. After cleaning the dinner dishes in a couple of large plastic tubs, we set off on our own canoe ride around the lake, at ease in each other's company. It was hard to believe that, only twenty years before, this same water flowed red with blood. The lake was a scene of mass killings; many people drowned trying to escape the blood-shed. The water was still and serene, with just a few locals out fishing.

Everyone else was just waking up as we paddled back to shore. To honor the day, Bill made us all breakfast lakeside—strong French-press coffee and omelets for the ladies, French toast for the boys. The five of them consumed two entire loaves of bread drenched in powdered sugar. Our leisurely breakfast soon rolled into lunch. After more water sports and a late-morning beer, we indulged in Julia's homemade pasta and sauce topped with fresh Parmesan.

Returning to the city surprisingly refreshed, each of us resumed our regular Sunday activities: Kai had his weekly Hebrew lesson via Skype; Bill and Eli went shopping for dinner; Sam, as usual, was engrossed in his computer. I walked the mile or so to the shopping mall to run a few errands. When I came home, the boys all surprised me with Mother's Day gifts. Kai made his own card; Eli had bought a rotating digital picture frame and loaded it up with photographs from our recent adventures; Sam made a video compilation of the beautiful flower photos he'd taken in South Africa. It was set to "All You Need Is Love" and dedicated to the "best mom in the world." The tears were streaming down my checks before I could stop myself. I must have watched the video half a dozen times.

Though I've celebrated International Women's Day for many years, Mother's Day *is* special. Almost from the time my children were born, I had struggled with the idea of being a good mom. It wasn't so much that I regretted my choice of career as I wondered if the boys felt cheated because my work often took me so far away from them, whether they ever wished for a different kind of mom.

And yet, the women in Rwanda and around the world had shown me time and again that there was no single or right approach to motherhood. It, too, differed from country to country, woman to woman. Soviet women did not love their children less, as that public opinion poll all those years ago suggested, and neither did South Sudanese, Congolese, Afghan, Iraqi, Nigerian, Bosnian, Kosovar, or Rwandan women. We just needed to look past the otherness. We all loved our children, sometimes more than life itself. That Mother's Day was the first time I felt I had really earned the day.

I had come to Rwanda in search of inspiration, hoping to find a better place. My place. I found it that late afternoon, not only in the mementos of our year in Rwanda and all that they symbolized, but in my own sons.

24

Out of Africa

In early June, about three weeks before Bill and the boys were due to leave Rwanda, we decided to take Sam and Eli to the Kigali Genocide Memorial. I'd been the one hesitating for months, uncertain whether to expose them to the very worst of humanity. The boys, and Kai in particular, were still so young and impressionable. Maybe I was being overly protective, but what happened in 1994 was so beyond the bounds of rationality or normal emotion, beyond anything they had ever confronted. Their innocence, itself a privilege in many ways, was not something to take lightly.

We went on a Friday afternoon when the boys had early release from school. We met first for a quiet lunch at the memorial's outdoor café so Bill and I could prepare Sam and Eli for what they were about to see. There we were joined by Freddy Mutanguha, the country director of Aegis Trust, the genocide-prevention group that runs the memorial. Freddy, who has a gentle yet commanding presence, lost both of his parents and four sisters in the genocide. He then worked his way through school to become a leading peace and human rights advocate before joining Aegis. Everyone who met Freddy could attest to his big heart. Bill and I considered him a friend.

The cluster of off-white buildings that house the memorial sat near the top of a long and steep hill. We met our guide, a survivor from Remera—a neighborhood adjacent to ours—in the reception area just inside the entrance. We followed him outside first for a silent walk around the mass graves. The remains of more than 250,000 victims were buried beneath the thick slabs of concrete. We each left a small stone on the grave as is the Jewish custom, as my mother had done for David each year, and then went through the simple yet poignant gardens of unity, division, and reconciliation. Moving inside, we slowly made our way around the inside of the memorial, stopping at each exhibit so the boys could absorb the history and ask questions.

Dr. James Smith, the cofounder of Aegis, and others describe the genocidal process as having eight distinct stages: classification, symbolization, dehumanization, organization, polarization, preparation, extermination, and denial. While war, Smith said, is based more on hostility and aggression, genocide is about "the deliberate and systematic targeting of a certain group of people for extermination, just because of who they are." It is the most extreme version of exclusion.

The "enemy" must first be demonized before they can be destroyed. As we walked through a room at the memorial devoted to other crimes against humanity—in Bosnia, Armenia, and Cambodia, and during the Holocaust, when six million Jews and others were exterminated—the demonization associated with each mass atrocity was clear. So were the bystanders.

The boys had learned about the Holocaust in Sunday school. They visited the United States Holocaust Memorial Museum with their youth group and later had the chance to talk with a survivor. Bill and I each had friends whose parents were survivors. The Holocaust felt personal to us, integral to our family history and the history of our people.

Standing in front of an exhibit that depicted the time leading up to the genocide, we talked about what Rwanda's foreign minister called the "mismanagement of diversity." Radio broadcasts and newspapers portrayed the Tutsi as cockroaches and snakes that did not deserve to live. "People were drugged by ideology, manipulated psychologically and socially," said Father Borile, the Catholic priest who ran the Centre Saint Antoine Orphanage.

We entered a carpeted, dimly lit room with walls covered with personal photographs of the dead that had been donated by their loved ones. Sam lingered on a cube seat there for several minutes. Eli stood in horror before a room filled with skulls and bones and tattered, stained clothing. He shuddered and quickly moved on to the next exhibit. In another room, the children's hall, several enlarged photographs of children were on display. Below each was a plaque that stated the child's name; age; favorite toy, food, or sport;

and how they were killed: some by machete, others like two-year-old Fillette by having their heads smashed against a wall. Fillette was described as a "good girl" who loved rice and chips and to play with her doll; she considered her dad her best friend. Eli and I both lost it then.

I'd seen the bloodstained walls of the church at Ntarama where five thousand men, women, and children seeking safety had perished. More than 30 percent of the killings took place in and around churches, at the hands of civilian-led militias trained to kill a thousand Tutsi in twenty minutes. Some even bribed their killers so they could go more quickly, by gun instead of a club or machete.

I thought of Violette, who joined the program in 2004. Her story came to my attention through her American sponsor. Violette was alone with her two children in the small village of Gahini as the country disintegrated into chaos. Her husband was working three hours away in Kigali, where he could earn a better living. Violette knew they were in grave danger. Carrying her two children in her arms, she fled to a nearby church where she thought she and her family would be safe. Instead, the church came under attack by machete-wielding militia.

"There was shooting going on and people were falling on each other and dying everywhere," she'd told her sponsor-sister.

Violette lay down in the aisle and smeared blood on herself and her children. Pretending to be dead, they hid among the corpses. Afraid to move, they lay there for a week, until the Rwandan Patriotic Army liberated the area. She estimated that there were seven hundred people in that church. Only twenty survived.

Violette later started a business, harvesting sorghum to make a popular local drink and beans to eat and sell. Though she never finished high school, she was determined to educate her children. "My business allowed me to pay school fees, to send my children to school," she said. She became president of a women's craft cooperative that united all members of her community, those victimized by the genocide and others who confessed to genocide crimes or had family members in prison.

It was women like Violette who inspired hope that such an atrocity might never come to pass again. But the median age in Rwanda was just under twenty; many had no direct memory of the genocide. Families still wrestled with how to talk about it, cope with it. There were teachers and community leaders who avoided the subject altogether. Children grew up being told there were certain things they shouldn't ask about or question—rape being one of them. Trauma, shame, and stigma all fed into the mores of silence.

Despite the progress toward peace and reconciliation, the mixed marriages, workplaces, government offices, and the intense efforts to remake a nation blind to ethnicity, deep-seated ethnic tension persists in the country and across the region. If the economy falters—and with this tiny country already bursting at the seams—the youth could become disaffected, as has happened in many other countries. And unless this next generation is able to talk about and learn from a past not of their own making, they face a potential time bomb.

Back at the museum entrance, we thanked our guide and said good-bye to Freddy, making a small contribution toward the memorial's upkeep on our way out. Sam and Eli were unusually somber on the ride home. There was none of the normal backseat shoving or horseplay.

Over dinner that night, Sam, surprisingly, spoke up first. "You see the peoples' pictures and faces and then you look at the skeletons and bones . . . it made me angry at the people who committed these crimes. We could have done something and we didn't do it. We just stood there and let those people die."

Eli nodded in agreement. "It's scary, the amount of pain that people can cause other human beings."

The visit was still on Eli's mind as he went to bed that night, but we were glad we'd taken them. I was so proud of the boys for their openness and bravery, their willingness to experience real life, its beauties as well as its brutalities. Contemplating your own humanity through the lens of a genocide was not easy. It could well be one of the hardest things, ever. And yet the boys had to know, had to see, the true cost of otherness to be able to think and act differently; to learn that they are the ones responsible for their humanness, for the kind of person they choose to be.

Along with the Holocaust, the genocide would now be woven into our own family narrative. No longer a horror experienced by unknown people a world away, it was real, it happened, in our backyard. Freddy, Joseph, Innocent, Paula, and all the other survivors we knew lived with it every day. We would remember it, too. Once you know something, there is no unknowing.

For several months now, Bill had been consulting with the United States Holocaust Memorial Museum as they planned their participation in the twentieth commemoration of the genocide against the Tutsis the following year. They had sent a small delegation to Kigali to conduct interviews on the causes and legacy of the genocide, and I'd arranged for them to meet Angelique, the head of the brickmaking cooperative, and several other co-op members one afternoon in one of the new training pods at the center. The group wanted to understand what, if anything, had changed since 1994.

"Do you think the genocide could happen again?" asked the director of the Center for Genocide Prevention at the museum.

"No!" the women volunteered at once.

"Before the genocide, the country was divided," said one woman. "There was no trust among people. Now everyone is working together, doing business."

"The young generation is not connected to our bad history. All kids are in school," declared another.

"Women were more isolated before. We are out in the open now," stated a third. "Women would not let it happen."

"There is less division now," Angelique agreed. "Our fates are more intertwined."

Angelique would be the featured speaker at the center's ribbon cutting. After all she'd been through and done, she'd earned her place in the spotlight.

While we were racing to finish the Women's Opportunity Center, we were starting to pack up our house in Kigali. What we couldn't take with us, we planned to sell or give away. The year had gone by so fast. It would have been nice to have another year here, but Bill's work was in the States and the boys were ready to get back. They would be leaving right after school let out for the summer. I would follow a week later, after the center opened.

Transitions are never easy, but this one was more than that. Wrapping up, handing things off, letting go, saying good-bye. This was my most traumatic departure yet in terms of its finality. I had known it was coming, known it from the time the news was delivered that a new CEO had been chosen. Knowing it, though, didn't make it easier. Still, I was grateful for the honor, the privilege, of doing this work over those ten years, and for this last one in Rwanda.

While the year here had been one that challenged everything I believed about my role, my purpose, my family, and relationships, it had also been a year of discovery. Whereas I had been looking for the big gesture, the recognition I felt I had earned, these survivors taught me that it is really the smallest gestures, those heart-catching moments that remind us of who we are and of our humanity, that matter the most. If I had gotten the CEO role, Rwanda would never have happened for us. Given that choice now, I would have chosen Rwanda.

Though it was time to move on, the work itself felt so unfinished. While there were more girls in primary school than ever before, 130 million girls were still not in school. Sub-Saharan Africa was still home to the largest gender gap in education. And forty million African women and girls still married before their fifteenth birthday. "When girls are socialized in the framework of certain cultural practices to lower their eyes, to have sex and learn to please a man, their rights to education and personal dignity go out the window at an early age," wrote Malawi's former president Dr. Joyce Banda. African women were also more likely to be murdered by family members or intimate partners than women anywhere else in the world. At least the next generation of women on the continent had a decent chance at a different life. Less so for their mothers.

There was so much more to be done to help women survivors everywhere make the difficult journey along the path to self-sufficiency. It sometimes seemed as though, for all of the progress for women worldwide—and there *had* been progress—the gulf between places where women had real choices and those where they didn't was just too wide. On the most frustrating days, that gap seemed nearly impossible to bridge.

Between site checks at the opportunity center in Kayonza and packing up, my last couple of weeks in Rwanda were spent saying good-bye to friends and colleagues. Amy and Julia were also leaving at the end of the school year: Amy was moving for a new job in Zambia, where there were good school options for Muriel, and Julia and her boys to Zimbabwe, her next country posting. I was going to miss them and my Rwandan colleagues; we'd come to know each other during long car rides to the field and shared time in the office. We'd celebrated birthdays, births, weddings, and holidays together. We knew each other's families.

The staff was genuinely touched that my family had come to Rwanda. They always asked after Bill and gave hugs to the boys whenever they dropped by the office. I found the staff's deep commitment to the women in the program equally touching, along with their well-deserved pride in the country and the organization's accomplishments, including the new center. It hadn't been easy.

Through a series of farewell parties, I was being loved out of the country and Women for Women. The staff invited me onto the balcony one morning for coffee and pastries, then surprised me with their heartfelt tributes and a beautiful piece of fabric. The senior management team hosted a goat feast for our family at a local restaurant. Kai wowed everyone over dinner by singing the Rwandan national anthem in Kinyarwanda.

The pièce de résistance was a souvenir cooking party at our home, organized by Clemence, the income-generation manager. She brought over several bags full of supplies and ingredients and proceeded to take over the kitchen for the next few hours. The boys and I, along with the senior team, learned to prepare East African *pilau*, *chapatti*, and several other regional dishes. Paula, Joseph, and Bill all joined us.

If one had to go, this was absolutely the best way: with good cheer and high spirits. My belly was filled with delicious food, my heart with love.

The last few days before Bill and the boys left were a whirlwind. We managed to host an impromptu birthday party for Kai, his twelfth, inviting his whole class and their parents over for pizza, cake, and ice cream. Kai, all of us, had the chance to say good-bye to new friends. And just like, that they were gone. I still had a hundred things to do, so there was no time for feeling lonely or sad. Somehow the construction project looked like it was going to pull together in the nick of time—at least to be presentable for the grand opening.

Bill had been especially solicitous before he left. He came home with a big bunch of calla lilies one day, other little gifts the next. Most nights we sat on the front patio after work, the equivalent of our green chairs by the window, to debrief each other on the day. Under the glow of candlelight, we started to talk through our plans for the summer and into the fall. He made me feel grounded, like it was all going to turn out just fine.

We were still working furiously through the construction punch list at the center. We had more bricks to point, ceilings to paint, and furniture and equipment to install, so that the place wouldn't look so deserted. The solar water pump had yet to arrive onsite, and no one actually knew how to use the compost toilets. Those expensive safari tents we'd purchased in Kenya had also been poorly installed and threatened to collapse if anyone leaned too hard against one of the metal poles. The main thing was to get the toilets functioning in time for the opening.

We also had to prepare for the grand opening itself: protocol and security for the VIPs; stage construction, a steel structure with a wooden floor and carpet; registration and souvenirs for the guests; decorations, entertainment, and a working sound system; and press, videographers and photographers. The week of the opening, I divided my time between the scheduled events with donors and board members in the city and Kayonza, where we were trying to clear the site enough to erect a large, circus-type tent to hold close to four hundred guests. Several program graduates were enlisted to help us scour the grounds and remove the remaining debris.

We went to the site early the day of the opening to make sure everything was set. It wasn't, but it was darn close, and only a handful of us could tell the difference. Hopefully, no one would look too closely at the unfinished ceilings or paint-splattered floors during the post-ceremony tours.

For the second time that year, I donned a borrowed *mushanana* and took my seat among the crowd waiting for the ceremony to begin. In the end, President Kagame sent his regrets but dispatched the new minister of gender in his stead to open the center. Inyumba, the beloved gender minister who had passed away, would have been proud. Zainab, Women for Women International's founder, would have as well. It was too bad neither was there to see the center become a reality. With a plaque engraved with Inyumba's name and mounted on a brick wall near the entrance, the Women's Opportunity Center was formally dedicated to her legacy.

It was late morning when the master of ceremonies stepped up to the podium to deliver his opening remarks. A local women's dance troupe wearing identical *mushanana* then entertained the crowd, followed by more speeches and another performance by a flamboyantly costumed troupe of women drummers that wowed the audience. The star of the day, though, had to be Angelique, who was called to the stage to speak for the more than fifty thousand women survivors of war who had graduated from the program in Rwanda.

"Distinguished guests, our leaders and all invitees gathered in this place, I first and foremost extend my greetings on behalf of other women.

"I am called Mukankubana Angelique. I am a widow and a family of three people.

"Before joining Women for Women I was a farmer just like my colleagues, digging for others for the survival of my family. After joining I acquired knowledge and managed to develop economically, I am on the level of employing other people as day labors. Not only that, I bought cows, goats and chicken.

"After Graduation Women for Women took me for further trainings at Goldman Sachs so that I can gain more skills.

"We were trained on following topics: family planning, small business management/ entrepreneurship, agribusiness, and brickmaking.

"As women, we were taught brickmaking by Women for Women International. We managed to produce more than five hundred thousand bricks that were used in the construction of the Women Opportunity Centre that has gathered us here. We are very grateful for the construction of the Women's Opportunity Centre, especially Kayonza District and the entire Country.

"We have formed a cooperative of brickmaking which has made us to be whom we are today. I am able to earn sixty thousand Rwandan Francs (60.000Rwf) on a monthly basis. Our cooperative is called KATWICO and our objectives are as follows:

- To continue brickmaking as a skill for construction in Kayonza and elsewhere;
- To buy a machine that will facilitate us to make tiles;
- To request a loan in the bank that will assist us in our business.

"Without taking much time, we thank Women for Women International for their continuity in empowering women towards their developing.

"We also thank our country leaders for their good collaboration in making partnership with other countries.

"Thank you."

When the minister of gender pronounced the center officially open, I was beaming with pride and crying at the same time. It had been an emotionally charged week, sad yet satisfying in its own way. "This is an achievement of women and it will last forever," Angelique had said of the center. She was right. Of course Angelique was right. Nothing and no one could ever take that away from her and her fellow brick makers.

I celebrated that night, first at a teary dinner with the staff, board, and donors, then at a boisterous party at an Indian place up the road with the architects and team from Sharon Davis Design. Everyone who attended the opening had been blown away by the center's innovative design and eco-functionality. It was the firm's first-ever project in Rwanda, but it likely would not be their last. Our family's contribution: a handmade brick-fired pizza oven for the café, which we hoped would employ more women and generate revenue for the center.

The Women's Opportunity Center was now a piece of my own story; a place of industry where women and others in the community could come together to learn and work, whether they were looking to expand their business or were still in need of a helping hand. Claudine was one of those women.

A 2011 program graduate, Claudine was part of a women's pineapple-growing cooperative that had failed due to lack of interest and people stealing the pineapples. She was selling beer now just to survive but had a new baby girl to think about and aspirations for them both. Claudine was interested in the business training so that she could start a new enterprise. The center could hopefully help Claudine, and women like her, lift themselves up again, with the support of other women.

Women by women. Brick by brick. That was the reason; that was the goal. Professionally speaking, nothing else really mattered.

25

A Better Place

A small flatbed truck arrived early the next morning to cart away the rest of the furniture, kitchenware, beds, and bedding, all sold cheap to the ex-principal of ISK, who was moving as well. Except for some appliances that were left behind for the new World Bank family moving in, the house looked just as it did a short year ago: completely empty, aside from our three tiny lizard friends that had been there since the beginning. I spent the rest of the day packing up, making giveaway boxes for Paula and Joseph, both of whom were unemployed now despite our best efforts to find them work. Not only was Joseph losing his job, he was losing his home, as the bank insisted on bringing in their own security. That room beside the gate would belong to someone other than Joseph for the first time.

Joseph told Bill before he left that he hoped to return to Byumba and buy a piece of land. "If I have land and can farm my own crops then I will feel like a man," he'd said. He also shared that we were the first tenants to tell him in advance that we were leaving. Paula looked forlorn, standing there in the house, when Kai left. "I will miss you so much, Kai," she cried. We were sad, too, and concerned for them both, with no income or prospects. They were part of our extended family now.

At dusk, I found the one and only glass I'd saved for the occasion and poured myself what was left in the icy bottle of vodka in the freezer. With my back against the white, bare wall in the living room, earbuds in, I sat listening to the "Happy Birthday Karen" playlist, then rose to my feet and started to dance around the cavernous space, calm and more at peace than I'd been in a long while. Amy stopped by, and we went out for one last meal together. She would also be leaving soon, off to spend a few weeks in the States before her new job started in Zambia. Sometime, somewhere, our paths would cross again. Julia, as well. They, too, had become my sisters.

It was dark when the plane took off for the United States, but in my mind's eye, Rwanda's gentle green hills were gradually fading from view as we rose higher in the night sky. At some point over the long-haul flights, it occurred to me that I was on a one-way ticket. For the first time in twenty years, I had no plans to travel, no idea when and where my next trip would be. That I was, in fact, grounded.

It felt strange to be back in Bethesda. In some ways, it was like we'd never left, and in others, it was almost new. Somewhere between Kigali and Yei . . . . Like Stella, I finally got my groove back—Karen's personal reinvention as a better wife, mother, and daughter, a better woman, or at least I'd like to think so.

The boys were happy to be back in familiar surroundings. They spent their first couple of weeks at home devouring their favorite foods, riding their bikes around Bethesda, catching up with friends. They'd had to adjust some as well. Like Bill and me, they had been altered by their experiences in Rwanda, by the people they met and those they came to know and love—Joseph and Paula, their new friends from ISK. Sam and Eli in particular seemed well on their way to becoming those good men I hoped for.

Two days after I got home, my parents came for a visit. It had seemed like a good idea months ago when they'd first suggested it. Yet when I found myself, jet-lagged and disoriented, frantically cleaning the house and weeding the yard to prepare for their arrival, I asked myself why I hadn't just told them to come later. I took a few deep breaths and decided to embrace it. They were making an effort, and so should I.

It all turned out just fine. Dad said the backyard looked the best he'd seen it, even if the front was overgrown. Mom sat at the kitchen table for hours, playing endless card games with her grandsons. We also talked. Really talked. She's better now at expressing her love; like my father, she has softened with age and time. She's toughened up some as well, but perhaps needed to, doing what she had to do to survive. Never effusive, I knew both of them were proud of the work I was doing, of the woman I had become.

Later in the summer, I tagged along with Bill on a short work trip to Boston. Our second morning there, my brother Ken and I met for breakfast at one of the local coffeehouses. Like so many times before, we started to reminisce about our childhood, how terrorized he felt by our father, how angry I was for many years, how neither of us felt loved or protected in the family. The same stories we'd told over and over again. But this time felt different. We told them now with a little less fervor, a little more distance. Both of us, for our own reasons and in our own time, were ready to leave those hurt children behind.

Running along the Charles River later that day, the warm sun on my face, the same place where, the summer before, my family and I decided to spend a year in Rwanda, it occurred to me that, perhaps unconsciously, both Ken and I had chosen to work with survivors. He as a therapist working with traumatized war veterans and those who have suffered various forms of abuse. It all somehow made sense. In helping to heal others, we had in fact been working to heal ourselves.

We sent the boys off to Camp Sangamon, the rugged all-boys camp in Vermont where they'd gone for years. Sam and Eli were to be counselors in training for the first time. It was a few firsts for me as well—the first time without work in more than twenty-five years; the first in ten that my head wasn't constantly in another country, worrying about how the latest threat or outbreak of violence would impact the women in the program. I now had time for some of the little things I'd missed out on through years of nonstop work and frequent travel, like shopping in real stores as opposed to airports, or running when the sun was already up. I didn't have to cram a week's worth of laundry in on the weekends but could parse it out during the week. For the first time in years, I wasn't juggling work, overseas travel, and the rest of life. It felt good to bask in the rareness of down time as Cheryl had predicted.

I spent a lot of time reflecting on our year in Rwanda, my time as a solo parent. Without Bill there to handle things, I had to do for myself, and in so doing, learned how to be more self-sufficient but, also, how to ask for help. No woman is an island, nor should she be. Having a family and a community for support didn't make you weak. It made you fortunate. It was their love, their "tethers," that had given me the ability, the freedom, to be so independent. Letting others in had not only become a source of strength but also one of healing.

Bill and I still divvy up household and parenting responsibilities based on affinity and proximity. At the highest level, we both want the same things, meaningful work and a meaningful life. Sharing the tasks of daily life, irrespective of gender roles, has allowed each of us to pursue those dreams. But now, after Rwanda, I can embrace all the facets of my womanhood, the roles of wife and mother, more completely. I'm in love with those jobs as well.

The lessons from our year in Rwanda continue to sustain me: Debora's resiliency after losing her entire family to genocide, Grace's compassion and courage, which led her to pick up baby Vanessa and raise her as her own. Euphraise's relentless tenacity, which enabled her to survive war, poverty, and years of abuse to go on to become a successful businesswoman and teach all of her children a trade. Yvette's constant struggle to rise above her circumstances. Calm and deliberate Tereza, who, in the face of obstacle after obstacle, showed her husband, her neighbors, and her entire community that one woman can indeed change many things. *Shag za shagom*, step by step, brick by brick. Forgiveness. Fortitude. Hope.

These women, and so many others, helped me to see just how much we have in common: a shared desire—no, the right—to be treated with respect, to support and educate our children, to live a life free from violence and abuse, in peace and with dignity, to believe in a better future. Beyond continents and cultures, war and peace, what separates us, truly, is choice—the ability to choose, from the simplest expression of our daily preferences to the more profound, life-changing choices that shape us as women and human beings.

In many ways, our time in Rwanda surprised me. It deepened my sense of perspective and appreciation for my work and family, and for what it takes to be a woman almost anywhere today, even when that womanhood is threatened or diminished by one's family, culture, or society. It gave me the courage to look inside, to forgive and accept who I am, and to do some things differently for the sake of my family. While making tough choices can be daunting, even debilitating, as it was for me at first, that very act of choosing is really the great privilege of our lives.

Rwanda was special to all of us, but it may have meant the most to me and my marriage to Bill. By making the best of a challenging year of commuting, both of us were forced to step outside of our normal routines, confront our fears and boundaries around risk and change. We both had had to adjust our lens to see each other, and our relationship, in a new light. Sometimes you have to put it all on the line to mend your own wounds of the past, to actually will yourself, to find or hold that better place. It was yet another thing I had learned from women survivors, who continue to inspire me every single day.

Gradually I began to sort through options for the next phase of my career. Though I didn't have another job lined up, I knew that it was going to be okay. I still had choices. I still had a lot more of myself to give. Whatever came next, I would continue working to advance women. I'd taken a long, broken path to become, in the truest sense, a woman for women. I had no desire to go back now.

Epilogue

It has been six years now since we returned from Rwanda, practically a life-time ago, or so it seems. So many transitions have happened, starting with me. After intensive, back-to-back jobs for twenty-five years, I still wanted to do work that felt meaningful but didn't require me to be away so much from Bill and the boys, that didn't require so much of my heart.

Five years ago, I joined the Akilah Institute, Rwanda's only women's col-lege, initially as a consultant to help with strategy. Akilah, a female name that means *intelligent* in Arabic and Swahili, was founded a decade ago to create opportunities for women's higher education. Its unique approach to educa-tion resonates even more with me today. Rather than starting with the sup-ply—underserved women in need of skills and employment—we start with the demand—the skills gaps in the current and future labor market—and work backward, so that young women graduate ready to assume leadership roles in the workplace and society. When I discovered that Akilah's small but entrepreneurial team was just as committed to women's economic indepen-dence, I was all in.

When I came on board full time as its president, Akilah had 355 students and 95 alumni, 90 percent of whom secured jobs within six months of gradu-ation. My goals were to enhance the quality and impact of our academic pro-grams and, at the same time, build the infrastructure and staff for growth. It wasn't easy. We struggled with capacity, systems, and resource challenges. In spite of our focus on technology, business, and entrepreneurship, many in the education sector dismissed us as a cooking or sewing school for poor girls.

Over the next few years, as our reputation and impact grew, we made strategic investments in a new competency-based, blended (online and in-person) education model to drive higher student outcomes and scale. The model's key pillars: twenty-first-century skills, personalized learning, innovation, ethical leadership, and sustainability, enable learners to address complex global challenges and launch their own meaningful careers.

The young women who study at Akilah are almost all from Rwanda, the majority from rural areas; most are the first in their families to go to college. Their stories are truly inspiring: Nadine, who barely survived the genocide as a three-year-old and was raised by a single mother. "Sometimes she didn't have a job, so we'd go without food for several days. I wanted to get an education so I could help us and move on to a better life." And Aisha, who begged and begged her father, a practicing Muslim with several wives, to be allowed to go to school. She became the only girl in her family to study at a university. And Sandrine, who parlayed her love of computers into an information systems degree and a career as a software engineer.

Today, with more than a thousand students on campus, near 90 percent employment rates, and graduate incomes that average twelve times the national median, hundreds of young women are leading productive and purposeful lives and are able to invest in their families, communities, and country. They take on senior roles in companies, start their own businesses, develop new apps, and design programs. These women are the next generation of female leaders in Rwanda: the metaphorical daughters of Women for Women's graduates.

Still, after a decade of pioneering women's education, we knew it was time to do more. Millions of learners across Africa and Asia, young women and men, are all clamoring for a market-relevant, personalized, and affordable education. We pivoted again, this time to launch Davis College, a new global network of coed universities that leverages the latest technology and learning methods to meet that demand. Internalizing those lessons from Rwanda, we weren't paralyzed over the decision, and we didn't ask for permission. The team jumped without knowing right where we would land.

My commitment to advancing women hasn't wavered. Akilah continues to grow and thrive as its own all-female campus within the Davis College network. Why? Because I know, I've learned, that when women are educated and earn incomes, when they have access to knowledge and resources, whole societies benefit.

The work allows me to travel to Rwanda every few months and to stay in touch with Paula and her son, Kai. It took her more than a year to find a new job after we left Rwanda, but she has work now, and her little boy is in school. Paula is going back to school herself, to study hospitality management at a local university near her home. We've tried to track down Joseph but have yet to find him.

And the boys? Kai is about to finish high school, plays varsity sports and drives! That one still makes us laugh at his spot-on impersonations of a Slovenian gangster. Sam and Eli are about to graduate from college; one is on the East Coast, the other in the west. Eli is majoring in global studies, sings a cappella, and interned in Rwanda last summer for field experience. Sam studies engineering and spent two summers in Swaziland building footbridges to help struggling communities gain access to medical care, schools, and markets. Bill has begun to step back from his leadership position at his consulting firm. I could not be more proud of all of them.

Everyone was home for Thanksgiving this past year. The house was crowded, with twenty-five guests squeezed in around three long tables. We didn't care. All of us were exactly where we wanted to be, surrounded by family and friends. Bill fed us smoked and roasted turkey, Eli made three pies, and I prepared the vegetable sides. Sweeta, my former Afghan colleague, and her husband joined us, having canceled other plans when they received our invitation. "You saved my family, Karen," Sweeta said simply. Her children are also thriving. Her daughter is now a teenager and plans to return to Afghanistan to help other students once she completes her own education. Her son is in college and intends to fulfill his parents' dreams of becoming a doctor like his grandmother.

Last December, Bill and I marked another milestone: our thirtieth wedding anniversary. We took the whole family to the island of Anguilla to celebrate. Life is not perfect, nor is our relationship. Yes, our marriage could have easily fallen apart. Those issues that had to do with my past are still there, still a challenge; they probably always will be. The pretense, though, is gone. Those lessons from the women finally allowed us to meet each other where we were, not where we wanted or expected the other to be, while also learning to give more full-heartedly. That, combined with a deep respect, has made all the difference.

I suspect many marriages fail when one or both partners feel stuck in the roles they may have defined for themselves, when there is too little room to maneuver, rebalance, or reinvent. I felt that way. I know now that it's possible to change that dynamic, and that it's worth it, on so many levels, for life and work. Progress, not perfection. Progress, not paralysis, as Mika had advised.

It hasn't gotten much easier to balance a demanding job, a marriage, and contemporary parenting, but that *is* life, and it's how so many of us women have chosen to live it. It may not always be pretty, but it can be very satisfying. That power, that ability to choose, has become even more precious with time. We have to make many choices in a lifetime—about career, about family, about whether to combine work and family and all the trade-offs involved. Embrace your choices wholeheartedly, for they are luxuries not shared by many women around the world. Choose because it is the right decision for you, because it is your right, and because that right is also a gift.

What a world it would be if every woman, every person, could have a life of their own choosing. No one could ask for more.

Acknowledgments

When I started to write this book more than six years ago, I had no idea what I was taking on. I was an international development professional, not a writer. All I knew was that, as someone who cares deeply about women's issues and straddles the developed and developing worlds, I wanted to share what I had learned about the lives of women in countries affected by war and conflict, hoping their stories might touch and inspire others as they had touched and inspired me. It seemed disingenuous to share the personal stories of these women without being willing to share my own.

There are so many people to thank for giving me their time, their wise counsel, their prompts and encouragement over the years. First, the editors. Barbara Brownell Grogan, who believed in this book from the start and coached me through its birthing. Steve Marvin, who let me know that my writing still had a long way to go. John Thompson, who helped to shape the manuscript in so many ways. Tara Weaver, whose careful coaxing got my personal story on the page. Lisa Shannon, whose editorial advice and friendship were a constant source of inspiration. Coralie Hunter, whose deft guidance and steady pen took the book to a new level. And Michelle Hamilton, the minimalist, who pushed me to think in terms of scenes and to better balance the personal and professional.

I'm also grateful to my friends, and a few agents, who took the time to read and provide invaluable comments on various versions of the manuscript:

Karen Barr Engel, Cheryl Battan, Katherine Borsecnik, Stephanie Cabot, Coleen Carone, Sharon Davis, Phebe Macrae, Kate Johnson, Sean Kleier, Anne Mosle, Connie Sommers, Melanne Verveer, and Mary Zients.

Special thanks to:

Susan McEachern, vice president and senior executive editor at Rowman & Littlefield, for believing in the manuscript and seeing its promise, and to the rest of the team at R&L, including Alden Perkins, Katelyn Turner, and Barb Stark.

My colleagues at Women for Women International (past and present), for your continued support, and to my colleagues (past and present) at Akilah. You are truly changing the face of global education. Particular thanks to Aline Kabanda and Linda Mukangoga, for their keen insights about Rwanda, Elizabeth Dearborn Hughes and Cristi Ford for their constructive feedback on the manuscript, Anne DeGiovanni, for her deep wisdom and unwavering belief in this narrative, Jean Mulroy, whose development lens was instrumental to the revision process, and Sean Huff, for his unfailing dedication to me and this book.

My sisters around the world, for your strength and courage and for trusting me with your stories. And to the Rwandan people, for making me feel so at home in your country.

My parents, Marge and Allan Sherman; my sister, Laura; my brother, Ken, for their love and willingness to share some difficult memories. My sons, Eli, Sam, and Kai, for being the best boys ever and the loves of my life.

Bill, for always, always, always having my back. Your love and friendship mean the world to me.

Selected Bibliography

"Africa's Singapore?" *The Economist*, February 25, 2012. https://www.economist.com/business/2012/02/25/africas-singapore.

Alam, Mayesha, Ségolène Dufour-Genneson, and Rebecca Turkington. *Security, Basic Services and Economic Opportunity in South Sudan: Perspectives of Women Post-Independence and Pre-Civil War*. Washington, DC: Georgetown University School of Foreign Service, 2014.

Alfred, Charlotte. "How South Sudan's Conflict Is Killing Women Far from the Battlefield." *Huffington Post*, July 10, 2015. https://www.huffingtonpost.com/2015/07/10/women-in-south-sudan_n_7707560.html.

"A New Country Rises from the Ashes." *The Economist*, May 4, 2013. https://www.economist.com/middle-east-and-africa/2013/05/04/a-new-country-rises-from-the-ruins.

Banda, Joyce. "Africa's Women Belong at the Top." *Gates Notes* (blog). September 14, 2018. Accessed September 24, 2018. https://www.gatesnotes.com/Development/Joyce-Banda-on-the-value-of-empowering-women.

Banda, Joyce, and Priscilla Agyapong. "An Agenda for Harmful Cultural Practices and Girls' Empowerment." *Center for Global Development*, December 12, 2016. https://www.cgdev.org/publication/agenda-harmful-cultural-practices-and-girls-empowerment.

Bertelli, Michele, and Javier Sauras. "A Woman's Burden in War-Torn South Sudan." *Al Jazeera*, September 30, 2017. https://www.aljazeera.com/indepth/features/2017/07/woman-burden-war-torn-south-sudan-170730132806188.html.

Blackney, Elizabeth. "Dr. Denis Mukwege: Congo's Nobel Nominee." *Huffington Post*, October 10, 2013. https://www.huffingtonpost.com/elizabeth-blackney/dr-denis-mukwege-congos-n_b_4080518.html.

Bloomberg Philanthropies and NoVo Foundation. *Social Investment Report: A Look at Women for Women International.* Amstelveen, Netherlands: KPMG, 2012.

Boseley, Sarah. "Rwanda: A Revolution in Rights for Women." *The Guardian*, May 28, 2010. https://www.theguardian.com/world/2010/may/28/womens-rights-rwanda.

Buvinic, Mayra, Rebecca Furst-Nichols, and Emily Courey Pryor. "A Roadmap for Promoting Women's Economic Empowerment." Slideshow, United Nations Foundation, 2013.

Cavell, Anna. "Q&A: South Sudan Moves Towards Forming Unity Government." *Al Jazeera*, January 13, 2016. https://www.aljazeera.com/news/2016/01/qa-south-sudan-moves-forming-unity-government-160113163129399.html.

Chamberlain, Gethin. "South Sudan's Battle for Cattle Is Forcing Schoolgirls to Become Teenage Brides." *The Guardian*, June 8, 2017. https://www.theguardian.com/global-development/2017/jun/08/south-sudan-battle-for-cattle-is-forcing-schoolgirls-to-become-teenage-brides.

Constable, Pamela. "Proposed Law to Protect Afghan Women Faces Backlash." *Washington Post*, May 25, 2013. https://www.washingtonpost.com/world/asia_pacific/law-to-protect-afghan-women-faces-backlash/2013/05/25/3b47d1ea-c49f-11e2-9642-a56177f1cdf7_story.html.

Desai, Lisa. "Why Women Are Economic Backbone of Rwanda." *CNN News*, July 24, 2010. http://www.cnn.com/2010/WORLD/africa/07/22/rwanda.women.business/index.html.

"DR Congo: Senior UN Officials Relay Hopes for Latest Great Lakes Peace Effort." *UN Daily News*, June 4, 2013. https://news.un.org/en/story/2013/06/441362-dr-congo-senior-un-officials-relay-hopes-latest-great-lakes-peace-effort.

"Dr. Mukwege, Panzi Hospital, and PHR's Partnership." *Physicians for Human Rights*, n.d. https://phr.org/issues/sexual-violence/program-on-sexual-violence-in-conflict-zones/networking-and-partnerships/phrs-partnership-with-dr-denis-mukwege-and-panzi-hospital-drc/.

Duany, Julia A., and Wal Duany. "War and Women in the Sudan: Role Change and Adjustment to New Responsibilities." *Northeast African Studies* 8, no. 2 (2001): 63–82. Michigan State University Press.

Duflo, Esther. "Women Empowerment and Economic Development." *Journal of Economic Literature* 50, no. 4 (2012): 1051–79.

Enough Team, The. "Not Just 'Lost Boys,' but 'Lost Girls'—in War-Torn South Sudan." *Christian Science Monitor*, October 2, 2014. https://www.csmonitor.com/World/Africa/Africa-Monitor/2014/1002/Not-just-Lost-Boy-but-Lost-Girls-in-war-torn-South-Sudan.

Evans, Tom. "Bosnian Leader: 'Ethnic Cleansing' Continues 15 Years after War." *CNN News*, March 2, 2010. http://www.cnn.com/2010/WORLD/europe/03/01/bosnia.herzegovina/index.html.

Gettleman, Jeffrey. "After Years of Struggle, South Sudan Becomes a New Nation." *New York Times*, July 9, 2011. https://www.nytimes.com/2011/07/10/world/africa/10sudan.html.

Government of Rwanda. *National Scaling-Up Strategy for One Stop Centers in Rwanda.* Kigali: Government of Rwanda, 2012.

Hartung, William D., and Bridget Moix. *Report: U.S. Arms to Africa and the Congo War.* New York: World Policy Institute, 2000. Accessed July 20, 2017. https://worldpolicy.org/2009/11/13/report-u-s-arms-to-africa-and-the-congo-war-world-policy-institute-research-project/.

Hunt, Swanee. "The Rise of Rwanda's Women." *Foreign Affairs*, March 30, 2014. https://www.foreignaffairs.com/articles/rwanda/2014-03-30/rise-rwandas-women.

Hunt, Swanee, and Laura Heaton. "Women in Post-Genocide Rwanda Have Helped Heal Their Country." *National Geographic*, April 4, 2014. https://news.nationalgeographic.com/news/2014/04/140404-rwanda-genocide-parliament-kigali-rwandan-patriotic-front-world-women-education/.

Kabeer, Naila. "Resources, Agency, Achievements: Reflections on the Measurements of Women's Empowerment." *Development and Change*, no. 30 (1999): 435–64.

Kanyesigye, Frank. "Rwanda Ranks Top in MDGs Progress." *New Times*, May 29, 2013.

Killian, Dan. "Mind the Gender Justice Gap." *Peace Direct* (blog). May 16, 2013. https://www.peaceinsight.org/blog/2013/05/mind-the-gender-justice-gap/.

Klugman, Jeni, and Sarah Twigg. "Gender at Work in Africa: Legal Constraints and Opportunities for Reform." *Oxford Human Rights Hub* (2015): 1–46.

Kuo, Lily. "Rwanda Is a Landlocked Country with Few Natural Resources. So Why Is China Investing So Heavily in It?" *Quartz*, November 22, 2016. https://qz.com/africa/827935/rwanda-is-a-landlocked-country-with-few-natural-resources-so-why-is-china-investing-so-heavily-in-it/.

Kwibuka, Eugene. "World Bank, UN Chiefs Hail Rwanda's Gender Politics." *New Times*, May 24, 2013.

Lacy, Marc. "Since '94 Horror, Rwandans Turn Toward Islam." *New York Times*, April 7, 2004. https://www.nytimes.com/2004/04/07/world/since-94-horror-rwandans-turn-toward-islam.html.

Leithead, Alastair. "South Sudan Conflict: 'Soldiers Will Kill You for No Reason in Yei.'" *BBC News*, March 9, 2017. https://www.bbc.com/news/world-africa-39209280.

Lemmon, Gayle Tzemach. "Entrepreneurship in Postconflict Zones." Council on Foreign Relations, 2012.

McNeish, Hannah. "South Sudan: Women and Girls Raped as 'Wages' for Government-Allied Fighters." *The Guardian*, September 28, 2015. https://www.theguardian.com/global-development/2015/sep/28/south-sudan-women-girls-raped-as-wages-for-government-allied-fighters.

Mednick, Sam. "South Sudan Violence against Women Is Twice Global Average." *Associated Press*, November 29, 2017. https://apnews.com/10449fd23da1461e9feb21d9b732db68.

Moyo, Dambisa. "The African Threat." *Project Syndicate,* November 23, 2018. https://www.project-syndicate.org/onpoint/the-african-threat-by-dambisa-moyo-2018-11?barrier=accesspaylog.

Musaka, Daniel. *PANZI Hospital Annual Report.* PANZI Hospital, 2015.

Muscati, Samer. "South Sudan's War on Women." *Human Rights Watch*, August 5, 2015. https://www.hrw.org/news/2015/08/05/south-sudans-war-women.

Nsengimana, Simon, Robertson K. Tengeh, and Chux Gervase Iwu. "The Sustainability of Businesses in Kigali, Rwanda: An Analysis of the Barriers Faced by Women Entrepreneurs." *Sustainability* 1372, no. 9 (2017): 1–9.

Nyiramutangwa, S., O. Katengwa, A. Mukiga, and N. Abrahams. *Exploring Community Perceptions and Women's Experiences of Violence against Women and Use of Services in Bugesera District, Eastern Province, Rwana.* Kigali: Rwanda Women's Network, 2011.

Pelley, Scott. "Fighting Famine in War-Torn South Sudan." *CBS News*, March 19, 2017. https://www.cbsnews.com/news/fighting-south-sudan-famine/.

"Rape and Cannibalism in South Sudan, African Union Says." *BBC News*, October 29, 2015. https://www.bbc.com/news/world-africa-34657418.

Republic of Rwanda. *Gender Impact Assessment of the Law No. 22199 of 12/11/99 to Supplement Book One of the Civil Code and to Institute Part Five Regarding Matrimonial Regimes, Liberalities, & Successions.* Kigali: Republic of Rwanda, 2011.

Republic of Rwanda. *National Evaluation Report on Implementation of the Beijing Declaration and Platform for Action (1995) and the Outcome of the Twenty-third Special Session of the General Assembly (2000).* Kigali: Republic of Rwanda, 2009.

Republic of Rwanda. *Rwanda Vision 2020.* Kigali: Republic of Rwanda, 2000.

"Rwanda 'Gacaca' Genocide Courts Finish Work." *BBC News*, June 18, 2012. https://www.bbc.com/news/world-africa-18490348.

Santora, Marc. "As South Sudan Crisis Worsens, 'There Is No More Country.'" *New York Times*, June 22, 2015. https://www.nytimes.com/2015/06/23/world/africa/as-south-sudan-crisis-worsens-there-is-no-more-country.html.

Sen, Amartya. *Development as Freedom.* Oxford: Oxford University Press, 1999.

Sen, Amartya. "Many Faces of Gender Inequality." *Frontline*, October–November, 2001. https://frontline.thehindu.com/static/html/fl1822/18220040.htm.

Shapiro, Danielle. "Congo Rape Crisis: Study Reveals Shocking New Numbers." *Daily Beast*, May 11, 2011. https://www.thedailybeast.com/congo-rape-crisis-study-reveals-shocking-new-numbers.

Sherman, Karen. "Eyewitness Report: Violence Growing as South Sudan Preps for Independence." *ABC News*, June 4, 2011. https://abcnews.go.com/

International/violence-growing-south-sudan-region-plans-declare-independence/ story?id=13737151.

Sherman, Karen. "Josephine's Story: A Remarkable Woman in Congo." *Africa. com* (blog). June 14, 2012. Accessed March 12, 2013. www.africa.com/blog/ josephine8217s_story_a_remarkable_woman_in_congo/.

Sherman, Karen. "Legal Marriage." *Huffington Post*, November 6, 2012. https:// www.huffingtonpost.com/karen-sherman/legal-marriage_b_2080914.html.

Sherman, Karen. "Rwanda Making Strides for Women." *Africa.com* (blog). January 11, 2012. Accessed February 29, 2012. http://www.africa.com/printblog?id=499.

Sherman, Karen. *Twenty Years Post-Genocide Women Engender Change in Rwanda.* Washington, DC: Georgetown Institute for Women, Peace & Security, 2014.

Sherman, Karen. "Women and War." *Huffington Post*, November 30, 2012. https:// www.huffingtonpost.com/entry/women-and-war_1_b_2217906.

Sherman, Karen. "Women Build Nations." *Global Entrepreneurship Week* (blog). November 27, 2012. Accessed March 12, 2013. http://www.unleashingideas.org/ blog/women-build-nations.

Sherman, Karen. "Women's Economic Empowerment and the Future of South Sudan." *Women's Economic Participation in Conflict-Affected and Fragile Settings* (January 2016): 16–25.

Sieff, Kevin. "At Least 15 U.N. Peacekeepers Killed in Attack in Congo." *Washington Post*, December 8, 2017. https://www.washingtonpost.com/world/africa/at-least-14-un-peacekeepers-killed-in-attack-in-congo/2017/12/08/614d69ca-dc2a-11e7-a241-0848315642d0_story.html?noredirect=on&utm_term=.314a4534f368.

Skarlatos, Theopi. "'The job of Rebuilding Rwanda Fell to Us Women.'" *BBC News*, December 27, 2012. https://www.bbc.com/news/world-africa-20727127.

Slegh, Henny, and Augustin Kimonyo. *Masculinity and Gender Based Violence in Rwanda.* Kigali: Rwanda Men's Resource Centre, 2010.

Sommers, Marc. "The Darling Dictator of the Day." *New York Times*, May 27, 2012. https://www.nytimes.com/2012/05/28/opinion/Paul-Kagame-The-Darling-Dictator-of-the-day.html.

South Sudan. *South Sudan's Constitution of 2011.* Juba: South Sudan, 2011.

"South Sudan Keeps Buying Weapons amid Famine: UN." *Al Jazeera*, March 17, 2017. https://www.aljazeera.com/news/2017/03/south-sudan-buying-weapons-famine-170317200215330.html.

"South Sudan Profile—Overview." *BBC News*, August 27, 2015. https://www.bbc.com/news/world-africa-14069082.

Turkington, Rebecca. "Champions for Change: Dr. Denis Mukwege." *Council on Foreign Relations* (blog). October 11, 2018. Accessed October 19, 2018. https://www.cfr.org/blog/champions-change-dr-denis-mukwege.

United Nations. *Central Equatoria State Profile*. New York: United Nations, 2010.

Vagianos, Alanna. "Domestic Violence Is the Most Common Killer of Women Around the World." *Huffington Post*, November 26, 2018. https://www.huffingtonpost.com/entry/domestic-violence-most-common-killer-of-women-united-nations_us_5bfbf61ee4b0eb6d931142ac.

Vogt, Heidi. "World's Newest Country Struggles to Survive." *Wall Street Journal*, June 10, 2015. https://www.wsj.com/articles/worlds-newest-country-struggles-to-survive-1433977300.

Warner, Gregory. "It's the No. 1 Country for Women in Politics—But Not in Daily Life." *NPR News*, July 29, 2016. https://www.npr.org/sections/goatsandsoda/2016/07/29/487360094/invisibilia-no-one-thought-this-all-womans-debate-team-could-crush-it.

World Bank Group. *Gender at Work*. Washington, DC: World Bank Group, 2013.

World Bank Group. *Voice and Agency: Empowering Women and Girls for Shared Prosperity*. Washington, DC: World Bank Group, 2014.

Index

Note: Individuals who are identified by pseudonyms in the text are indexed under those same pseudonyms.

240; and domestic life, 57–58, 80–81, 175, 227; and genocide memorial, 229–33; and Kilimanjaro, 159, 207–9; later life, 247; and Model UN, 185, 203; and move to Rwanda, 3, 5–6, 15, 38; relationship with, 163, 168; and running, 16, 171; and school, 20; and travel, 49–50, 108, 194. *See also* boys
Wilkens, Carl, 88
women, ix, 205; in Afghanistan, 78–79; in Bosnia, 34; commonalities of, 195–96; in Congo, 61–64; gap-toothed, 107–8; Kagame and, 91; in Russia, 33, 35; in Rwanda, 10–11, 47, 91–98, 112, 195, 233; and social networks, 121–26; in South Sudan, 75, 146, 149, 177–78, 179f, 180, 218; value of, 76, 95–97, 189–90, 219; war and, 136, 138. *See also* survivors
Women for Women International, 6, 34, 110–12, 139; CEO of, 111, 119, 183; holiday party, 152–53; HQ-field dynamic in, 118; ID cards, 220–21;

and International Women's Day, 191; Kigali offices, 23–28; logo, 23; practices of, 42; sponsorship program, 197; staff, 23–24
Women's Opportunity Center, Kayonza, Rwanda, ix, 6, 139, 171, 202; construction of, 43–45, 222–24; Inyumba and, 150; opening of, 235–38; services, 45
work-life balance, 35, 83, 107–20, 226; CEO search and, 14; international development field and, 54; reflections on, 248; and social networks, 125
World Bank, 54, 239

Yei, South Sudan, 146–47, 175–82, 179f, 187–94, 191f, 217–22
Yom Kippur, 52, 66
youth, in Rwanda, 82
Yvette, 197–200, 199f

Zulatkha, 25

About the Author

Karen Sherman has spent the past thirty years working in conflict-affected and transitional countries around the world and raising three children. Prior to joining the Akilah Institute, an award-winning women's college in Rwanda, she served as chief operating officer at Women for Women International and held senior leadership positions at other international organizations where she focused mainly on women's economic development and participation. Sherman studied political science at the University of Oregon and earned a master's degree in Russian and East European studies at the George Washington University. She has served on multiple boards and is the founding chair of Everywoman.org, calling for a global treaty to end violence against women. A native of Portland, Oregon, she lives in Bethesda, Maryland, with her family.